CORSETS:
A Visual History

CORSETS:
A Visual History

Compiled by and Notes by
R.L. SHEP

R.L. Shep
Mendocino

Published by:

R.L. Shep
Box 668
Mendocino, CA 95460

Library of Congress Cataloging-in-Publication Data

Shep, R.L., 1933-
    Corsets: a visual survey / compiled by and notes by R.L. Shep
        p.   cm.
    Includes bibliographical references.
    ISBN 0-914046-20-9 : $26.95
    1. Corsets--History--19th century. 2. Corsets--History--20th
century.   I. Title.
GT2075.S54 1993
391′ .42--dc20   93-21419
                                                       CIP

CONTENTS

NOTES

Corsets are intriguing, mysterious, shocking, and slightly naughty (look at what Madonna has done with them). To understand period clothing it is essential to know what was worn underneath the dresses and how the 'look' was achieved. For the Victorian and Edwardian eras, corsets were the most important undergarment and certainly the one which influenced the ultimate shape of the wearer.

One does not wear a corset, one wears corsets or more properly a 'pair of corsets.' Corsets have a long and varied history and have been called by many names: stays, bodices, a pair of bodies, waspie, corse, foundation garments, etc. The term corsets was used in the 14th century to refer to a breastplate as worn by a soldier: "un corset de fer," "vi corsets de feer," "2 cor d'acier." The word corslet was also used for a breastplate at one time.

Planche refers to stays as follows: "The injurious practice of tight lacing, 'a custom fertile in disease and death,' appears to have been introduced by the Normans as early as the twelfth century; and the romances of the Middle Ages teem with allusions to, and laudation of, the wasp-like waists of the dames and demoiselles of the period."

Stays or Bodices, *temp.* 1700.

"The stays that retained their original character of 'a pair of boddies,' are seen in an old print, undated but clearly about the year 1700, which represents the front and back view of a young woman, whose stays are composed of two pieces laced together before and behind; and a 'pair of stays' they continued to be called, notwithstanding subsequent incorporation. The monstrous 'whalebone prisons' of the time of George II, are delineated in several of Hogarth's most instructive engravings." (George II, 1727-60; Hogarth, 1697-1764).

The *Encyclopedia Britannica* traces corsets back to the Cretans of the Minoan Bronze Age (2nd century BC). They were fairly universal from around 1810 (after the Empire fashions) to the end of World War I, then they went out of fashion during most of the 1920s. But there was an attempt by clothing designers to bring them back in the '30s, which World War II put an end to.

When you read fashion dictionaries and corset histories you realize that corsets or stays were worn by men as well as women throughout most of history. And it is not until you start looking at advertisements and catalogs that you realize that they were also worn by children and even babies!

We are not attempting to present an overall history of corsets here. That has been done a number of times and many of those books will be found listed in the Bibliography following these notes. Unfortunately most histories are not very well illustrated. But if you are interested in the many forms that corsets have taken over the ages you might like *Freaks of Fashion: The Corset & the Crinoline (1868)* which we have recently reprinted. It has many illustrations of early historical corsets which have not been included in this work.

What we are attempting to do is present a visual survey of corsets as seen through advertisements, department store catalogs, and corset company catalogs. In doing this we are restricted by the fact that there was not a lot of material to draw from before 1870. But then as it became all right to talk about and show corsets there is almost a flood of material to draw from right up until the end of World War I. However, it must be born in mind that these sources were often printed on very cheap paper which discolored easily. Then after about 1900 when half-tones were widely used there are added problems in reproducing them. Because of this we excluded some illustrations that were in really bad condition and at other times put them in because there was nothing else that illustrated that particular type corset.

By presenting a wealth of visual information it is possible to trace the development of corsets during these periods. It is also possible to follow various corset companies and in many instances to trace the changing prices over the time span. A case in point is comparing the two copies of the *Royal Blue Book Corset Catalog* which we were able to find, namely the one for 1907 and that for 1916. These catalogs illustrate Royal Winchester and Bon Ton corsets.

Corsets were considered a necessity by most people throughout the Victorian and Edwardian eras. But it was also obvious to a number of people that they were dangerous and unhealthy. Aside from those far-sighted and more radical people few advocated completely doing away with corsets, but there were movements to make them less rigid and constricting and you will find many references to 'dress reform corsets.' In fact the real dress reformers did want to do away with corsets, but they were only a small if very vocal group who were also interested in Women's Rights and, in many instances, were often interested in the Temperance movement.

Corsets were blamed for any number of women's health problems, and rightly so. Among these were deformed ribcages and spines, shortness of breath, and compressed genitalia which weakened a woman's ability to have healthy children. Also they could cause a woman to have a prolapsed or sagging uterus, causing it to invert and protrude from the vagina. There were a number of remedies for this, the major ones being devices called 'pessaries.'

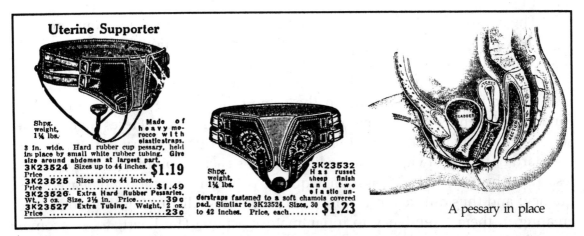

Uterine Supporter

Shpg. weight, 1¼ lbs.
Made of heavy morocco with elastic straps.
3 in. wide. Hard rubber cup pessary, held in place by small white rubber tubing. Give size around abdomen at largest part.
3K23524 Sizes up to 44 inches. $1.19
Price ....
3K23525 Sizes above 44 inches. $1.49
Price ....
3K23526. Extra Hard Rubber Pessaries.
Wt., 3 oz. Size, 2½ in. Price........39c
3K23527 Extra Tubing. Weight, 2 oz. $1.23
Price 23c

Shpg. weight, 1¼ lbs.
3K23532 Has russet sheep finish and two understraps fastened to a soft chamois covered pad. Similar to 3K23524. Sizes, 30 to 42 inches. Price, each........ $1.23

A pessary in place

These were made of various materials and were worn at all times except when the woman went to bed. They relieved the condition but in no way cured it.

It is still common to talk to women who remember their mothers and grandmothers wearing corsets even after they were out of fashion because they were 'used to them' and felt more secure and better with them on. It almost runs parallel to Chinese footbinding! It was horrible and painful, but after they had been worn for so long women could not feel comfortable without them.

The following are excerpts from articles about corsets showing how attitudes changed over time.

The Penny Magazine (1833)

"At first, laced waistcoats are used rather for the convenience of suspending other parts of the dress than with any view of giving support to weak muscles, or of influencing the shape; and confined to such use they would be perfectly harmless. In time, when weakness becomes inferred, not from any evidences of actual debility, but merely from the girls not being able to maintain the unnatural and constrained posture which fashion and false taste enjoin, the advantage of compressing the chest by means of the waistcoat, so as to give support to the muscles of the back, becomes discovered, and the mechanical power supplied by the lace affords but too effective means of accomplishing this compression. The effect pleases the mother, promoting, as it does, her dearly-prized object—a good carriage; it is endured by the girl as the lesser of two evils, for though at first irksome, it releases her from the pain of endeavours which she has not power to continue to the extent required.

"As years advance, various causes combine to render this practice more inveterate and more pernicious; and still the potent instrument, the lace, lends its ready and effectual aid. Now a taper waist becomes an object of ambition, and the stays are to be laced more closely. This is still done gradually, and, at first, imperceptibly to the parties. The effect, however, though slow, is sure, and the powers of endurance thus exercised come in time to bear almost unconsciously what, if suddenly or quickly attempted, no heroism could possibly sustain.

"The derangements to which this increased pressure gives rise must now be considered. The first is the obvious impediment to the motions of the ribs which this constriction of the chest occasions. For perfect respiration these motions should be free and unrestrained. In proportion as respiration is impeded, is the blood imperfectly vitalised; and in the same ratio are the nutrient and other functions dependent on the blood inadequately performed. Here, then, is one source of debility which affects the whole frame, reducing every part below the standard of healthful vigour. According, also, as each inspiration of air becomes less full, the wants of the system require, as a compensation, increased frequency; and thus quickened respiration commences, disturbing the lungs, and creating in them a tendency to inflammatory action. The heart, too, becomes excited, the pulse accelerated, and palpitation is in time superadded. All these effects are capable of resulting from mere constriction of the chest; they become fearfully aggravated when, at a more advanced stage, additional sources, of irritation arise in flexure of the spine, and in derangements of the stomach, liver, and other organs subservient to digestion. The foregoing disturbances are formidable enough, and sufficiently destructive of health, yet they are not the only lesions (injuries) which tight lacing induces. The pressure, which is chiefly made on the lower part of the chest, and to which this part most readily yields, extends its malign influence to the abdominal viscera also. By it the stomach and liver are compressed, and, in time, partially detruded from the concavity of the diaphragm, to the great disturbance of their functions; and being pressed downwards too, these trespass on that space which the other abdominal viscera require, superinducing still further derangements. Thus, almost every function of the body becomes more of less depraved. Nothing could have prevented the source of all this mischief and misery from being fully detected and universally understood, but the slow and insidious process by which the aberration from sound principle effects its ravages.

"The mere weakness of back, so often adverted to, becomes in its turn an aggravating cause of visceral lesion. The body cannot be always cased in tightly-laced stays—their pressure may be endured to any extent under the excitement of the evening display, but during the day some relaxation must take place. Under it, the muscles of the back, deprived of their accustomed support, and incapable of themselves to sustain the incumbent weight, yield, and the column of the spine bends, at first anteriorily, causing round shoulders and an arched back; but eventually inclines to one or other side, giving rise to the well-known and too frequently occuring state of lateral curvature. This last change most frequently commences in the sitting posture, such females being, through general debility, much disposed to sedentary habits. As soon as lateral curvature commences, the lungs and heart become still more disturbed; anhelation (difficulty of breating) from slight exertion, short cough, and palpitation ensue; and at this time, chiefly in consequence of the pulmonary derangement, alarm begins to be entertained, and the approach of phthisis apprehended."

The following figures, taken from a valuable work in German, by the late professor *Soemmering, on the Effects of Stays,* cannot fail to make an impression on the mind of every parent and guardian of youth.

We are assured by medical men of the first authority that there is no exaggeration in these outlines. Such melancholy specimens are daily to be met with, both living and dead.

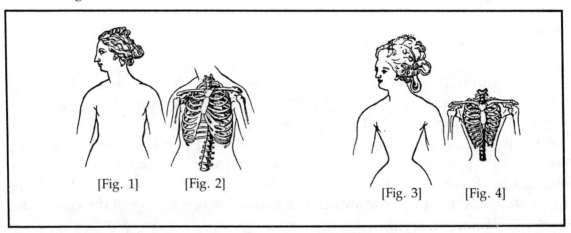

[Fig. 1]   [Fig. 2]   [Fig. 3]   [Fig. 4]

Fig. 1 is an outline of the famous statue of the Venus de Medici, and may be considered as the *beau ideal* of a fine female figure.

Fig. 2. is the skeleton of a similar figure, with the bones in their natural position.

Fig. 3. is an outline of the figure of a modern "boarding-school miss," after it has been permanently remodelled by stays.

Fig. 4. is the skeleton belonging to such a figure as No. 3.

Harpers Bazar 1871

Now that waspish waists are no longer admired, the plump, supple figures that fashion dictates require easy-fitting corsets, shaped to adapt themselves readily to the figure, and give the necessary support. To secure an accurate, and withal a stylish fit, the corset must have great fullness for the bust and hips, and ample length, both back and front, to fall in with the natural taper of the waist. The improved glove-fitting corsets possess these requisites, and are now preferred by most ladies to any other kind. They are filled with very flexible bones, and are moulded over steam, to show the beautiful roundness of the bust and hips. Their price has been the objection hitherto, but they are now made of substantial coutil, and sold at $1.50, in as good shape as the qualities that cost much more. There are ten qualities of these corsets. Handsome ones of fine coutil, with many thin, light bones, and prettily embroidered on the bone-cases, are $5. Ladies who are fond of wearing scarlet woolen corsets in winter will be pleased with the new pale rose-colored corsets, made of cotton coutil, for summer wear. Misses' corsets, in sizes ranging from sixteen to twenty-four inches, are made of white coutil, with the gores and graceful curved seams of the glove-fitting principle. The new ventilating corsets have the centre gore, that passes around the waist to stay the body and permit the strain, made of coutil, while the upper and lower gores are of open-worked material. A luxury for midsummer is the gossamer perfumed corset, made of perforated canvas, with the few elastic bones shielded by light corded goods. These corsets are put through an elaborate fumigating process, and those made a year ago retain their faint, pleasant odor. Price $2.

Women's Home Companion 1912

How would it do to have a little talk about corsets? It is really the thing nearest to our hearts, you know, and the most important thing, too, in securing the ideal figure of today. And what is the ideal figure we all are striving for? It is the youthful figure, therefore it must be supple and slender. There is nothing rigid or stiff, you know, about buoyant, smiling youth. So away, and very far away, with the heavy, uncomfortable, vise-like corset of the past. Flexibility, freedom, and comfort—these are the words that are descriptive of the best of the new corsets.

With but slight variations, demanded by the latest styles, the corset is now molded to the figure. It is made not to bind, to compress, nor to pinch, but to follow the graceful lines of the human form and to support it.

But there is no doubt that the corset is a difficult and troublesome thing to handle—that is, adjusting it to our individual needs. It must be sometimes coaxed and sometimes driven, and all the time controlled; and we must not forget that it is the arch upon which the whole figure depends. It either weakens and distorts or strengthens and beautifies.

But now let us take up our own different corset needs. To begin with, one of the big strides shown in the corset industry today is that corsets are now made for individual types of figures. I am not refering to the made to order corsets, but to the manufactured corsets. Whatever your need, there is a corset to supply it; in fact, the majority of the best American corsets are made with a purpose. They have something to accomplish, and they are designed so that they successfully accomplish that something.

Of course it goes without saying that it is the fat woman who has the most troubles. This much-harassed woman must learn that flesh has got to be accepted. She cannot push it aside, because that only makes it the more prominent in a place where it ought not to be. However, there really is a place for all flesh, but all flesh must be kept in its place. Be sure to remember this when you start to reduce your figure. Don't try to move your abdomen up and then compress it in a place where it does not belong. The flesh is adaptable in its place, but it is more than perverse and obstinate where it does not belong.

Then, above all else, every stout woman must stop thinking that she can wear a corset two or three sizes smaller than she needs by actual measurement. What earthly difference does it make whether a large, well-built woman's waist measures twenty-six or thirty inches? It is how she looks in her corset, and how she feels in it, that counts. Let me tell you that the fat woman looks much better in a corset an inch or so too large for her, where her fat can sink down into it, rather than in a corset two or three inches too small which presses her fat up and out until it appears in many unsightly bulges and bumps. A safe rule to follow is to wear a corset in a size three inches smaller than the waistband of your dress. For instance, if your waistband measures thirty-two inches, you can safely and correctly wear a corset size twenty-nine. I am referring, you see, to the stout woman.

There are many types of fat women, and in selecting a corset it is necessary to cater to the special part of the figure which needs attention. For instance, there are stout women with rather slender hips, but with an abdomen that is most prominent. For this type of figure there is a specially designed corset, with straps which not only reduce the abdomen but hygienically support it. Right here let me give a word of advice to the thin woman who happens to have a large bust in proportion to the rest of the lines of her figure. It may be a temptation for her to wear a low-bust corset that is nothing more than a girdle, but this she must not do. She must be careful to confine her bust, and so help to give symmetrical lines to her figure. It does not matter at all how low a corset she wears and how few bones it has, if she wears with it a brassiere.

It is the wise woman who looks askance at the table piled high with bargain corsets. There is something alluring, there is no doubt, about a dainty-looking corset which is marked down to seventy-five cents, but there is apt to be something disastrous about the effect upon the figure of these bargain corsets that are picked up at random. If you are absolutely sure that a marked-down corset is a model which fits the special needs of your own figure, then of course it is a little economy worth considering. If not, pass it by. It is the wise woman who decides in the beginning just what corset suits her figure best, and also what corset best improves the lines of her figure. Then it is this corset that she clings to. Wearing one make of corset for a certain time, and then changing to another, is fatal to the fit of your different gowns, throwing their lines entirely out. In selecting this right, suited-to-the-figure corset, be sure that it is a reliable corset. Don't buy too cheap a corset, and don't wear the corset you do buy, so continuously that it loses its shape and strength, and therefore does not accomplish its purpose. Corsets like clothes need rest, and every woman should of course have more than one or two pairs of corsets.

The woman who has perfect corset sense is she who wears a corset right in size, right in shape, and so perfectly fitted that corset and figure seem one.

ACKNOWLEDGEMENTS

I would like to thank the following who provided us with materials to be used in this work:

Helen Barglebaugh
Stan Dufford
Joy Emery
Holly Hollinger
Irene Lewisohn Costume Reference Library, The Costume Institute of
    The Metropolitan Museum of Art
Bob Kaufman
Kevin Seligman
Fred Struthers
Betty Williams
Judy Wood

BIBLIOGRAPHY — Further Reading

The Art of Beauty. Mrs. Haweis. 1877
The Corset and the Crinoline. Nora Waugh. 1954
Le Corset a Travers Les Ages. Ernest Leoty. 1893
Le Corset dans L'Art. F. Libran & H. Clouzet. 1933
Cyclopedia of Costume. J.R. Planche. 1876
Dictionary of English Fashion. C.W. & P.E. Cunnington & C. Beard. 1960
Dress As Fine Art. Mrs. Merrifield. 1854
The Encyclopedia Britannica. 1986
Fashion in Underwear. E. Ewing. 1971
Fairchild's Dictionary of Fashion. Charlotte Calasibetta. 1975
Foundations of Fashion. C. Page. 1981
Freaks of Fashion: The Corset & The Crinoline (1868). William Berry Lord.
    Reprinted by R.L. Shep. 1993
Health & Beauty, or Corsets & Clothing. Mdme. Caplin. 1855
The History of Corsets. M. Crawford & Guernsey. 1951
The History of Ladies Underwear. Cecil Saint-Laurent. 1968
History of Underclothes. C.W. & P. Cunnington. 1951
In Her Own Right. Elizabeth Griffith. 1984
Language of Fashion. Mary Brooks Picken. 1939
The Light of the Home. Harvey Green. 1983
Never Satisfied. Helen Schwartz. 1986
The Undercover Story. exhibit catalog. N.Y. & Kyoto. 1982
Unmentionables: From Figleaves to Scanties. Robert Holliday. 1933
Victorian Costume & Costume Accessories. Anne Buck. 1984

Pre-1870

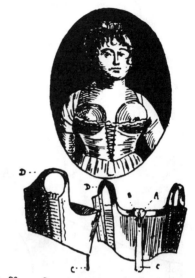

Fig. 90. — Corset de Moreau de la Sarthe (1803)

Fig. 91. — Effets merveilleux des lacets (1807)

Fig. 92. — La fureur des corsets (1809)

Un porteur d'eau lace une cuisinière avec un billion. — Le vieux mari se sert de ses lunettes pour lacer sa jeune femme. — L'amant emploie l'amour pour lacer son amie. — Un jeune jockey lace sa vieille maitresse bossue.

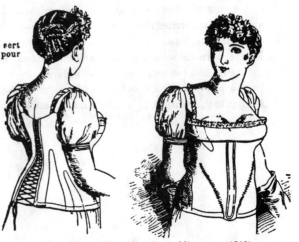

Fig. 93. — Corset à la « Ninon » (1810).

PATTERN FOR STAYS.

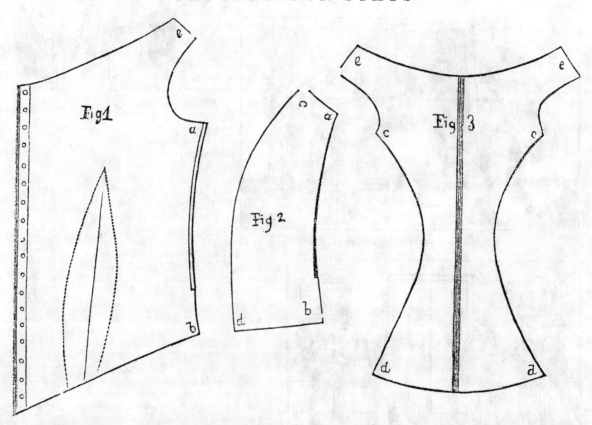

A CORRESPONDENT who has kindly furnished the above pattern writes respecting it as follows:—

"I have inclosed a pattern of a pair of stays, that I have worn for some time past, and can answer for their ease and convenience. I had suffered severely from a pain in my side, but since I have worn stays similar to this pattern, I have been much better. One yard and a quarter of satteen is sufficient to make them; and three lengths of whalebone, one on each side of the front, and another down the middle of the back, should be used. Hooks and eyelet-holes, or buttons, for fastenings."

Fig. 1. Front.   Fig. 2. Side-piece.
Fig. 3. The whole of the back.

1853

MADAME CAPLIN'S CORSETS.

No. 1.

We have before alluded to the establishment of this lady, at 58 Bemers Street, Oxford Street, London, and have now procured some cuts of those peculiar inventions, founded on physical investigations and principles, which have made her so famous.

No. 1.—The Registered Coporiform Child's Bodice offers many advantages, and is valuable for infants and children, affording ease and comfort, supporting the frame, and directing the growth. It is arranged so as to follow the prominent and receding lines of the body; a smooth and comfortable fit is thus obtained, but without the slightest pressure. A pair of straps passes over the shoulders, which cross in the back, and are fastened similarly to a gentleman's brace. We can at once accord the advantages that this bodice possesses over those usually made for children—namely, the straight-corded bodice, which Madame Caplin states, from a want of shape and adaptation, slips off the shoulders on to the arms, causing the head and shoulders to bend forward; thus producing a stooping position, round shoulders, contraction of the chest, and a flattening of the ribs.

No. 2.

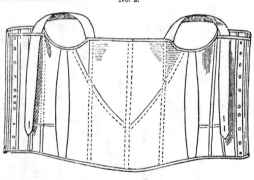

Madame Caplin has introduced another invention, called "The Invisible Scapula Contractor." (No. 2.) This we were very much pleased with, and consider it an ingenious contrivance. She explained its use by stating that, in many cases, the child's bodice has not sufficient power of itself to counteract the stooping of the body, and particularly where this evil has been of long standing. In such instances, the contractors cannot fail to be of the greatest utility. We were also much gratified in inspecting the models and numerous inventions which were exhibited by Madame Caplin at the Great Exhibition, and where she received the only prize granted in the United Kingdom for adaptations of this kind. They are twenty-three in number, commencing with infancy, and following the different phases of woman's life up to old age.

No. 3.

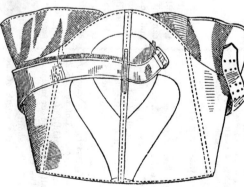

The Contracting Belt (No. 3), among others, is strictly anatomical in its construction. The front is composed of elastic materials, in which are inserted medical plates, thus combining perfect support and elasticity.

1854

PRACTICAL INSTRUCTIONS IN STAY MAKING.

Materials necessary for making a Pair of Stays.—Half a yard of material; a piece of stay-tape for casing; some whalebone, either ready prepared, or in strips to be split and shaved to size; a steel busk; wash-leather sufficient to cover it, and webbing to ease it; a paper of 8-between needles; a reel of 25-cotton; a box of French holes; and a punch for putting them in.

DIRECTIONS FOR TAKING THE MEASURE.

Measure round the waist as tightly as possible, noticing the number of inches; deduct two as an allowance for the clothes. Next take the measure of the bust by placing the measure in the middle of the chest, at No. 1 (see engraving), and pass it over the bosom to No. 8, not tightly, and no allowance here to be made for the clothes.

Then, from No. 8, passing the measure closely under the arm, to No. 1 of the back, which is not to reach the middle of the back by an inch and a half; next place the measure at the bottom of the busk, and pass round stomach and hips, allowing about four inches for clothes, and then take the length of the busk.

It must be remembered that stays ought NOT TO MEET when they are laced on.

It will be found to simplify the directions very much if a form, similar to the following, be first prepared, and the number of inches written against each as the part is measured; and then no confusion can possibly take place in the cutting out:—

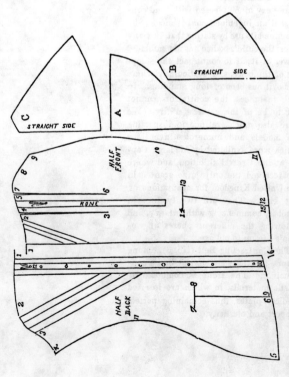

Waist
Bust
Back
Hips
Length of Busk.

DIRECTIONS FOR CUTTING OUT.

A pattern must now be prepared according to the directions given in the engraving, which can easily be done by enlarging the design, and adding the requisite number of inches between each figure.

THE BACK.—Double the material sufficiently wide to take two whalebones, the holes, and to turn-in for felling-down, as marked in the engraving; then lay on the pattern, and cut out the two parts of the back together, allowing, for turnings-in, about half an inch at the seam under the arm.

THE FRONT is cut out by placing the pattern so that the straight way comes in the direction of the little bones up the bosom, leaving a good turning-in up the front seam, which crease off in pattern on the double material, as it is better to cut out every part in the double; that you may have each side exactly alike.

Should you desire to increase the size of the stays, it must ALWAYS be done by allowing the required additional size on the front and back at the seam under the arm, and by proportioning the armhole to the increased size.

When the bosom gores are to be put in, the material is merely cut from No. 2 to No. 3, and from No. 5 to No. 6, in a direct line, *cutting none away*. In cutting places for stomach and hip-gores, in front and back, cut straight up, and then from No. 7 to No. 8 in back, and from No. 13 to No. 14 in front. Then cut out all the gores, as directed in the engraving.

DIRECTIONS FOR MAKING.

1st.—Stitch a place for the first bone at back, and for the holes, the width of half an inch, keeping the line perfectly even, and fell down a place for the second bone on the wrong side.

2d.—Fit the bosom-gores by making a narrow turning-in from No. 2 to No. 3, and from No. 3 to No. 4; fix the gore at 3, the straight side of the gore next the busk, tacking it very closely up to No. 2; then fix the other gore in like manner at No. 6, the straight side next the armhole, tacking up to No. 7.

3d.—With a measure, make the required size across the bust, by increasing or diminishing the gores at the top; tack the other sides very firmly from No. 3 to No. 4, and from No. 6 to No. 5, shaping them prettily, narrow at the bottom, and of a rounded form towards the top; then stitch them very neatly; and, cutting away superfluous stuff on the wrong side, hem down, beginning each side from No. 3 to No. 6.

4th.—Hem a piece of stay-tape at the back, for little bones, and stitch down the middle of it on the right side.

The other half front to be done in a similar manner.

5th.—Put in the stomach-gores, turning in from 14 to 15, and tacking the straight side of the gore under it; and fix the hip-gores in the back in like manner, the straight side to the holes.

6th.—Join the seams under the arm by pinning No. 10 of half-front to No. 11 of half-back, to half the size of waist required, wrapping the front on to the back. Everywhere face each piece to its fellow piece, and crease it, that it may be exactly the same size and shape. Then do the other half in the same way.

7th.—Having closed the seam, finish the stomach and hip-gore by measuring and making to the size required round the hip, by letting out or taking in, rounding them to fit the hip; face and crease the gores for the other half, which is to be finished in the same manner.

8th.—Take a piece of webbing wide enough to case the busk when covered with wash-leather; double it exactly, and tack down the half-front, the double edge being scrupulously down the centre of the stays; fell it on very closely; then stitch the two halves together at the crease down the middle; turn the other half of the webbing on to the unfinished side, and fell it down as before, turning in a little piece top and bottom, and finish.

9th.—Bind the stays very neatly, top and bottom.

10th.—Put in the holes, two near each other at the top of the right side, and two near each other at the bottom of the left side—the rest at equal distances.

Proceed now to the boning, which do by scraping them to fit nicely; then, having covered them with a piece of glazed calico, cut, at the bottom of each bone place, a hole, like a button-hole, and work it round like one; put the bones in, and drill a hole through the stays and the bone, about an inch and a half from the top and bottom of each bone, and fasten them in with silk by bringing the needle through the hole to the right side, and passing it over the top of the bone, as marked at No. 12. Then put in the busk; and, if a hook is required at the bottom, put that in before the busk, which is best done by leaving a short hole in the seam, and passing the hook through, fastening it securely at the back. The busk must be stitched in very firmly, top and bottom.

Should the stays have become soiled in the process of making, they are easily cleaned with bread inside and out, and, when cleaned, must be nicely pressed, taking care to make *no creases* anywhere.

If these simple directions be strictly adhered to in the making up, a pair of well-fitting stays, at a trifling cost, will reward the pains of the worker.

1857

DOUGLAS & SHERWOOD'S CELEBRATED TOURNURE CORSET.

(Front view.)

(*Patented January 4, 1859.*)

DOUGLAS & SHERWOOD'S CELEBRATED TOURNURE CORSET.

(Back view.)

(*Patented January 4, 1859.*)

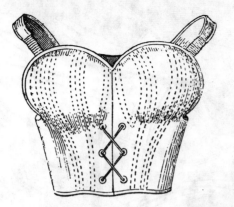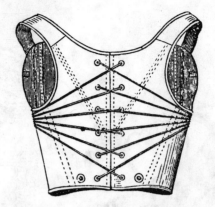

CORSET: BACK AND FRONT.

1861

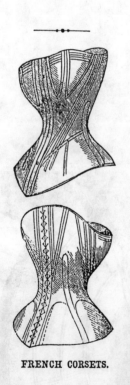

FRENCH CORSETS.

1862

1866

CORSET FOR GIRL FROM 10 TO 12 YEARS OLD.

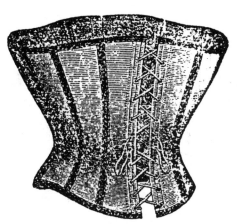

CORSET WITHOUT GORES.—BACK.

WHITE DRILLING CORSET.

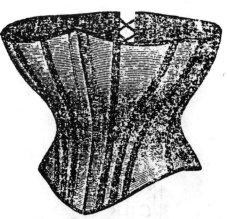

CORSET WITHOUT GORES.—FRONT.

BROWN DRILLING CORSET.

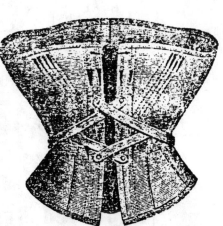

ENGLISH LEATHER CORSET WITH STRAPS.—BACK.

1868

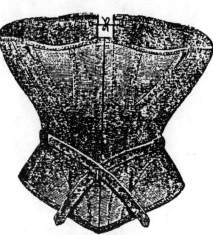

ENGLISH LEATHER CORSET WITH STRAPS.—FRONT.

1866

1869

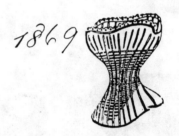

Improved Breast Protectors.

The three illustrations represent the Breast Protectors and Supporters, in the different styles made. Figure 1 is the "Single" style—that is, without a division in the center. Figure 2 is the "double" style, with hinges. Either style is excellent, and make the dress fit smoothly and elegantly, as seen in Figure 3, which gives the shape imparted by these new and convenient accessories to the perfection of a lady's *tournure.*

THIS new invention, patented in 1866 and 1867, has already won its way to the confidence of ladies, and supersedes Spring Pads, and all other Breast Protectors and Supporters, in

Its Natural Shape, its Perfect Adjustment to the Form, Its Lightness, and means of Ventilation.

It is secured by an elastic and clasp around the waist. It can not slip from its position. Ladies who require an improved bust will find this exactly what is needed. No lady who has had a dress fitted with one will do without it. Made in three sizes. Also, the Double Breast Protector, with Elastic hinges. Sold, wholesale and retail, by MME. DEMOREST, No. 838 Broadway, and all furnishing, skirt and corset stores. Price $1.50 each.

1869

1870s

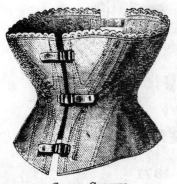

COUTIL CORSETS.

1872

JEAN CORSETS.

1872

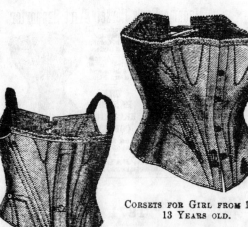

CORSETS FOR GIRL FROM
5 TO 7 YEARS OLD.

CORSETS FOR GIRL FROM 11 TO
13 YEARS OLD.

CORSETS FOR GIRL FROM 14 TO
16 YEARS OLD.

CORSETS FOR
GIRL FROM 4 TO
6 YEARS OLD.

1874

THOMSON'S PATENT
GLOVE-FITTING
CORSETS.

SURPASSES ALL OTHERS FOR COMFORT.

THE BEST YET INTRODUCED.

The Friends of this
Famous Corset are
now numbered by
MILLIONS,
and the immense Sale of
them is astonishing
They give complete
satisfaction
FOR SALE BY ALL
FIRST CLASS DEALERS.
SEE THAT THE NAME OF THOMSON
AND THE TRADE MARK A CROWN.
ARE STAMPED ON EVERY PAIR.

FITS THE FIGURE EXQUISITELY.

1874

NOVELTIES IN LADIES' UNDERWEAR.

As the cold weather approaches, the need of thicker garments makes itself felt. Ladies who are about to replenish their stock of fall and winter underwear, will find it to their advantage to carefully examine the following garments before deciding on what they will purchase. If the goods are not to be found at the stores where such things are usually kept, then let them send a memoranda of their wants to GEORGE FROST & CO., 287 Devonshire St., Boston, and their orders will be promptly filled and sent by mail, postage prepaid, on receipt of price; or, by express, C.O.D. The first garment offered to their consideration is the

EMANCIPATION UNION UNDER FLANNEL.
Patented August 3d, 1875.

Fig. 1.

By reference to the Drawing Fig. 1, it will be seen that the vest and drawers are in one, being knitted together in process of manufacture, forming a continuous garment from the neck to the wrists and ankles, clothing the whole body evenly, and fitting it closely. Particular attention is called to the full bosom form, which adds greatly to the comfort of the wearer. These flannels are manufactured expressly for us from the finest white cashmere and merino, and also in a cheaper grade, and sold at the following prices: Cashmere, full fashioned, per suit, $6.50. Merino, full fashioned, $5.25. Merino, cut and seamed, $4.00.

THE EMANCIPATION WAIST.
Patented August 3d, 1875.

Fig. 2.

This waist is universally acknowledged to be one of the best of the strictly hygienic Dress Reform garments. It is adapted for ladies and children, and when properly fitted to the form takes the weight of the outer clothing from the hips, doing away with skirt-supporters of all kinds, and distributing the strain over the shoulders. By the peculiar cut and fit of the front, the breasts are supported and freed from compression, and also from the "drag" from the shoulders that many complain of who wear other Dress Reform garments. This waist takes the place of the chemise, corset and corset cover, and is so arranged that the bands of the outer skirts do not lay over one another, and, although fitting the form closely, leaves every nerve, vein, and blood-vessel free to act, thus securing the recommendation and endorsement of all our leading physicians.

It is manufactured from fine white cotton cloth, with a lining of the same. As a ready-made garment, we make it with a lacing on the side, both plain and handsomely trimmed, short and long sleeves, at the following prices: Plain, short sleeves, $2.50; long sleeves, $2.75. Trimmed, short sleeves, $3.75; long sleeves, $4.00.

THE DRESS REFORM CORSET WAIST AND SKIRT-SUPPORTER.
Patented April 6th, 1875.

Fig. 3.

In this Waist is furnished an article of dress that meets a long felt want, viz: something of a corset kind for those who can not wear corsets. Not only is this want satisfied, but a garment is also provided that is a compromise between the extreme waist and the ordinary corset, and one that is favorably received by those interested in Dress Reform. It is suitable alike for children, misses, young and elderly ladies. Being constructed without a steel, and almost entirely without bones, and as the skirt attachment is easily removed, the whole garment may be readily washed, thus making it the most economical corset known.

It is a corset and corset cover combined, and by its peculiar construction secures at once to its wearer health, comfort, and freedom of movement, as well as grace and beauty of form.

In sending measurements for flannels, give the chest or under-bust measure. For the other garments, the waist measure over the dress. Remember, if they can not be found at the stores, to send to

GEORGE FROST & CO., 287 Devonshire St., Boston, Mass.

It can be made full or large at pleasure. The skirts are supported at fixed points by an easily adjustable attachment.

It is made from a fine soft-finished jean, and trimmed with a patent everlasting trimming warranted to wash. Ladies', $2.50; Misses', $1.75; Children's, $1.50.

For those who feel a corset is indispensable to their comfort, the best there is made is the

COMBINATION SHOULDER-BRACE CORSET.
Patented October 27th, 1874.

The special merits of which may be summed up as follows:

Fig. 4.

1st.—In this Corset is provided a support or form for the bosom, without the use of bones or wire in the construction of this part to retain its shape.

2d.—The healthful advantages are perhaps more strongly embodied in the office of the Shoulder-Brace. Running, as it does, from the outer side of each bosom form, over the shoulder and crossing in the back, not only is a firmer support given to the bosom, but by the peculiar manner in which it is made, is a brace to the shoulders, expanding the chest, as well as being a support to the whole garment.

3d.—By means of a very simple and easily adjustable attachment of a detachable hook with rings, the skirts are supported at fixed points, bringing the weight thereof directly upon the shoulders.

4th.—In connection with the above, and by the peculiar cut of the different parts, together with the manner in which the bones are distributed, not only is a most perfect-fitting corset obtained, but one that gives to its wearer a symmetrical figure, without interfering in the least with any of the movements of the body or the circulation of the blood.

Made from Satteen and English Jean. In colored and white Satteen, $1.75; English Jean, $2.50.

No ladies wardrobe is complete without a pair of the

WARREN STOCKING SUPPORTERS.

The superiority of stocking supporters over the old-fashioned blood-strangling garters is now a well recognized fact by every intelligent person. Many devices for taking the place of the button and button-hole in fastening the stocking to the straps of the supporter have been put upon the market, but none so simple, neat, and serviceable as

THE WARREN PATENT,

to the merits of which particular attention is called.

By glancing at the figure it will at once be seen there are no sharp teeth to tear the stocking; no intricate complications of springs, slides, and bows to aggravate the wearer by getting out of order; nothing to scratch or irritate the limbs. It is made from a single piece of metal, having a wedge-shaped opening pointing downward, into which is inserted a small fold of the stocking which, by crowding into the narrowest part of the wedge, is held firm and fast. It is the most economical fastening known, there being nothing to wear out, and by the manner of its hold upon the stocking compresses the fibres of the fabric, thereby causing less wear.

For children it is especially adapted, as there is nothing to stick into them in case of a fall, and any child can adjust it as readily as a button to a button-hole.

Ladies with belts, 50c.; side-pads and button-holes, 45c. Children's side-pads and button-holes, 35c.; hooks, 20c.

1874

Fig. 9.—EMBROIDERED CORSET COVER.

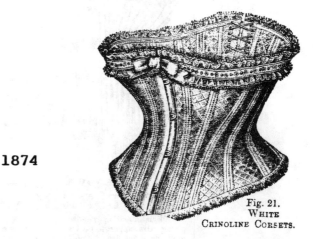

Fig. 21.
WHITE
CRINOLINE CORSETS.

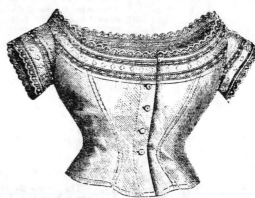

Fig. 8.—MUSLIN CORSET COVER.

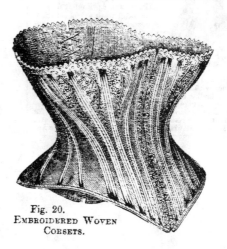

Fig. 20.
EMBROIDERED WOVEN
CORSETS.

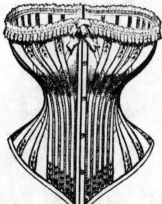

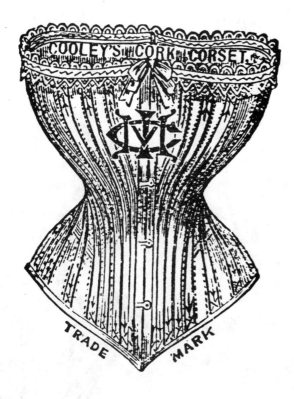

COOLEY'S CORK CORSET.

TRADE MARK

1875

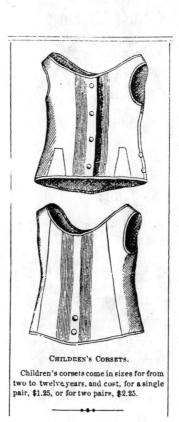

CHILDREN'S CORSETS.

Children's corsets come in sizes for from two to twelve years, and cost, for a single pair, $1.25, or for two pairs, $2.25.

Fig. 1.—Shoulder-Braces with
Corsets for Girl from 13 to
15 Years old.—Back.
[See Fig. 2.]

Shoulder-Braces for Girl from 5 to 7
Years old.

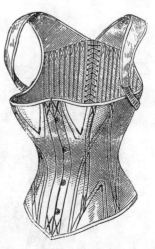

Fig. 2.—Shoulder-Braces with
Corsets for Girl from 13 to
15 Years old.—Front.
[See Fig. 1.]

Jean Corsets.

1877

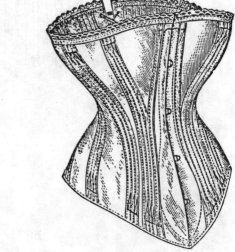

Coutil Corsets.

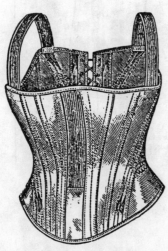

Corsets for Girl from 5 to 7
Years old.

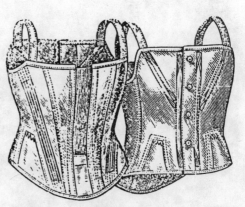

Corsets for Girl from 3 to 5 Years old.—Front
and Back.

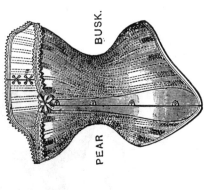
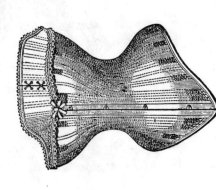

MME. DEMOREST'S "ARTISTIC" CORSETS.

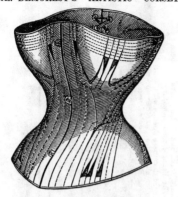

FRONT.

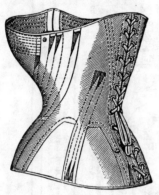

BACK.

1878

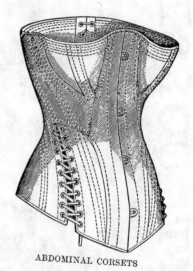

ABDOMINAL CORSETS

1878

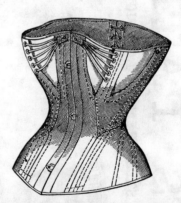

NURSING CORSETS

1878

1879

1880s

Dress Reform Corset Waist.

Patented April 6 and Nov. 16, 1875.

1880 catalog

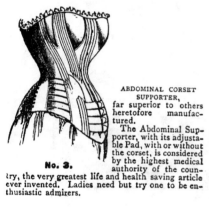

No. 3.

ABDOMINAL CORSET
SUPPORTER,
far superior to others
heretofore manufac-
tured.

The Abdominal Sup-
porter, with its adjusta-
ble Pad, with or without
the corset, is considered
by the highest medical
authority of the coun-
try, the very greatest life and health saving article
ever invented. Ladies need but try one to be en-
thusiastic admirers.

1880

The Comfort Waist.
PRICE, $1.75.

FOR LADIES. FOR LADIES.

1880 catalog

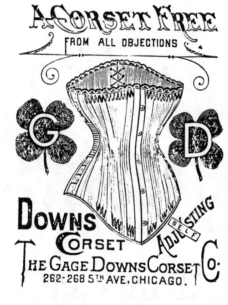

A CORSET FREE
FROM ALL OBJECTIONS

G D

DOWNS
CORSET SELF ADJUSTING CO.
THE GAGE DOWNS CORSET
262-268 5TH AVE, CHICAGO.

early 1880s

Centennial Waist.
FOR MISSES AND CHILDREN
Patented 1876.

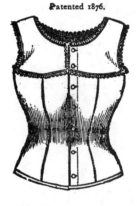

1880 catalog

WILSON'S CORSET WAIST,
For Children.

Unequalled for neatness, simplicity and convenience. This waist is made of two thicknesses of the
best quality of satin jean, strengthened by thirty
rows of cable cord stitched into five groops, as
shown in the illustration. By means of this cording, the right amount of firmness is secured without
bones or stays, and the waist retains its shape until
worn out. This corset waist is adapted to all children two years old and upward. Price, post-paid,
$1.00. The same, with Stocking Supporter, $1.25.

1880

THE "BON TON" CORSET
(REGISTERED).
SIMPLICITY and PERFECTION.

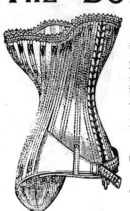

This new Corset supersedes anything yet introduced, and
is especially adapted to the prevailing fashion. By it the
figure can be reduced to symmetrical proportions, without
unsightly overlapping in front, or prejudicial to health.
The principle consists in the side-seams being left open from
the bottom of the corset to nearly the waist, to which are
affixed graduated straps, terminating in a buckle at the
back, by which the corset can be reduced to the size required. The "Bon Ton" Corset is made in all sizes, from
19 in. to 30 in., of the best materials in all colours, modelled
on copper lay figures heated by steam, and is sold at prices
within the reach of all.

To be had of all drapers, outfitters, and wholesale only of
LAMPRELL, ANDREWS, AND EMERSON,
12, CANNON STREET, LONDON, E.C.

Quality No. 1 in White		Quality No. 2 in White	
" " Drab	} 7/6	" " Drab	} 10/
" " Black		" " Scarlet	
		" " Black	

1880

IZOD'S PATENT CORSETS.

PEAR   BUSK

HONI SOIT QUI MAL Y PENSE

DIEU ET MON DROIT

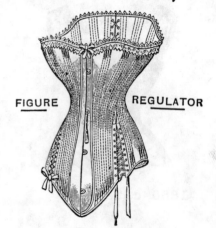

FIGURE   REGULATOR

1880

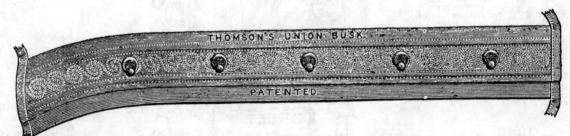

THOMSON'S UNION BUSK.

PATENTED

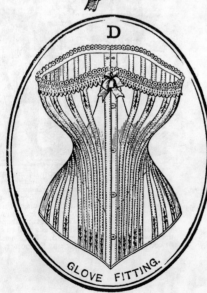

D

GLOVE FITTING.

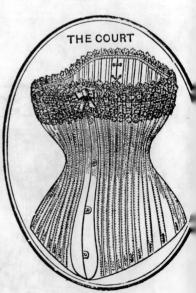

THE COURT

HEALTH CORSETS.

THOMSON'S IMPROVED GLOVE-FITTING,
TRUE-FIT AND CUIRASSE PRIZE MEDAL
STEAM MODELLED CORSETS,

*So well known and highly esteemed throughout the
civilized world, are so perfect in construction, and
so admirably adapted to Nature's model, that they
produce a perfect figure, never get out of shape, and
by their use tight lacing is wholly unnecessary.*

Can be obtained of all the best Drapers and Retailers in town
or country by simply giving waist measurement and stating letter
or name of Corset required. None genuine without the Name
and Trade Mark—a Crown.

1880

THE "DUCHESS" CORSET.
THOMAS'S PATENT.

Is constructed on a graceful model for the present style of dress; the shape being permanently retained by a series of narrow whalebones placed diagonally across the front, gradually curving in and contracting the Corset at the bottom of the busk, whereby the size of the figure is reduced, the outline improved, a permanent support afforded, and a fashionable and elegant appearance secured.

THOMAS'S NEW ENLARGING "DUCHESS."

This highly important invention has been added to the Duchess Corsets, by which married ladies can, from time to time, enlarge them without trouble, This may be repeated on each side three times, graduated from one quarter of an inch at the top to one inch and a quarter at the bottom, increasing the size to the extent of nine inches, the Corset still retaining its graceful shape, giving the wearer the utmost comfort and support ; requiring neither *Buckles, Belts, Elastics, Straps, or Laces*, all of which are useless, give much trouble, and cause a bulky appearance.

The bones being placed sideways, their ends cannot press into the wearer on stooping, sitting, &c.

The Celebrated Patent Taper Busk in these Corsets is the most comfortable of all busks ; *it is perfectly free from pressure at the top*, strong at the bottom, each half is made of two plates of the finest silver steel, and it cannot be broken.

CAUTION.—The universal approval by Ladies of this Corset has caused many worthless imitations. Ladies are requested to see that the Patentee's name, W. THOMAS, is stamped on the Corset.

PATENTEE—W. THOMAS, 128 & 129, CHEAPSIDE, LONDON,
And may be procured through respectable Drapers and Milliners.

1880

Dr. Warner's Nursing Corset.

This corset embodies the well-known excellent features of the Dr. Warner Health Corset, viz. : the Skirt-Supporter and improved Tampico Bust. But in the center of each bust there is an opening, with adjustable cover, which admirably adapts it to the wants of mothers who are nursing. It may be had in white or drab. Price, postage paid, $1.75.

Dr. Warner's Misses Corset
And Skirt-Supporter.

This corset is designed for misses from twelve to fifteen years old. At this age, when the body is rapidly developing, it is especially important that the weight of the clothing should be supported from the shoulders. This is conveniently accomplished by the use of this corset. The skirt-supporter is the same as arranged in the Health Corset. Price, postage paid, $1.00.

1880

FLEXIBLE HIP CORSET.

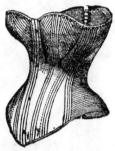

This corset is constructed after the analogy of the human body, the bones over the hips passing, like the ribs, around the body. By this arrangement severe strain across the bones is avoided, so that it is IMPOSSIBLE for the corset to break down over the hips. The point of greatest weakness in other corsets becomes in this the point of greatest strength. At the same time this construction secures a perfect-fitting corset, so comfortable that a lady can lie down in it with ease ; so flexible that it yields readily to every movement of the body, and yet so firm that it gives the requisite support at the sides. No corset ever introduced has in a single season had so large a sale, and met with so great popular favor as the Flexible Hip Corset. Price, post-paid, $1.25.

THE PERFECTION CORSET.

This corset combines the Tampico Bust of Dr. Warner's Health Corset with the sides and back of the Flexible Hip Corset, thus making, as its name implies, the most perfect corset that can be constructed. It is made of the best materials, is highly ornamented. Ladies desiring the very best of everything will be delighted with this corset. Price, postage paid, $1.50.

Dr. Warner's Abdominal Corset,
With Extension Front.

This corset extends about two inches below the bottom of the steel in front, while upon each side of the steel a gore is inserted, made of the best quality of silk elastic. By this arrangement the corset is made to give all the support needed without at the same time so cramping and confusing the movement of the body as to make it uncomfortable. Ladies who cannot wear an abdominal corset with a long, stiff steel, can wear this with ease.

By mail, postage paid, on receipt of $2.00.

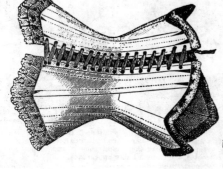

Fig. 2.—Lady's Corset.—Back. [See Fig. 1.]

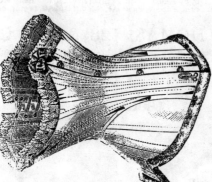

Fig. 1.—Lady's Corset.—Front. [See Fig. 2.]

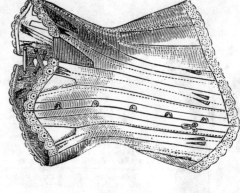

Spoon-bill Corset.

LORD & TAYLOR, NEW YORK.

29 Domestic ; hand-made, well boned, double steel, white and drab, 0.50
30 Domestic; hand-made, double steel, white and drab, 0.75
31 "Little Beauty," waist, 20 to 27 inches, 0.45
32 "Our Own" waist, heavily corded, 3 to 14 years, 0.65

BUSTLES.

Bustles are now universally worn. Parisian ladies wear them of immense size. A short, or long, bustle of moderate size, however, is more worn in this country. Bustles of French cordelette have reeds run in them, so they can be taken out and washed. They come in two lengths, the shorter one twenty-one inches. A few hoops are sold, but they are in reality only large bustles, having an apron front of tapes, the entire fullness being fastened back by elastics.

No. 1.   No. 2.

1 Tampico ; two rows of fluting, upper row extending to front; 12 inches long, 0.75
2 Tampico, two rows of fluting; 8 inches, 0.75; 9 inches, 1.00

No. 3.   No. 4.

3 Tampico ; 9 inches, with one row of fluting, 0.50; 12 inches, with two rows of fluting, 0.70
4 French hair-cloth; 9 inches, with five puffs, 1.00; 12 inches, with seven puffs, 1.35; tampico, 9 inches, 0.50; 12 inches, 0.70

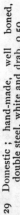

No. 24, 1.75

No. 25, 3.50

25 Moody's abdominal ; French coutil, white and drab, with "Welcome" clasp :
19 to 30 inches, 3.25
31   36   3.50
26 Moody's abdominal ; domestic satteen, white and drab,
19 to 30 inches, 1.65
31   36   1.85

No. 27, 1.25

No. 28, 1.45

27 Coutil, spoon steel, perfect fit, white and drab, 1.25
28 French coutil, "Olivette," medium length, narrow steel, and a perfect fit; extra good 1.45, (real value, 2).

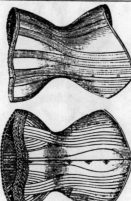

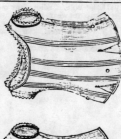

No. 31, 0.45

No. 32, 0.65

19 Boston comfort waist for children, with attachment for stocking and skirt supporter, buttoned at the back, 0.85

Boston comfort waist; each waist is stamped with two numbers, the first is size of waist and the second is the size around the shoulders. In ordering for children please state age, whether slender, etc.

20 Boston comfort waist, white and drab, jean, ordinary lacing at the back, well boned, 0.50; with cords in place of bones, 0.80

No. 20, .95.

No. 21, 1.15

21 Misses' corset, white and drab, jean, ordinary lacing at the back, cords instead of bones, 1.15

No. 23, .85.

22 Children's corset, ordinary clasp, lacing at the back, cords instead of bones, sizes 1 and 2 for children under 16, 0.85 size 3 for misses and ladies, .85

No. 22, .85.

23 Shoulder-braces:

24 Abdomen-supporter; elastic bands, front and back, support in the most comfortable manner; buckles and slides nickel plated; attachment for stocking-supporter, 1.75; improved supporter, 2.50

No. 11, 2.25

No. 12, 3.00

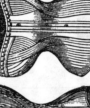

No. 13.

No. 14, 1.00

No. 15.

No. 16, 3.25

15 French woven; short, for evening dress or riding,
    about sixty bones,   1.15
    shorter,   1.75
    six hundred bones,   2.00

16 Bridal; white, with embroidery. 3.25

17 French woven ("Zonare"), nursing, 1.75.

18 Boston comfort waist; a corset for invalids, with shoulder-straps and rows of very stiff cords in place of bones, to give support and still yield readily to the movements of the person, laced at the side, 1.50 1.80

1882

The Boston comfort waist is recommended to invalids. The bones are replaced by heavy cords. The garment laces under the arms, and is supported at the shoulders by straps. These waists are made of jean, and are sold in long and medium lengths. Waists of London cord are used for children from two and a half years, up to fifteen. They are made with shoulder-straps, and without steels or bones, being simply buttoned at the back. A few heavy cords are stitched in to give the garment shape, and straps are furnished at the hips for supporting the stocking suspenders.

Take the following measures over the corset under the dress waist; bust measure, length from under the arm to waist, length from under the arm to bottom of corset, length front and back. Half of an old corset is preferred.

1. Lord & Taylor's "Imperial," made to order; especially suited to stout figures, $10.

2. French coutil ("Bernhardt"), abdominal, with narrow clasps, extra heavy bones, and side steels, 6.00

3. French satteen, well boned, red, black, blue, cream, gray or white, 18 to 30 inches, 2.50

4. French coutil ("Lord & Taylor's Belt"), abdominal, broad side steels, laced, and with deep band of webbing for stout figures, 4.50.

5. French coutil ("The Jersey"), broad steels, 4.00

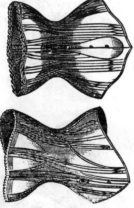

No. 2, 6.00

No. 3, 3.50

No. 6, 5.00

No. 7, 2.35

6. French coutil, according to quality and weight of bones, 1.75 2.50 3.75 4.50 5.

7. French coutil, broad steels, white or gray, 2.35

8. Thompson's glove-fitting, 1.25 1.50 1.75 4.

No. 8, 4.00

No. 9, 2.25

9. French woven, according to quality, 1. 1.35 1.75; embroidered, 2.25.

10. French woven, extra long, narrow steels, 1.50 1.90 2.25

11. French woven, broad steels, for stout figures, 2.00 2.25 2.75

12. French corset of red rep, stitched in black, 3.00

13. "Madeline," jean, white or drab, spoon steel: 18 to 30 inches, 1.25
    31 " 36 " 1.35

14. "Our Own," a good domestic corset, 1.00

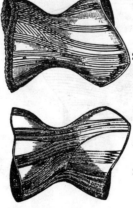

No. 5, 0.40

No. 4, 4.50

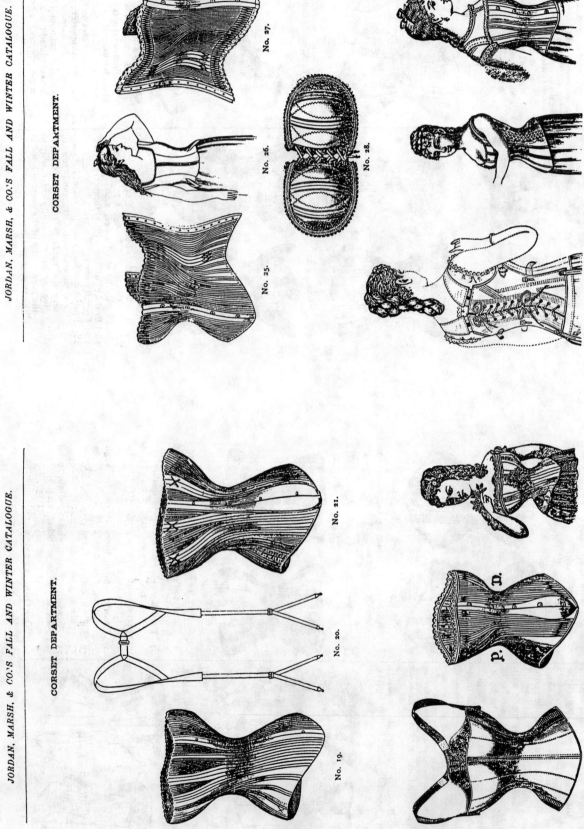

No. 27.

No. 26.

No. 25.

No. 28.

No. 31.

No. 30.

No. 29.

No. 21.

No. 20.

No. 19.

No. 24.

No. 23.

p.

p.

No. 22.

1882

CORSET DEPARTMENT.

No. 12.

No. 11.

No. 10.

FERRIS' PATENT

No. 15.

No. 14.

MADAM FOY'S
PATENT
SKIRT SUPPORTING
CORSETS

No. 13.

No. 16.

No. 18.

No. 17.

CORSET DEPARTMENT.

No. 3.

No. 2.

No. 1.

No. 6.

No. 5.

No. 4.

No. 9.

No. 8.

No. 7.

P.

D.

1882

1882

CORSET COVERS.

1885

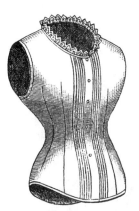

No. 651. Hamburg edging and tucks, 45c.

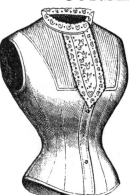

No. 653. Hamburg inserting and edging, 75c.

No. 655. Hamburg inserting and edging, 98c.

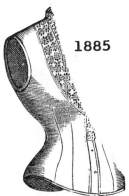

No. 657. Hamburg embroidery and edging, 95c.

No. 659. Real Torchon lace and Nainsook inserting, $1.25.

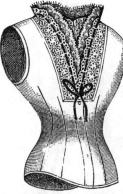

No. 661. Hamburg and Valenciennes lace edging, $1.75.

No. 663. Real Torchon lace and feather stitching, $1.48.

No. 665. Hamburg inserting and edging, 83c.

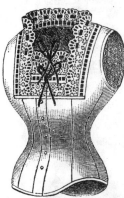

No. 667. Hamburg inserting, edging and ribbon, $1.63.

No. 669. Real Medici lace, 95c.

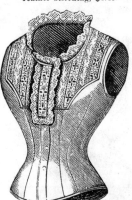

No. 671. Valenciennes lace an Nainsook inserting, $1.35.

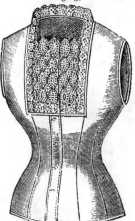

No. 673. Hamburg edging, 95c.

No. 675. Jersey cloth, in white, pink and blue, $1.25.

No. 677. Hamburg inserting and edging, $1.15.

No. 679. Real Florentine lace and ribbon, $1.98.

o. 681. Real Medici lace, $2.50.

CORSET COVERS.

1885

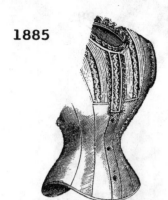

No. 683.   Real Torchon lace, $1.35.

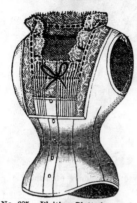

No. 685.   Plaiting, Platte lace and ribbon, $1.85; in low neck, $2.35.

No. 687.   Real Torchon lace, Nainsook inserting, $1.73.

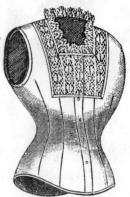

No. 689.   Real Medici lace, $1.35.

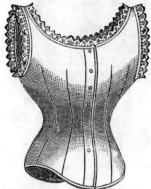

No. 691.   Hamburg edging, 54c.

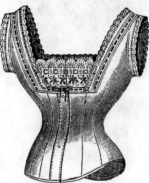

No. 693.   Hamburg edging and ribbon, $1.75.

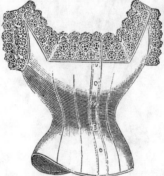

No. 695.   Hamburg edging, $1.15.

No. 697.   Hamburg inserting and edging, 98c.

No. 699.   Platte lace inserting, edging and ribbon, $1.85.

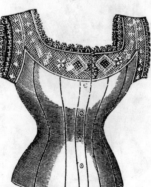

No. 701.   Real Torchon lace yoke, 98c.

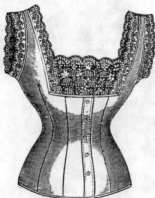

No. 703.   Hamburg edging, $1.65.

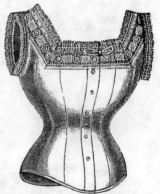

No. 705.   Real Medici lace and ribbon, $1.48.

No. 707.   Real Torchon lace inserting and edging, $2.45.
No. 709.   In Valenciennes Lace, $1.95.

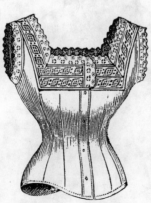

No. 711.   Hamburg inserting and edging, $1.35.

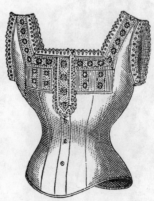

No. 713.   Hamburg inserting and edging, $1.85.

No. 715.   Real Medici lace and ribbon, $2.63.

1885

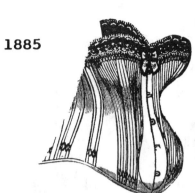

The Linda C. P. Fine French Coutille, 16 inches long, heavily boned; double side steels, $4.95.

The Cordelia C. P. Coutille, thoroughly boned, broad band of webbing to encircle the hips, broad clasps and side steels, low bust; specially adapted for stout ladies. $2.75.

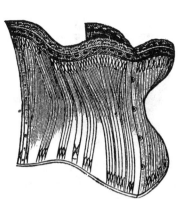

The Vicountess C. P. French Sateen, thoroughly boned, side steels; each bone stitched with silk, in white, pink, blue and black, $2.85.

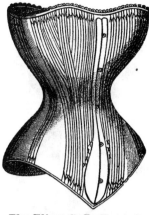

The Elisee C. P. French Coutille, very heavily boned, with side steels, extra length, low bust, superior finish; same style in grey, stitched with colors, $2.45.

Dr. Warner's "Health," $1.15.

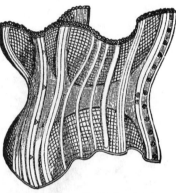

The Thomson Ventilating, $1.00.

The Wanda P. D. Ventilating; made of double net, $2.25.

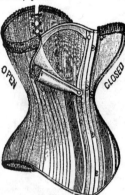

The Comfort Nursing, $1.25.

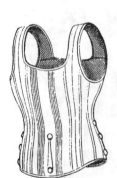

The Pet. Misses' Waist, 20 to 26 in., 32c.

The Pearl. Misses' Corset; steel in front; in white and colored, 45c.

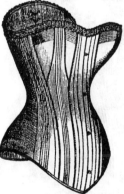

Dr. Warner's Coraline, 90c.

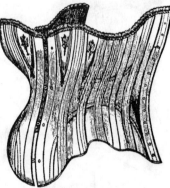

The Thomson Glove Fitting R. H., $1.00.

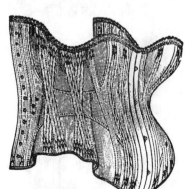

The Thomson Glove Fitting, F, $1.75.

Volanthe Ladies' Waist, $1.50.

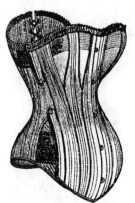

The Abdominal, $1.50.

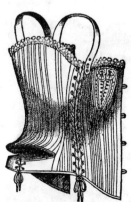

Madame Foy's Improved Corset Skirt Supporter, 96c.

French Hand Made Satin Corsets, in all colors, $4.25, 5.00, 6.35 to 25.00.

We direct attention to the fact that we are **the largest importers** of the **celebrated C. P. and P. D. makes of French hand made Corsets.** Styles illustrated are exclusively our own, and shapes will be found far superior to any other Corset imported.

1885

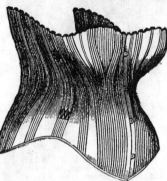
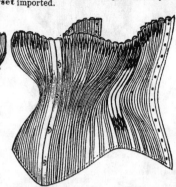
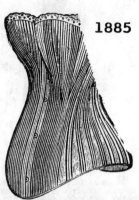

The Broadway, French Woven, in white and drab, 63c.

The Nettie, French Woven, double hip bones, stitched with silk, 91c.

The Nora, French Woven, double bones over hips, each bone stitched with silk, $1.39.

The Newport, French Woven, 100 bones, scalloped top, in drab and white, $1.00.

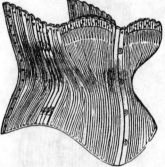
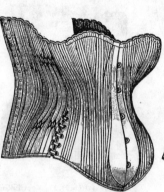
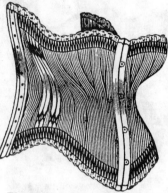
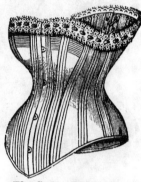

The Anna, French Woven, 11½ inches long, double side bones, each bone silk stitched, $1.25.

The Graphic, French Woven, extra long, laced on hips, $1.50.

The Boulevard, 500 bones, top and bottom, silk stitched, $1.69.

The Sadie P. D. French Sateen, heavily boned, corded bust, side steels, in pink, blue, black and white, $1.91.

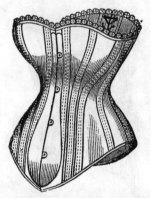

The Rival C. P. French Coutille, low bust, 12 inches long, $1.45.

The Lucille P. D. French Coutille, 13 inches long, heavily boned side steels, in white and drab, $1.35.

The Zephyr Ventilating, $1.25

The Lurline P. D. French Sateen, 13 inches long silk stitched, with side steels, $2.25.

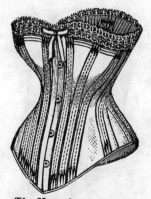
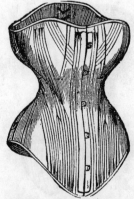

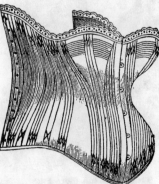

The Mercedes C. P. French Sateen, 13 inches long, boned bust, silk stitched, with side steels, in white, pink, black and blue, $2.45.

The Superior C. P. French Coutille, 14 inches long, very heavily boned, extra long waist, $2.50.

The Marie C. P. fine French Sateen, heavily boned, double side steels, bust richly embroidered, and trimmed with Valenciennes lace, Bridal Corset, $3.50.

Exhibition C. P. Coutille, extra long, double side steels, extra heavily boned, stitched top and bottom with silk, corded bust, $3.00.

CORSET DEPARTMENT.

1. Very good jean corset, white or drab, 18 to 30 inches,..........50c

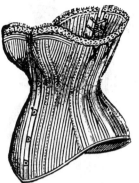

2. Extra heavy, double front steels, white or drab, 18 to 30 inches,..$1.00
3. 31 to 36 inches,..............1.25

4. American Coutille, hook clasp, linen band inside, 14 three-bone strips outside, boned bosom, edged with everlasting trimming, white drab, 18 to 30 inches,..........$1.00

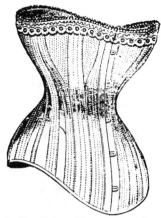

5. Heavily boned jean corset, perfect fitting, white or drab, 18 to 30 inches,..........................68c

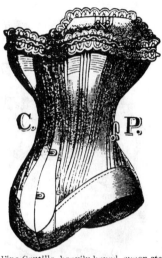

6. Fine Coutille, heavily boned, spoon steels, broad webbing band around bottom, suitable for stout ladies, white or drab, 20 to 36 inches,...............................$3.75

7. Mme. Clark's Hygeian Corset, double steels, elastic gores, white and drab, 18 to 30 inches, ...$1.25

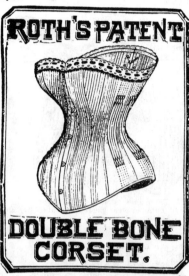

ROTH'S PATENT DOUBLE BONE CORSET.

8. Roth's Patent Double Bone Corset, whit or drab, 18 to 30 inches,...............$1.2

9. Nursing Corset made of jean and heavily boned, white or drab, 18 30 inches,...... ....$1.00

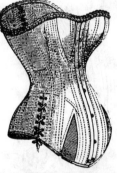

10. Thomson's Abdominable Corset, with elastic gores and side lacing, white or drab, 18 to 30 inches, $1.25. 10 A, 31 to 36, $1.68

11. Fine French Coutille, perfect fitting, boned bust and spoon steels, white or drab....... .$2.25

12. American Sateen Corset, with embroidered clasp and silk ribbon, colors white, drab, pink, blue, cardinal, black and old gold, 18 to 30 inches, ...$1.00

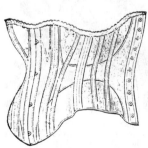

13. Thomson's "R. H." Corset, extra short, in white or drab, 18 to 30 inches, ...$1.00

14. Misses' Hand-made Corset, well boned, white or drab......................63c.

15. Ball's Health Preserving Corset, with wire elastic section, need no "breaking in," guaranteed perfectly satisfactory in every respect, or money refunded after three week's wear, white or drab, 18 to 30 inches...................$1 25

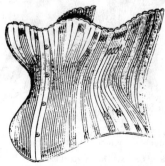

16. Short French woven corset, 11 inches long, 4 broad bones on each side.........................$1 35

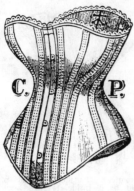

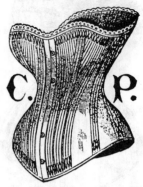

17. "P. D." French Coutille, side steels, white or drab, 18 to 30 inches.................$1.50

18. "C. P." French Coutille, with side steels, white or drab, 18 to 30 inches.................$1.50

19. Fine Sateen, trimmed with lace, in black, white, blue, pink cream and red, 18 to 30 inches......$2.25

20. French Coutille, perfect fitting, boned bust, white or drab, 18 to 30 inches................$2.45

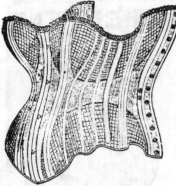

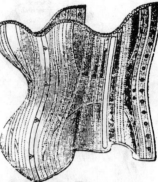

21. Thomson's Ventilating Corset for summer wear, perfect in shape. 98c

22. Fine Satin Bridal Corset, white, gold, black, cream, pink, blue and cardinal, 18 to 30 inches ... $3.25

23. R. & G. French Sateen Corset, trimmed with Russia lace and silk ribbon, white, drab, pink, blue, cardinal, cream, black and old gold, 18 to 30 inches..........$1.58

24. Thomson's Glove Fitting Corset, quality G, fine coutille, 18 to 32 inches, white or drab.......$1.25
2. 33 to 36 inches $1.50

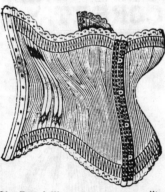

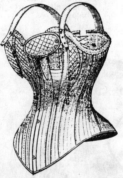

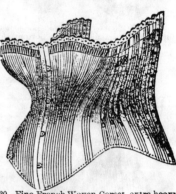

26. French Woven Corset, extra quality, fine bone, scalloped top and bottom, each bone fanned with silk, white or drab, 18 to 30 inches............$2.00

27. Misses' Fine French Woven Corset........73c
28. Better quality....$1.00

29. Dr. Warner's Nursing Corset...............$1.35

30. Fine French Woven Corset, extra heavy boned on each side, white or drab, 18 to 30 inches........................$1.25
31. Same style, better quality........$1.63

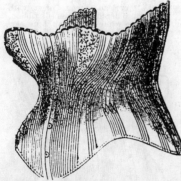

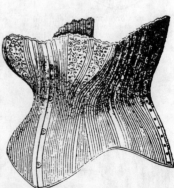

32. French woven corset, embroidered bust, double side bones, white or drab, 18 to 30. $1 00
32a. Same style, extra short........$1 00

33. Dr. Warner's Health Corset.....$1.25

34. Dr. Warner's Coraline Corset made throughout of superior material, and is warranted in every respect; side steels can be removed without injury to the corset in case they are not desired........$1.00

35. French Woven, with side steels, 18 to 30 inches, white or drab..............75c

Dr. WARNER'S UNBREAKABLE CORALINE CORSETS.

Over THREE MILLION Pairs already Sold. To be had of Drapers and Ladies' Outfitters.

Coraline cannot break, but will outlast the Corset. It is more pliable than whalebone, and adapts itself readily to the movements of the body. A new pair will be given in any case where the Coraline breaks with six months' ordinary wear. ☞ See each pair is stamped "Dr. Warner."

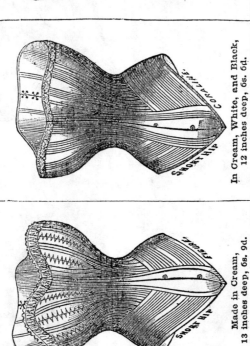

QUALITY M. CORALINE.

THIS Shape is designed for short flat figures, being made with beautifully rounded bosoms It gives all the natural curves and fulness of a well-proportioned bust.

Ladies with high Hips will find this Shape most comfortable because the stiff hip sections are cut away, and there is no possibility of Hip Bones breaking, a difficulty ladies have long had to contend against.

Made in Cream,
13 inches deep, 6s. 9d.

QUALITY D. CORALINE.

THIS Shape is for ladies with high hips, the rigid hip sections are cut away, relieving the wearer of the pressure caused by other styles of Corsets, making them most comfortable for ladies of fine contour or delicate constitution. The sides are flexible and well stayed, permitting tighter lacing without debilitating effects, and at the same time prevent wrinkling at the sides.

In Cream, White, and Black,
12 inches deep, 6s. 6d.

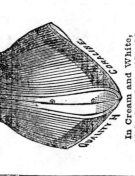

QUALITY H. CORALINE.

A durable and handsome Corset elegantly proportioned for medium figures, recommended with every confidence as being the best in the trade.

Great support is gained by wearing them, and they fit so well that the utmost grace of figure is obtained. They keep their shape better than other Corsets, as they are boned throughout with unbreakable Coraline.

In Cream and White,
13 inches deep, 12s. 6d.

QUALITY B. CORALINE.

THIS Corset is suitable for stout figures. The bones passing like the ribs around the body secure a perfect-fitting Corset, so comfortable that a lady can lie down with ease, so flexible that it yields readily to every movement, and yet so firm that it gives great support at the sides.

In White & Drab, 5s. 6d.,
Black, 6s. 6d. 12 inches deep.

THESE CORSETS are BONED with UNBREAKABLE CORALINE, WHICH is SUPERIOR to HORN or WHALEBONE.

1887

BALL'S

HEALTH PRESERVING

COILED WIRE SPRING
ELASTIC SECTION

CORSETS

BONED WITH KABO.

We confidently recommend Ball's Corsets to our customers for the following reasons:

They are boned with a material *which will not break, nor roll up at the hips.*

They afford perfect support *without injurious compression,* and are recommended by every physician who has examined them. *They need no "breaking in,"* fitting perfectly the first day they are worn, and yield to every movement of the wearer.

Every pair sold with the following

GUARANTEE ! *If not perfectly satisfactory in every respect, AFTER THREE WEEKS' TRIAL, the money paid for them will be refunded, even if so soiled as to be unsalable.*

1887

EQUIPOISE WAIST

For Ladies Misses, Children and Infants.

THIS WAIST is a perfect substitute for corsets and may be worn either with or without the bones which, owing to the construction of the bone pockets, may be removed at pleasure.

THE CUT represents the Waist as made for Ladies and Misses, boned and with full bust; the construction of inside of bust, under fulled piece, is that of a corset front, so that a corset and a perfect bust support is provided within a waist. In the Open Back Soft Waists, as made for Children and Infants, particular attention to the physical proportions and requirements of the growing little ones has been given in shaping the parts, and from the large variety of sizes, all ages can be perfectly fitted from stock.

PATENTED.

PRICES.

Style 600, Ladies' Whole Back, without Bones,	$1.75
" 601, " " " Boned Front only.	2.00
" 603, " Laced Back, Boned front & back,	2.25
" 610, Misses' Whole Back, without Bones	1.40
" 611, " " " Boned . . .	1.75
" 621, Children's—without Bones,	.75
" 631, Infants'	.75

DIRECTIONS FOR MEASURING.

For Ladies' and Misses, take a snug measure around waist over dress, and give it to us in inches.

For Children and Infants, take chest measure also, and state age of child.

We shall take pleasure in sending circulars to all who desire to learn more about this meritorious garment.

Waists sent by mail to any part of the U. S., postage prepaid, on receipt of price, and if not satisfactory, we will exchange or refund the money, if returned in good order. Mention LADIES' HOME JOURNAL.

☞ One good Agent wanted for every City and Town in the United States. Address:

GEORGE FROST & CO.,
279 Devonshire Street, BOSTON, MASS

1888

BEAUTIFUL WOMEN

In the United States, Canada and England wear

"GOOD SENSE"

CORSET WAISTS.

THOUSANDS NOW IN USE.
BEST FOR HEALTH,
Economy and Beauty.
Buttons at front instead of Clasps.

☞ Be sure your Corset is stamped "Good Sense."

SOLD BY
LEADING RETAILERS

everywhere. Send for Circular.

FERRIS BROS., Manufacturers
341 Broadway, NEW YORK.

1887

Fig. 156. — Corset de grossesse, modèle Barreiros.

1888

---

5 CLAIMS

FOR

MADAME FOY'S

Skirt Supporting

CORSET

Sold by Leading Dealers.

1. Skirt Supporter.
2. Health.
3. Comfort.
4. Perfect Fit.
5. Modern Shape.

BY MAIL $1.30.

Foy, Harmon & Chadwick,

NEW HAVEN, CT.

LATEST FORM

1888

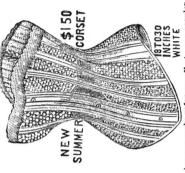
1888

The following illustrations are only a few of the many styles which we keep in stock of P. D.—Thoms
C. P.—Warner's—Z. Z. and French Woven Corsets. Other styles can be furnished on application.

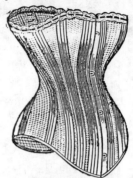

Sizes 18 to 30 inches.
No. 700. C. P. French Coutille, corded bust, 13 inches long, white or drab, $1.80.

Sizes 18 to 26 inches.
No. 701. P. D. French Sateen, double side steels, 13 inches long, white, $2.10.

Sizes 18 to 30 inches.
No. 702. Ventilating Corset, 95 cents.

Sizes 18 to 26 inches.
No. 703. "Z.Z." French Co corded bust, white on inches long, high bust.

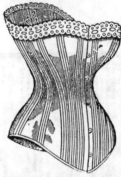
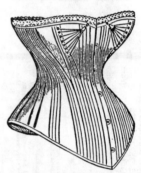

Sizes 18 to 25 inches.
No. 704. Z. Z. French Coutille, strapped with sateen, real whalebone, 14½ inches long, white, blue, ecru and gray, three side steels, $1.58.

Sizes 18 to 26 inches.
No. 705. P.D. French Coutille, 13 inches long, 5 hooks, double side steels, white and drab, $1.45; same shape in linen, $1.75; same shape in ventilating, $1.50 and 2.25.

Sizes 21 to 26 inches.
No. 706. C.P. "Nursing" French Coutille, $1.85.

Sizes 18 to 30 inches.
No. 707. P. D. French Co white and drab, extra three side steels, $2.50.

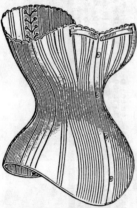
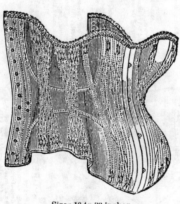
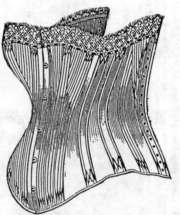
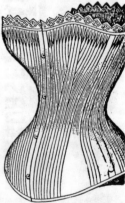

Sizes 20 to 26 inches.
No. 708. "Improved Nursing." French woven, heavily boned, $1.37.

Sizes 18 to 32 inches.
No. 709. Thomson's Glove Fitting F., $1.75; G., $1.25; Ventilating, $1.00. Sizes 34 and 36, 25c. extra.

Sizes 18 to 25 inches.
No. 710. Z. Z. French Coutille, 15 inches long, double side steels, extra high bust and long waist, $2.65.

Sizes 18 to 26 inches.
No. 711. C. P. French Satee inches long, boned bust, Same shape in linen, $2.25 tilating, $2.25.

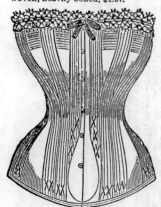
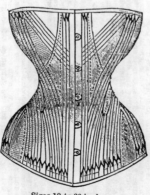
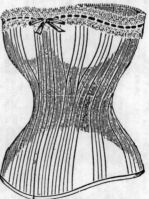
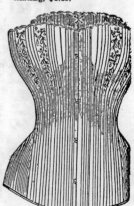

Sizes 18 to 34 inches.
No. 712. C. P. French Coutille, broad clasp, extra length, corded bust, white or drab, $2.35.

Sizes 19 to 30 inches.
No. 713. C. P. Superior French Coutille, 15 in. long, extra long waisted and heavily boned; sizes 22 to 25 have two side steels; 26 to 30 have three side steels, $3.00.

Sizes 18 to 30 inches.
No. 714. C. P. French Coutille, in white and drab, 13 inches long, side steels, $1.35.

Sizes 18 to 26 inches.
No. 715. Broadway "French Wo embroidered bust, scalloped 60c.

THE "FASSO" CORSET.

THESE Corsets, manufactured in France, and of which we are in constant receipt of large importations, _ARE SUPERIOR_ to any other Corset. They are well known throughout the principal cities of Europe (hand-sewn and made in the very best manner), are unequaled as to perfection of form, and guaranteed to be made of the best whalebone.

NONE GENUINE UNLESS STAMPED

THE "FASSO," AND

a L'ETOILE
S ✪ D
PARIS
DEPOSÉ   DEPOSÉ
TRADE-MARK.

200 bis. Sizes 18 to 24.

Ecru coutille, extra long waist, with perfectly sloping back, very heavily boned, stitched blue and cardinal, trimmed with plush to match stitching, 14¼ inches long, $8.50.

201 bis. White coutille, extra high bust, same shape as 200 bis, extra high back, which prevents the superfluous flesh from showing in the backs of dresses; very heavily boned, $9.50.

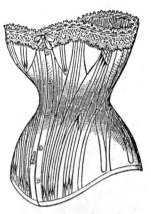

700.—Sizes, 22 to 30.

Extra fine coutille; 14 inches long; 5 hooks, 3 side-steels. Sizes 27 to 30 are heavily boned and 1 inch longer. For stout figures, $12.00.

750.—Similar in shape to 700, sloping more at waist and extra heavily boned. Sizes, 22 to 30, $12.00.

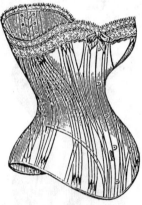

55.—Sizes 18 to 26.

14 inches long, high bust, long tapering waist, short over hips, for slender or medium figure; white and gray coutille, $6.25

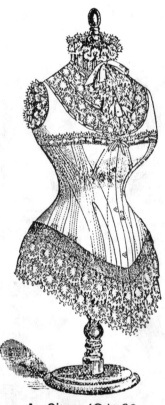

A.—Sizes, 18 to 30.

Black wool, 13½ in. long, high bust, long waist, for slender or medium figure; trimmed with plush to match stitching, $6.90.

C.—White coutille, 12 in. long, for all figures desiring a short corset. Sizes, 18 to 24, $4.50.

C.—Same as Style C, coutille, in linen and ventilating, $6.50.

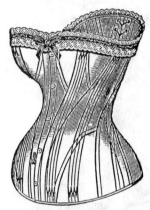

A.A.—Sizes, 18 to 30.

14 inches long, high bust, long waist, extra long over hips; for stout figure; double side-steels; white coutille, $6.90

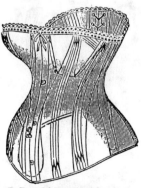

B.P.—Sizes, 22 to 30.

13 in. long, low bust, for short, stout figure; spoon steels, white and gray, $6.00. Sizes from 31 to 36 in., $6.90.

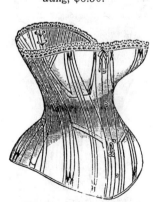

B.—Sizes, 22 to 30.

13 inches long, for short, stout figure. White and gray coutille, $4.00.

A.B.—Sizes, 18 to 26.

13 inches long, low bust, for medium stout figure; white and gray coutille, $5.00.

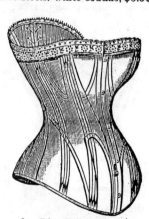

A.—Sizes, 18 to 26.

13¼ inches long, high bust, long waist, for slender or medium figure, white and gray coutille, $5.00.

A.—Same Style in linen, $7.50.

Front Steels to fit "Fasso" Corsets, 16c.; Spoon Shape, 35c. Side Steels, 14c. per pair. In ordering please state style Corset.

MISSES' AND CHILDREN'S CORSETS AND CORDED WAISTS.

We wish to call attention to our stock of Misses' Waists and Corsets, which is the largest in the city. We have numerous styles and can fit all ages. Only a few are illustrated, others can be furnished on application.

Sizes 22 to 26 inches.
No. 716. Corded Waist for girls from 3 to 10 years, 30c.

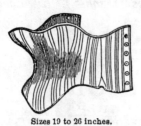

Sizes 19 to 26 inches.
No. 717. Sateen Corset, no opening in front, real whalebone, 10½ inches long, for tennis, riding, boating and all out-door sports, $1.25.

Sizes 20 to 26.
No. 718. Sateen Corset, buttoned front, shoulder straps, no bones or steels, corset does not extend below waist. Can be used as a breakfast corset, bust supporter, also for bathing, 95c.

Sizes 20 to 26 inches.
No. 719. "Baby" Waist, superfine material, soft and pliable, patented attached buttons that cannot fall off. For boys or girls. Ages, 1 to 4 years, 60c.; same shape, only longer, 4 to 8 years, 65c.

Sizes 18 to 25 inches.
No. 720. "Perfect-fitting" Corded Corset for Misses' first corset, steels in front, 45c.

Sizes 20 to 26 inches.
No. 721. Misses' Woven Corset, 11½ inches long, heavy bones on hips, 85c.

Sizes 18 to 25 inches.
No. 722. Improved Thomson's R. H. for Misses; 12 inches long, side steels, $1.00.

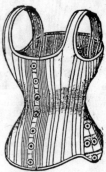

Sizes 22 to 26 inches.
No. 723. Misses' Waist, from 6 to 12 years, fine sateen, corded, in two styles, button front and back, 75c.; same style button front from 12 to 16 years, 85c.

Sizes 18 to 26 inches.
No. 724. "Warner's Health," $1.25.

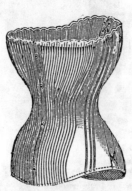

Sizes 18 to 24 inches.
No. 725. "Laurel," 12 inches long, $1.25.

Sizes 18 to 26 inches.
No. 72 "Common Sense," French Woven, 13 inches long, double hip bones, £38.
Same ste, 10½ inches long, $1.15.

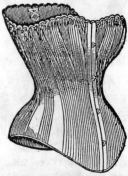

Sizes 18 to 30 inches.
No. 727. "Norma," French Woven, 13 inches long, double side bones, 95c.
"Unique," 10½ inches long, 92c.

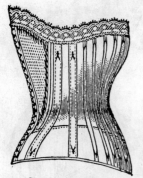

Sizes 18 to 26 inches.
No. 728. C. P. French Sateen, white, 13 inches long, double side steels, $2.75.

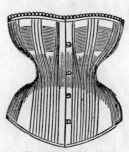

Sizes 18 to 26 inches.
No. 729. C. P. French Coutille, 11½ inches long, corded bust, $1.75; same style in sateen, $1.85.

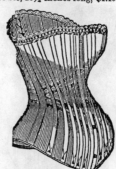

Sizes 18 to 24 inches.
No. 7. R. & G. French Sateen, extra high bt and long waist, 14½ inches long, wte only, $1.95.

Sizes 20 to 30 inches.
No. 731. Ladies' Corded Waist, button front, superfine material, pearl buttons, $1.50.

We cannot guarantee to furnish Linen, Ventilating, Tennis or Bathing Corsets after July 1st. If ordering after that date, please make another selection.

The following illustrations are only a few of the many styles which we keep in stock of P. D.—Thomps. C. P.—Warner's—Z. Z. and French Woven Corsets. Other styles can be furnished on application.

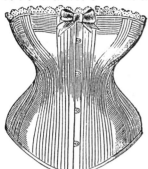

Sizes 18 to 30 inches.
No. 700. C. P. French Coutille, corded bust, 13 inches long, white or drab, $1.80.

Sizes 18 to 26 inches.
No. 701. P. D. French Sateen, double side steels, 13 inches long, white, $2.10.

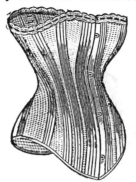

Sizes 18 to 30 inches.
No. 702. Ventilating Corset, 95 cents.

Sizes 18 to 26 inches.
No. 703. "Z.Z." French Cout corded bust, white only; inches long, high bust, $1

Sizes 18 to 25 inches.
No. 704. Z. Z. French Coutille, strapped with sateen, real whalebone, 14½ inches long, white, blue, ecru and gray, three side steels, $1.58.

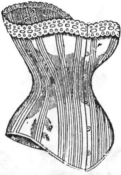

Sizes 18 to 26 inches.
No. 705. P.D. French Coutille, 13 inches long, 5 hooks, double side steels, white and drab, $1.45; *same shape in linen, $1.75; same shape in ventilating, $1.50 and 2.25.*

Sizes 21 to 26 inches.
No. 706. C.P. "Nursing" French Coutille, $1.85.

Sizes 18 to 30 inches.
No. 707. P. D. French Coutille, white and drab, extra long, three side steels, $2.50.

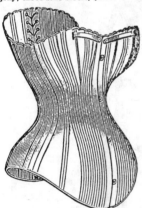

Sizes 20 to 26 inches.
No. 708. "Improved Nursing," French woven, heavily boned, $1.37.

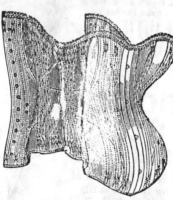

Size 18 to 32 inches.
No. 709. Tomson's Glove Fitting F., $1.75; G., $1.25; Ventilating, $1.00. Si 34 and 36, 25c. extra.

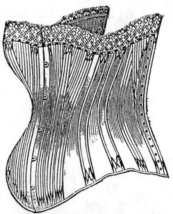

Sizes 18 to 25 inches.
No. 710. Z. Z. French Coutille, 15 inches long, double side steels, extra high bust and long waist, $2.65.

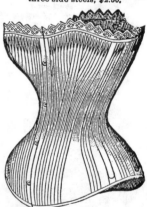

Sizes 18 to 26 inches.
No. 711. C. P. French Sateen, 13 inches long, boned bust, $2.25. Same shape in linen, $2.25.; Ventilating, $2.25.

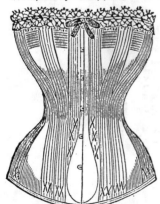

Sizes 18 to 34 inches.
No. 712. C. P. French Coutille, broad clasp, extra length, corded bust, white or drab, $2.35.

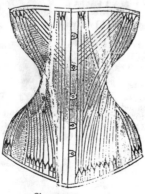

Sizes 18 to 30 inches.
No. 713. C. P. Superior French Coutille, 15 in. long, extra long corded and heavily boned, sizes 22 to 30 have two side steels; 26-30 have three side steels, $3.00.

Sizes 18 to 30 inches.
No. 714. C. P. French Coutille, in white and drab, 13 inches long, side steels, $1.35.

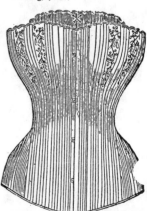

Sizes 18 to 26 inches.
No. 715. Broadway "French Woven," embroidered bust, scalloped top 60c.

Sizes 20 to 26.

No. 718. Sateen Corset, buttoned front, shoulder straps, no bones or steels, corset does not extend below waist. Can be used as a breakfast corset, bust supporter, also for bathing, 95c.

1889

1890s

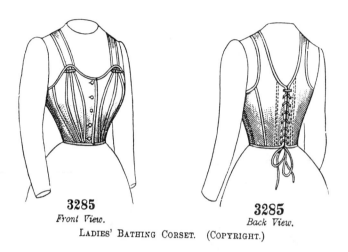

3285
Front View.

3285
Back View.

LADIES' BATHING CORSET. (COPYRIGHT.)

1890

SENSIBLE MOTHERS WEAR **GOOD SENSE** Buttons front instead of clasps.

A PERFECT HEALTH CORSET SUPERIOR to all OTHERS

BEAUTIFUL CHILDREN WEAR **GOOD SENSE** Tape-fastened Buttons. Ring Buckle at hip for hose sup't.

ALL SHAPES Full or Slim **Bust.** Long or short **Waist.** LADIES, MISSES, CHILDREN. *MARSHALL FIELD & CO.* CHICAGO. Wholesale Western Agents.

FERRIS' Good SENSE CORSET WAIST

FOR SALE By all Leading Retailers. Mailed free on receipt of price by manufacturers. **FERRIS BROS.** 341 Broadway, NEW YORK. Send for illustrated circular.

ca 1890

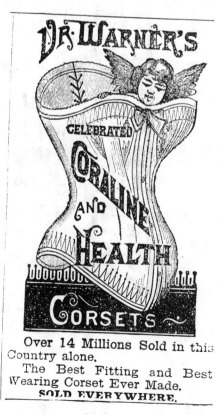

Over 14 Millions Sold in this Country alone.
The Best Fitting and Best Wearing Corset Ever Made.
SOLD EVERYWHERE.

1890

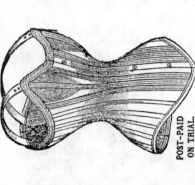
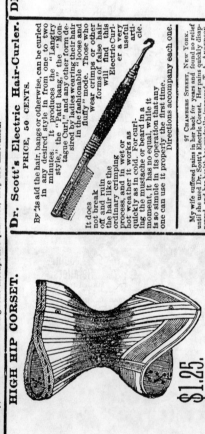

ca 1890

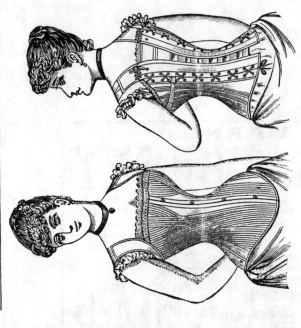

SAINT LOUIS, MISSOURI.

STYLE A.

LONG HIP AND BONED BUST.

ORDINARY SIZES, 18 TO 30.

Drab or White, A ....per pair,	$2	00
Cardinal, Blue, Pink, Old Gold, Black, "	2	50
Drab or White, Nursing .... "	2	50
Other Colors, Nursing .... "	3	00

5 and 9-inch Waists, 50 cents extra.

Extra sizes, 31 to 36, 25 cents.
" 37 up, 50 "

WITH AND WITHOUT STRAPS, SAME PRICE,

None genuine without the trade mark "Comet."

Comet
TRADE MARK

SKIRT SUPPORTERS.

The "Patti" Dress Supporter.

Price, ... **25 Cents.**

THE "PATTI" SKIRT SUPPORTER is attached to the Corset by Nickel Plated Hooks, which fasten firmly in the eyelets. No more convenient Skirt Supporter made.

The "Nilsson" Dress Supporter.

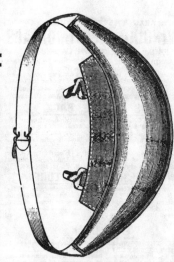

Price, ... **35 Cents.**

THE "NILSSON" has in addition to the Hooks, a Belt that is fastened in front with a Nickel Plated Buckle. The sizes of waists are: 22, 24, 26, 28, 30, 32, 34 and 36-inch.

ca 1890

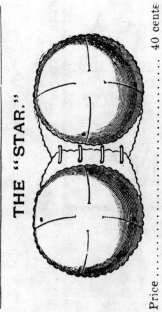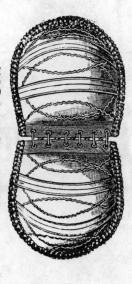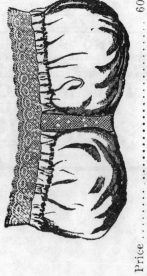

WILLIAMSON CORSET AND BRACE CO.

DRESS FORM BUSTS.

THE "STAR."

Price .... 40 cents

THE "BON-TON."

Price .... 50 cents

THE "DUCHESS."

Price .... 60 cents

WILLIAMSON CORSET AND BRACE CO.

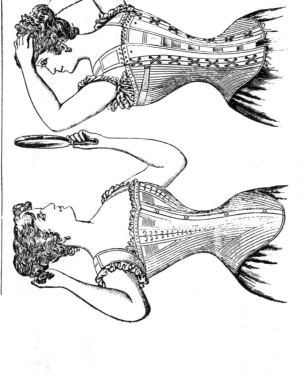

STYLE S. T.

Cutaway Over Hip, Embroidered Bust.

ORDINARY SIZES, 18 TO 30.

Drab or White. S. T. ....per pair, $2 00
Cardinal, Blue. Pink, Old Gold, Black, " .. 2 50
Drab or White. Nursing .... " 2 50
Other Colors, Nursing............ " 3 00
  5 and 9-inch Waists, 50 cents extra.
  Extra sizes, 31 to 36, 25 cents extra.
      " 37 up, 50 "

WITH AND WITHOUT STRAPS, SAME PRICE.

None genuine without the
trade mark "COMET."

TRADE MARK

SAINT LOUIS, MISSOURI.

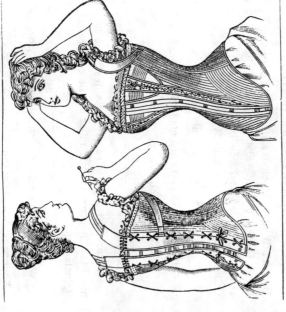

NURSING CORSET.

The above will give a full description of our Nursing

Corset, made in S.T., A. and B.S. style only.

50 cents extra.

WITH OR WITHOUT STRAPS, SAME PRICE.

None genuine without the
trade mark "COMET."

TRADE MARK

ca 1890

WILLIAMSON CORSET AND BRACE CO.

ABDOMINAL CORSETS.

ORDINARY SIZES, 18 TO 30.

Drab or White................per pair, $3 00
Other Colors................ " " 3 50
  Extra sizes, 31 to 36, 25 cents extra.
      " 37 up, 50 "
  5 and 9-inch Waists, 50 cents extra.
  We make the Abdominal in any style; the "ST"
is most generally worn.
  Our Abdominal Corset is the best "Binder Corset"
made; the front is 17 inches long; waist, 7 inches;
has 5 hook clasps; and is buttoned over abdomen
with two pearl buttons.

WITH OR WITHOUT STRAPS, SAME PRICE.

None genuine without the
trade mark "COMET."

TRADE MARK

WILLIAMSON CORSET AND BRACE CO.

SAINT LOUIS, MISSOURI.

SAINT LOUIS, MISSOURI.

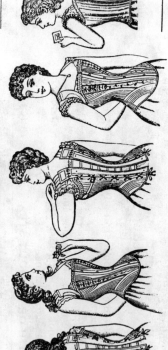

No. 1 TEDDIE WAISTS.

ORDINARY SIZES, 22 TO 27.

				per pair
6 inch length, front.	Drab or White	.	per pair,	$0 40
7	"	"	"	40
8	"	"	"	50
9	"	"	"	50
10	"	"	"	50
11	"	"	"	60
12	"	"	"	70
13	"	"	"	90

Other Colors, 20 cents extra.

28 up, 20 cents extra.

Some ladies send the ages of children for whom the "Teddies" are required, giving no length of front or size of waist; this is not sufficient. A child of seven years of age may have a larger waist than a child of 12 years, and many children of 7 are taller than others who are 8 or 9 years of age.

Always send FULL LENGTH OF FRONT FROM TOP TO BOTTOM, AND SIZE AROUND WAIST, WITHOUT ANY DEDUCTIONS.

None genuine without the trade mark "COMET."

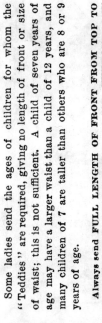

No. 2 TEDDIE WAISTS.

ORDINARY SIZES, 22 TO 27.

			per pair
8 inch length, front, Drab or White,	per pair,	$0 60
9	"	"	60
10	"	"	80
11	"	"	80
12	"	"	1 00
13	"	"	1 25

Other Colors, 20 cents per pair extra.

28 up, 25 cents "

The 8 and 9 inch have closed backs and buttoned fronts.

The sizes from 10 inch up lace in back and button in front.

Always send FULL LENGTH OF FRONT FROM TOP TO BOTTOM, AND SIZE AROUND WAIST, WITHOUT ANY DEDUCTIONS.

None genuine without the trade mark "COMET."

MISSES' CORSETS.

ORDINARY SIZES, 18 TO 27.

			per pair
Drab or White, 6 inch Waist......per pair,			$1 75
Other Colors, 6 inch Waist.........	"	"	2 00
Drab or White, 7 and 8 inch Waists .	"	"	2 00
Other Colors, 7 and 8 inch Waists...	"	"	2 25

28 up, 25 cents extra.

Our Misses' Corsets are made 6 inch Standard.

7 or 8 inch Waists, 25 cents extra.

Measure for Misses' same as Ladies', but bear in mind that a growing girl must not be compressed by tight lacing.

WITH OR WITHOUT STRAPS, SAME PRICE.

None genuine without the trade mark "COMET."

ca 1890

ca 1890

WILLIAMSON CORSET AND BRACE CO.

CENTER LACING, DOUBLE ELASTIC BACK CORSET

The Beau Ideal of Comfort, Grace and Durability.

THE ECLIPSE ABDOMINAL CORSET.

Drab or White, No. 1..............per pair, $2 50
Other Colors, No. 1............. "   3 00
Drab or White, No. 2............. "   3 00
Other Colors, No. 2............. "   3 50

Extra sizes, 31 to 36, 25 cents extra.
    "   37 up, 50 "   "
5 and 9-inch Waists, 50 "   "

Our Abdominal Corset is the best "Binder Corset" made; the front is 17 inches long; waist, 7 inches; has 5 hook clasps; and is buttoned over abdomen with two pearl buttons.

SAINT LOUIS, MISSOURI.

WILLIAMSON HEALTH WAIST.

THE "EMPRESS."

Drab or White....................$1 50
Black, Old Gold, Cardinal and Pink......... 1 75

ENGLISH SATTEEN.

Black, Old Gold, Cardinal and Pink......... 2 25
Extra sizes, 31 to 36, 25 cents extra.
    "   37 up, 50   "

The "Empress" has Back Supporting Steels only. No side steels. The sides are corded.
All made with buttons or steel clasp.
We make only 6, 7 and 8-inch Waists in these goods—no longer lengths.

None genuine without the trade mark "COMET."

Comet TRADE MARK

ca 1890

SAINT LOUIS, MISSOURI.

WILLIAMSON HEALTH WAIST.

"EMPRESS" OR "QUEEN."

Black, Old Gold, Cardinal or Pink..........$1 75

ENGLISH SATTEEN.

Black, Old Gold, Cardinal or Pink.......... 2 25

All made with buttons or steel clasps.
We make only 6, 7 and 8-inch Waists in these goods—no longer lengths.

The above represents the "Empress" and "Queen" in black or fancy colors.

None genuine without the trade mark "COMET."

Comet TRADE MARK

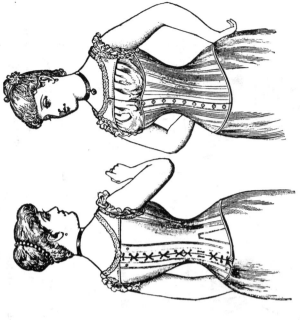

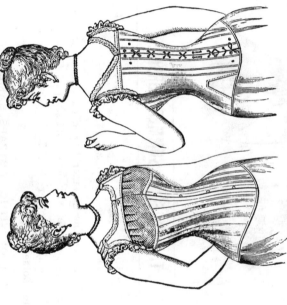

WILLIAMSON CORSET AND BRACE CO.

SAINT LOUIS, MISSOURI.

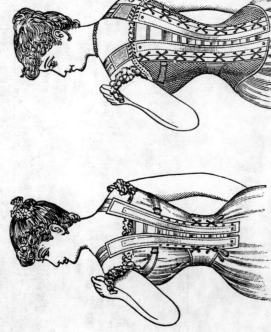

WILLIAMSON CORSET AND BRACE CO.

THE REGAL SUMMER CORSET.

ORDINARY SIZES, 18 TO 30.

White only............................per pair, $1 75

Extra sizes, 31 to 36, 25 cents extra.

" 37 up, 50 "

7, 8 and 9-inch Waists, 50 cents extra.

SPECIAL NOTICE.

We make this Summer Corset only in White, and only in one style, without straps.

We make no other than 9-inch Waist Specials in this Summer Corset. The waist measure and length of waist only, therefore, is necessary.

None genuine without the trade mark "COMET."

Comet TRADE MARK

THE IMPERIAL SUMMER CORSET.

White only............................$2 50

Extra sizes, 31 to 36, 25 cents extra.

We make this Summer Corset only in white, and only in one style, with or without straps.

We make no other than 7 and 8-inch Waists in this Corset.

WITH OR WITHOUT STRAPS, SAME PRICE.

None genuine without the trade mark "COMET."

Comet TRADE MARK

ca 1890

THE WILLIAMSON SHOULDER BRACE.

Nos. 1, 2, 3, 4 and 5.

Drab or White......................$1 50

INSTRUCTIONS FOR MEASUREMENT.

No. 1, for Children.........7 to 10 years.
12-inch Brace Steels.

No. 2, for Children.........11 to 14 years.
13-inch Brace Steels.

No. 3, Boys' and Misses'.........15 to 18 years.
14-inch Brace Steels.

No. 4, Youths' and Ladies'.........19 years or older.
15-inch Brace Steels.

No. 5, Men's.........25 years or older.
15-inch DOUBLE Brace Steels.

No waist measurement is necessary, as the Brace is not intended to close in front.

The height of the person for whom the Brace is intended is the best guide.

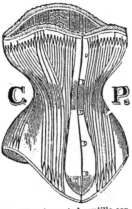

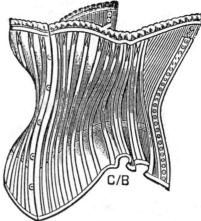

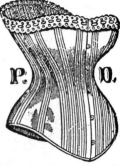

253. Fine French coutille; white or drab, 18 to 28 inches.. $1.75
254. In white, light blue or pink sateen, fine quality...... $1.75
255. Same, in black........ 2.00

256. Fine imported coutille corset, heavily boned, spoon steels, white or drab, 18 to 36 in., $3.90

257. "C B a la spirite," of English sateen, Venus back; in white, drab and black; sizes, 18 to 30 inches.................................... $1.59

258. Fine French coutille, white or drab, 18 to 28 inches. $1.75
259. Better quality, white, drab or black $2.50
260. Very best quality coutille, white or drab, 18 to 30 inches............... $3.00

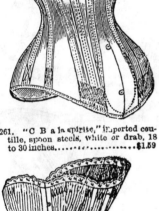

261. "C B a la spirite," imported coutille, spoon steels, white or drab, 18 to 30 inches................. $1.59

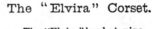

The "Elvira" Corset.

The "Elvira" is what nine-tenths of the women want —a perfect though moderate-priced corset. The result of years of close study and patient experimenting, it is conceded to-day to be the most satisfactory corset that woman has ever worn. It is an aid to grace and comfort.

Give every other corset its full measure of credit, and is there one among them that *combines* these three important features?

It is very fine coutille, with extra heavy bones, high bust and back, and is the only corset that will improve the figure without injurious or uncomfortable tight-lacing.

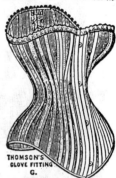

THOMSON'S GLOVE FITTING G.

266. Quality G, fine coutille, white or drab, 18 to 32 in., $1.25
267. Same, 33 to 36 inches, 1.50
267a. Quality E, white or drab, 18 to 30 inches,......... $1.50
267b. Black.................. 1.75

263. Fully guaranteed; white or drab, $3.50. Black, $3.98.
264. In extra fine coutille, white or drab......... $4.95
265. In extra heavy black satin................. $6.50

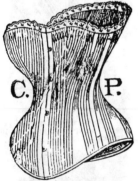

262. "C. P. Palma," French coutille corset, in white or drab, 18 to 28 inches.... .... $2.35
262a. In better quality, extra long waist and high bust...... $3.85

R & G

268. Imported coutille, long waisted, white or drab, 18 to 30 inches............ $1.29
269. Better quality.......... 1.50

270. Dr. Warner's health corset, in white or drab, 18 to 30 inches $1.25
271. Same style in satin, white, blue, cardinal, black.... $2.75

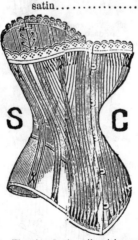

272. Fine hand-made satin strip corset, finest French sateen body, heavily boned, long waisted; used for bridal corset and other fine wear; white, drab or black, sizes 18 to 26 inches..... $2.25

273. Dr. Warner's abdominal. Elastic gores, which combine the support of this corset with the comfort and freedom of movement of a corset of ordinary length. It is adapted to all ladies who like a long corset, whether of stout or slight figure.
273a. 20 to 30 in., white or drab.. $1.50
273b. 31 to 36 inch............... 1.75

THOMSON'S GLOVE FITTING ABDOMINAL.

274. Thomson's abdominal corset white or drab, 20 to 32 in. $1.50
275. 33 to 36 inches........ 1.75

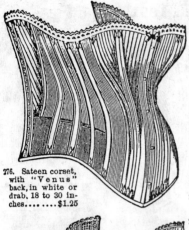

276. Sateen corset, with "Venus" back, in white or drab, 18 to 30 inches........$1.25

277. Dr. Warner's nursing corset, with shoulder straps, 18 to 30 inches.....................$1.25
278. Thomson's "G" nursing corset, white or drab, 18 to 30 inches, $1.25

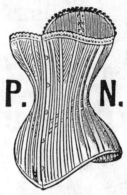

279. P. N. corset, double side steels with cork clasp protector, white or drab, 18 to 30 in...$1.00
280. Better quality...........1.25

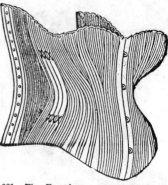

281. Fine French woven corset, embroidered top, white or drab, 18 to 30 inches, $1.00

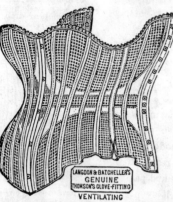

282. 18 to 32 inches.................$1.00
283. 32 to 36 "..................1.25
284. Featherweight ventilating corset, 18 to 30 inches, white or drab.............75c

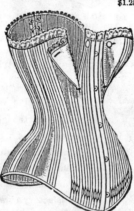

285. "C B a la spirite," nursing corset of coutille, in white or drab, 18 to 30 inches........$1.00

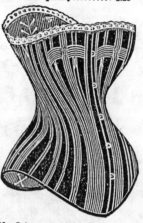

286. Sateen corset, top trimmed with embroidery, black only, 18 to 28 inches.......................$1.00
287. Better quality...............1.25

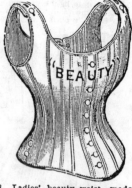

288. Ladies' beauty waist, made of satin jean, corded, buttoned front, laced back, in white............85c
289. In black..........................98c

290. Corset with sliding and detachable watch springs, white or drab, 18 to 30 inches, $1.25
291. Same, 31 to 36 inches................1.50

292. P. N. corset, side steels with cork clasp protector...........75c

293. Very good coutille corset, white or drab, 18 to 30 inches......$1.00

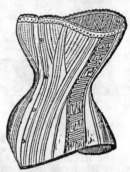

294. Ball's corset, guaranteed perfectly satisfactory; white or drab, 18 to 30 inches.......................$1.00

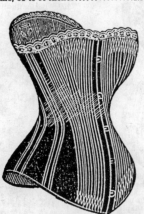

295. "C B a la spirite," of fine black sateen, handsomely finished...$1.25
296. Better, with spoon steels....2.25

297. Dr. Warner's sateen corset, white or drab, 18 to 30 inches $1.00

298. Jean corset, corded bust, side steels and double bust, white or drab, 18 to 30 inches..........50c

299. Madame Warren's dress form, unbreakable over hips, fills up any hollow part of the chest; in white or drab, 18 to 25 inches...........$1.25

1891

GOOD SENSE WAIST.
300.
Boys or girls, 1 to 4 years. Superfine material, buttons up the back, white.......50c

GOOD SENSE WAIST.
301.
Boys or girls, 4 to 6 years. Superfine material, buttons up the back, white and drab, 70c

GOOD SENSE.
302.
Misses' 7 to 12 years. Fine sateen jean, buttons front, laced back, white and drab.............75c

GOOD SENSE. 303.
Misses' 12 to 17 years. Fine sateen jean, buttons front, laced back. Fuller form than 302, and suitable for young ladies of slender form. White and drab.................88c

GOOD SENSE.
Ladies' medium form, long waist, buttons front, laced back, superfine material, extra fine pearl buttons, cloth-covered pliable steels, front and back, put in patent pockets and can be instantly removed. White and drab.
304. 18 to 30 in.............$1.50
305. 31 to 36 in.............1.75

306. Thomson's misses' glove fitting corset of coutille, white or drab.........75c
307. Better quality, R. H., $1.00

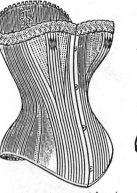

308. Misses' jean corset, heavily boned, white or drab, 18 to 26 inches.............59c

314. Best quality "Little Beauty" corset waist, made of double satin jean, with clusters of cording, 20 to 28 inches 35c
315. Cheaper quality....25c

309. Misses' corset made of jean, corded and boned, with shoulder straps...39c
310. Dr. Warner's misses' coraline corset, with shoulder straps.............65c

316. Children's summer waist, of very fine soft silesia, light and durable..25c

311. Beauty Waist, for misses' from 7 to 12 years, made of fine satin jean, buttons front and lace back, in white...63c

317. Ladies' dress forms of hair and springs, covered, per pair, 50c
Postage, 6c.

312. Child's muslin drawer waist, trimmed with embroidery. .280.
313. Same, untrimmed...........19c

318. Ladies' Sanitary Towels, per dozen, 60c

320. Dr. Warner's health dress forms of tampico grass....33c
Postage, 8c.

321. The above waist is made on a common sense principle, with extra strength at the points of greatest wear; it is soft and pliable, adjusting itself readily to the form of the wearer, and fulfilling in every particular the requirements of a perfect waist.........43c
322. For infants 1 to 3 years of age.....35c

DO NOT FAIL TO STATE SIZE AND COLOR WHEN ORDERING CORSETS.

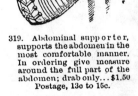

319. Abdominal supporter, supports the abdomen in the most comfortable manner. In ordering give measure around the full part of the abdomen; drab only...$1.50
Postage, 13c to 15c.

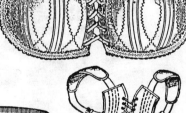

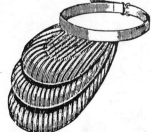 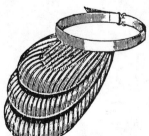

323. Ladies' safety belt; sizes, 24 to 36 inches waistband............25c

324. Shoulder braces for children, youths and adults..75c
Postage, 8c.

325. The "Grace" bustle, 2 coils, covered with sateen............18c

326. Tampico bustle, with 4 rows of plaiting.............35c

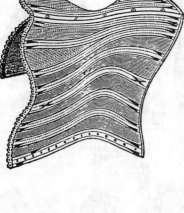

DR. WARNER'S CORSETS.

We make a special feature of fine French Corsets manufactured from the best imported materials. We guarantee these goods to be superior in shape and workmanship to any imported Corsets, and under the recent tariff laws they are much cheaper. Made in medium and extra long waists.

The Canfield Seamless Dress Shields are the only reliable water-proof Shield made. They have been worn by over 10,000,000 ladies.

WARNER BROTHERS,

359 Broadway, New York.

1891

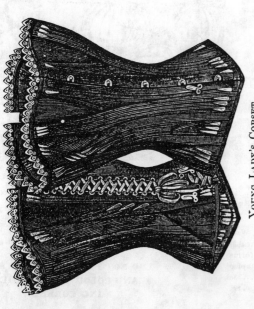

Young Lady's Corset.

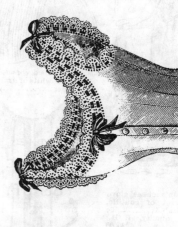

Corset Cover.

Corset for Elderly Lady.

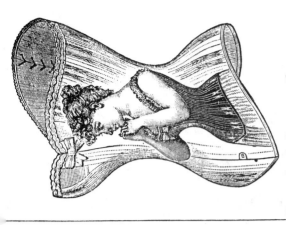

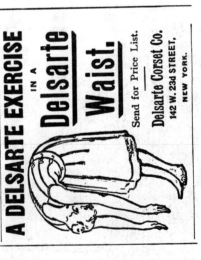

SENSIBLE CORSET WAISTS.

Combining Health, Comfort and Economy, together with Perfection in Shape.
They are made in six styles, to fit all ages, from Babies to Ladies.

Special Advantages
OF THE
**SENSIBLE
CORSET WAISTS.**

1. *The Buttons are fastened by our new patented flexible tape process and cannot pull out.*
2. *The Shoulder Straps are adjustable, so as to fit any size shoulder.*
3. *All steels are easily removed, and the waists washed without injury.*
4. *Soft and fine sateen is used in all waists, and the best workmanship.*
5. *The prices are much lower than any other first-class waists.*

SENSIBLE

WAIST.
STYLE A.
Boys or Girls, 1 to 4 years.
Sizes, 20 to 25 inches.
White or Drab.
Style A.............50c.
Same in Ferris Waist, 65c.

SENSIBLE WAISTS.

STYLE B.
Children, 4 to 7 years.
Sizes, 20 to 28 inches.
White or Drab.
Style B.................65c.
Same in Ferris Waist.................85c.

SENSIBLE

CORSET WAIST.
STYLE C.
Misses, 7 to 12 years.
Sizes, 19 to 28 inches.
White or Drab.
Style C.............85c.
Same, Ferris Waist $1.00

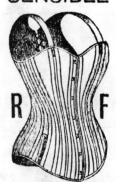

SENSIBLE

CORSET WAIST.
STYLE D.
Young Ladies, 12 to 17 years.
Sizes, 19 to 28 inches
White or Drab.
Style D........$1.00
Same, Ferris Waist 1.00

SENSIBLE

CORSET WAIST.
STYLE E.
Ladies—Long Waist.
Sizes, 19 to 30 inches.
White, Drab, or Black.
Style E.........$1.25

88. Ladies' Heavy Jean Corset, extra long waist, sizes 18 to 30 inches.......$1.00

R·F·EAGLE BRAND CORSET

Fine Fast Black Imported Italian Cloth, extra long waist, gauze on hip and bust, flossed top and bottom in silk; this Corset is a model of perfection.......................$4.50

89. Ladies' Corset, made of heavy jean, silk stitched, extra long waist.........$1.00
72. Fine Drab or Black Sateen Corset, long waist, double side steels, prettily stitched.............$2.00

SENSIBLE

CORSET WAIST.
STYLE F.
Ladies—Long Waist.
Sizes, 19 to 36 inches.
White, Drab, or Black.
Style F.........$1.75
Same, Ferris Waist, 1.75

CORSETS.

1. "Our Leader," Drab Jean, girdle waist, steel protector, 50c. each.
2. Raven, warranted fast black, steel protector, lace trimmed top, 75c. each.
3. Fast Black Sateen Corset, double side steels, silk stitched, warranted bone, $1.00 each.

4. Heavy Drab Jean Corset, girdle waist, double side steels, silk stitched, $1.00 each.
5. Heavy Black Sateen Corset, long waist, steel protector, nicely stitched; also in drab Jean, $1.50 each.
6. Extra Long Waist, heavily boned Corset, made of black sateen, $1.75 each.

CORSETS—Continued.

893. Fast Black, English sateen, all French horn, extra long waist, sizes 18 to 30, made in black only, $1.00 each.

893a. Heavy Drab Jean Corset, girdle waist, double side steels, silk stitched, $1.00 each.

933. Extra Long Waist, extra heavy materials, perfect shape, white, drab and ecru, $1.25 each.

924. Longest Waisted Corset, made of fine black sateen, triple side steels, beautifully stitched, Venus back, $3.00 each.

924a. Royal Worcester, made similar to above, of fine drab or black sateen, perfect fitting, $3.00 each.

924b. Same, in cheaper grade, $2.50 each.

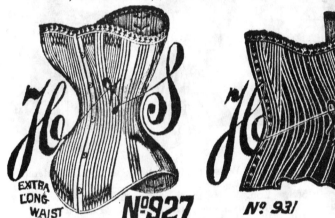
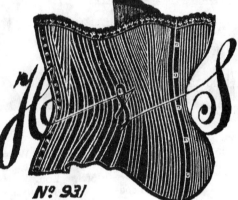

927. Extra Long Waist, made of black sateen, 85c. each.
940. Long Waist, made of drab coutille, 75c. each.

931. Extra Long Waist, fast black sateen, silk embroidered silk stitching in gold, cardinal, blue and black, $1.25'

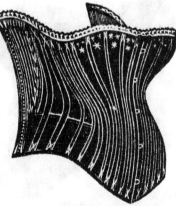
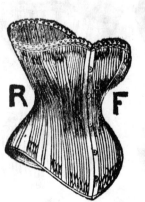

903. Long Waist, sizes 18 to 30, perfect shape, best French horn, $3.00 each.

849. Imitation French, perfect shape, fast color, made in black, drab and white sateen, sizes 18 to 30, $1.75.

849a. Wide bones, Venus back, heavily stitched, $2.00 ea.

This catalogue mailed free to your friends upon application.

92. Made of Fast Black and Drab Sateen, extra long waist, same shape as P. D., sizes 18 to 30, $2.00 each.

930. Fast Black, all French Horn, extra long waist, also made in white and drab, $1.75 each.

930a. Extra Long Waist, heavily boned Corset, made of heavy black sateen, $1.75 each.

CORSETS—Continued.

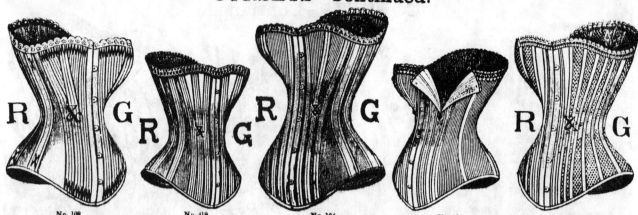

108. Ladies' Heavy Black Sateen Corset, long waist, steel protectors, nicely stitched, $1.50 each.

108a. Same, in drab jean, $1.50 each.

419. Young Ladies Corset, drab coutille, sizes 18 to 26, 75c. each.

104. Extra Long Waist, black and drab, extra heavy bones, sizes 18 to 30, $1.75 each.

104a. Nursing Corset, made in drab jean, sizes 18 to 30, $1.00 each.

104b. Long Waist, Ventilating Summer Corset, $1.00.

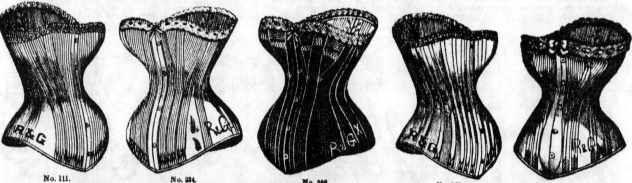

111. Extra Long Waist, made of sateen, in black and grey, heavily boned, silk embroidered, sizes 18 to 30, $1.00 each.

594. Long Waist, spoon busk, made of French drab coutille, sizes 18 to 36, $2.50 each.

594b. Same in Black Princella Cloth, sizes 18 to 36, $2.50.

284. Long Waist, made of black satin, embroidered top, $3.00 each.

558. Long Waist, made of French coutille, grey only, very heavily boned, sizes 18 to 30, $1.25 each.

105. Black Prunella and Drab, French coutille, sizes 18 to 20, $2.25 each.

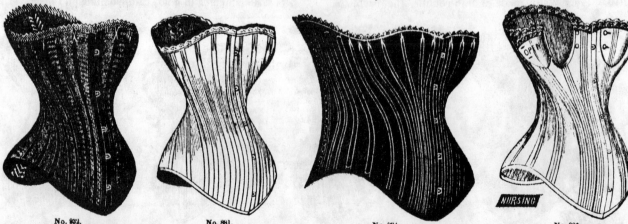

932. Imitation Coutille, 4 colors, perfect fit, 50c. each.

932a. "Our Leader," drab jean, girdle waist, steel protectors, 50c. each.

894. Extra Quality Sateen, fast black, sizes 18 to 36, extra heavy bone, $1.50 each.

All Corsets over 30 inch cost 25 cents per pair extra.

881. Extra heavy bone, made of best coutille, all French horn, perfect shape, white drab and ecru, sizes 18 to 36, $1.00 each.

896. Imitation French, all horn, white or drab, sizes 18 to 36, $1.00 each.

896a. Heavy Drab Jean Nursing Corset, $1.00 each.

1892

BEAUTY ACCOMMODATION WAIST, No. 7,

gives perfect form with ease of movement, develops bust, while not enlarging waist. Tampico Dress Forms with each Waist. Removable Steels, Adjustable Shoulder Straps, Laced at Back, Buttoned Front, Curved at Back to the Figure. In White and Black, 18 to 30 in. By mail, for **$1.50.** Little Beauty Waists for children, *the best.* Catalogue free.

E. H. HORWOOD & CO., 51 MERCER ST., N.Y.

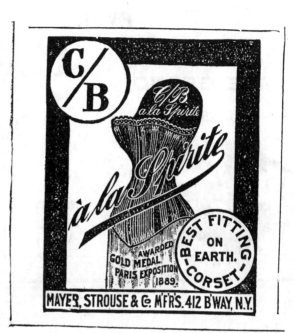

C/B

C/B à la Spirite

à la Spirite

AWARDED GOLD MEDAL PARIS EXPOSITION 1889.

BEST FITTING ON EARTH. CORSET

MAYER, STROUSE & Cº. MFRS. 412 B'WAY, N.Y.

A NICE THING TO FIT A DRESS OVER.

Patented Feb. 23, 1886.
See Patent Stamp on each Waist.

Take no Other.

FRONT.

BACK.

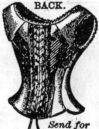

THE GENUINE

Jackson

Corset

Waists

Are made ONLY by the
Jackson Corset Co.,
Jackson, Mich.

The manufacturer's name is printed upon the boxes, and stamped upon inside of clasp in each Waist.
They are the *most popular* articles of the kind now on the market.
You should have one of them.

Be sure and get the right thing.

Send for Circular.

IF YOUR DEALER HASN'T IT, WRITE TO US,
Or to the E. T. CORSET CO., Sherbrooke, Prov. Que., Canada.

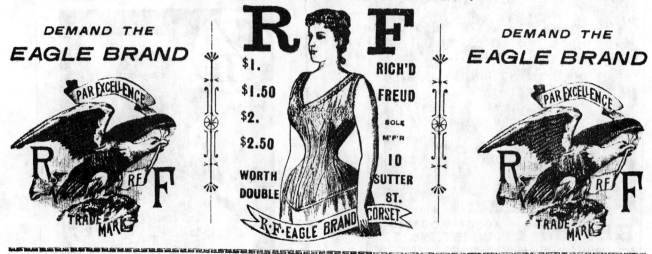

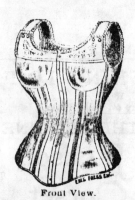

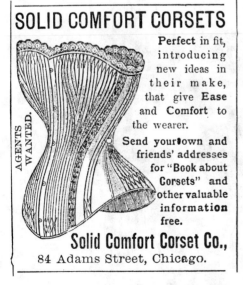

Royal Worcester

ca 1894

Extreme Light Weight,

SUMMER CORSETS AND WAISTS

Challenge the World!

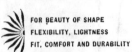

FOR BEAUTY OF SHAPE
FLEXIBILITY, LIGHTNESS
FIT, COMFORT AND DURABILITY

Received
Highest Award
at
World's Fair
1893.

STYLE 319—Summer. Lightest, finest, strongest, perfect fit and most comfortable; excellently boned. Spanish girdle encircles waist. Colors: White, drab. Lengths: Double extra long, extra long, long, medium and short. Retail price, $1.00. Extra sizes 31 to 36.

EVERY PAIR WARRANTED.

STYLE 318—Exquisite Specialty, French Lawn. Extra long and long; sizes 18 to 30. Retail price, $1.50.

STYLE 608—Pongee Silk, whalebone filled, extremely light. Extra long, long, medium, short. Ecru, white, black; sizes 18 to 30.
Retail price { Ecru, $3.50. White, 3.75. Black, 4.00.

STYLE 319—The favorite summer corset. Worn the year 'round.

The Merchant
POCKETS
the **MIDDLEMAN'S**
PROFIT
well as his own for
we don't sell
Jobbers.

STYLE 467—Summer Nursing, fine scrim, patent fasteners. Long and medium; sizes 18 to 30. Retail price, $1.25.

STYLE 443—High bust, summer, superior netting; long. Color: White; sizes 18 to 30. Retail price, $1.00.

STYLE 367—Ladies' Summer Waist, very light scrim; long. Color: White, only; sizes 18 to 30. Retail price, $1.00.

STYLE 419—Young Ladies' summer ventilated cloth, scant hip and bust. Length: Long. Color: White; sizes 18 to 26. Retail price, $1.00.

When reaction sets
in against the
VAGRANTLY CHEAP
Summer Corset
please remember
that the
WORCESTER CORSET
COMPANY
manufactures
only
RELIABLE
SUMMER CORSETS.

STYLE 667—Feather weight, long. Colors: White and drab; sizes 18 to 30. Retail price, $1.00.

STYLE 159—Summer, extra long, six hook steel; white, only; sizes 18 to 30. $6.50 a dozen, wholesale.

STYLE 157—Summer, extra long, six hook steel. Color: White; sizes 18 to 30. $4.50 a dozen, wholesale.

STYLE 154—Summer, long, white; sizes 18 to 30. $4.00 a dozen, wholesale.

WORCESTER CORSET COMPANY,

186 Market Street, Corner Adams.   CHICAGO, ILL.

New

Ferris' **Good Sense** Waists

in addition to our Standard Styles, ready to supply every need of the trade.

Styles 247 and 248,

Soft Well-made

Childs Waists,

to Retail at

25 cents.

Style 247—9 inch front, fits ages 2 to 4 yrs.
Style 248—10½ in.   "   "   " 4 to 6 "

Style 214—A soft Waist with no cords, for Misses 7 to 12 yrs. Retails at **70 cents.**

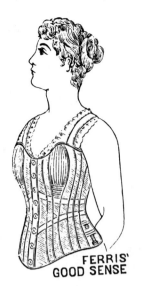

FERRIS' GOOD SENSE

Style 226. $1.00.

Plaited Bust for

Young Ladies,

a little fuller form than

Style 223.

The **Style 281,** Clasp Front, Soft Bust, introduced last year, is in great demand.

Soft Material throughout

and

Fits to a nicety.

Retails at $1.00.

Style 282 is the same

as **281** except that it is

Button Front.

FERRIS' GOOD SENSE

1894

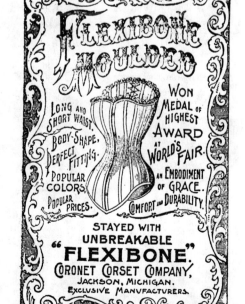

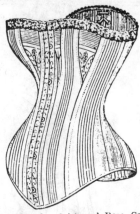

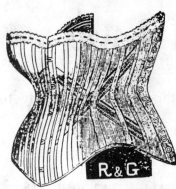

No. 127. H. & S. Corset, extra long waist, superior quality French sateen, well boned, embroidered top and silk flossed, in drab only. Sizes, 18 to 30 inches. 75c.

No. 128. Our Celebrated Rose Corset, made of heavy quality jean, corded bust, and silk embroidered; steel, white or drab. Sizes, 18 to 30 inches. 50c.

No. 129. The R. & G. Corset, heavy coutil, sateen finish, white or drab. Sizes, 18 to 30 inches. 95c.

No. 130. S. C. Corset, French sateen, extra long waist, double side steels, white or drab. Sizes, 18 to 30 inches. 95c.

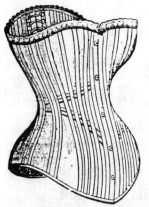

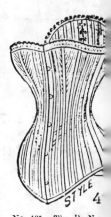

No. 131. The C. B. French Coutil Corset, silk embroidered top, white, black or drab. Sizes, 18 to 30 inches. 95c.

No. 132. C. B. Featherweight Ventilating Corset, for Summer wear. Sizes, 18 to 30 inches. 75c.

No. 133. Thomson's Glove Fitting Young Ladies' Corset, white or drab. Sizes, 18 to 26 inches. 75c.

No. 134. C. B. Corset, black only. French sateen, embroidered edge. Sizes, 18 to 30 inches. $1.00.

No. 135. The P. N. French coutil, sateen finish waist, has cork clasp protector, white or drab. Sizes, 18 to 30 inches. $1.00.

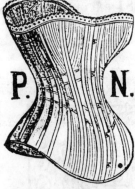

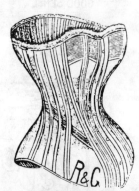

No. 136. P. N. Corset, long waist, superior finish and quality, black or drab. Sizes, 18 to 30 inches. $1.25.

No. 137. The R. & G. Extra Long Corset, heavy French coutil, corded bust, lace edge, white or drab. Sizes, 18 to 30 inches. 75c.

No. 138. The R. & G. Corset, heavy material, corded bust, white or drab. Sizes, 18 to 30 inches. 75c.

No. 139. Handsome Imported Corset, full of bones and embroidered, white or drab. Sizes, 18 to 30 inches.

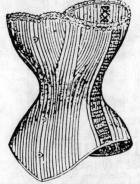

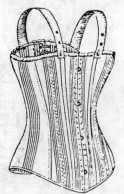

No. 140. Dr. Ball's Patent Corset, containing sectional wire coil in the side, instead of bone. This device renders it impossible for the corset to break down, and it is positively guaranteed to give satisfaction. We refund the price in each case that

No. 141. Little Daughter Misses' Corset, with shoulder straps, good

"THE PEARL" CORSET SHIELD
PATENT
MADE WITHOUT STEELS OR BONES.
DOES NOT INCREASE THE WAIST.
PREVENTS CORSETS BREAKING

No. 113. The P. N. Corset

No. 114. Thomson's Glove

No. 145. The Double Ve Waists, fine finish cloth. The weight of the underclothing is evenly distributed over the body by means of buttons sewed to bands stitched on the waist. For Infants, 50c.
No. 146. For Ladies, sizes 20 to 30 in. $1.00.
No. 147. For Children, sizes 20 to 26 in. 65c.

No. 148. The Little Beauty Corded Corset Waist, fine material and finish. Sizes, 20 to 27 inches; white only. 39c.

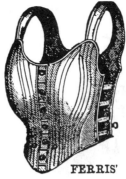

FERRIS'
BUST SUPPORTER.
Is particularly adapted to those who desire a shapely form without wearing a corset.
No. 149. $1.00.

No. 150. Madam Foy's Impr__ Skirt Supporter; white or drab. S__ 18 to 30 inches. $1.25.

No. 151. Plaited Pads. Interlined with Tampico, which can be instantly removed and cover washed. 50c.

No. 152. Small Bustle or Dress Pad, of best curled hair, sateen covering; white, drab or black. 25c.

No. 153. Dress Form, of best w__ curled hair, sateen covering; w__ only. 25c.

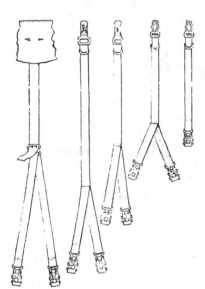

No. 154. Hose Supporters. Size D. Children's Single Clasp. 8c per pair.
Size C. Children's Double Clasp. 12c per pair.
Size B. Young Ladies'. 12c per pair.
Size A. Ladies'. 14c per pair.
Size E. Ladies', with belt. 21c per pair.

156   157   158   159   160

No. 156. Good Sense Corset Waist, best material and shape; children from 4 to 6 years. 70c.
No. 157. Good Sense Waist for Ladies, button front. $1.50.
No. 158. Good Sense Baby Waist, for infants under 3 years. 65c.
No. 159. Good Sense Waist for Young Ladies; 13 to 17 years. $1.00.
No. 160. Good Sense Waist for Misses; 7 to 12 years. 75c.

ROTH'S PATENT
DOUBLE BONE
CORSET.

No. 155. Roth's Double Bone Corset, sup__ quality. French coutil, silk flossed, white or __ Sizes, 18 to 30 inches. $1.25.

No. 161. Benefit Shoulder Brace, constructed on scientific principles. Adapted to both sexes. No. 1, suitable for ages to 5 years; No. 2, suitable for ages from 5 to 13 years; No. 3, suitable for ages __ years and up. 75c.

No. 162. Tampico Pads. 25c. Two sizes.

Madam Thomson's Breast Support.

No. 163 With knitted bosoms, is recommended to nursing mothers, also as a Breakfast or Bathing Corset for ladies of extra full form. $1.50.

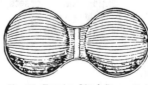

No. 164. Tampico Lined Bosom Pads. Medium size. 35c.

No. 165. Abdominal Supporter, best material, drab __ the measure should be taken from the lower part of around under the abdomen. No. 1, 30 to 35 inches; __ 40 inches; No. 2, 40 to 45 inches; No. 4, 45 to 50 inches.

No.   382.

MISSES' WAIST.

This garment has been manufactured and sold by us for years, thus proving itself to be a good seller and well adapted to the wants of a large class of trade.

It is well made, strong and durable.

**SUITABLE FOR MISSES FROM
10 TO 15 YEARS OF AGE.**

Made in strong soft jean.

Colors—Drab and White.

Price, $4.25 per Dozen.

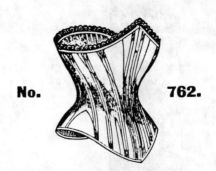

No.   762.

OUR LATEST CYCLING CORSET.

We have produced this new and beautiful model with special reference to the wants of lady cyclists. While enjoying the freedom of this exhilirating exercise the regular corset will be found too severe, and consequently wearisome.

A shorter garment, allowing more opportunity for chest expansion and freedom of motion to arms and shoulders, is a necessity, and all will appreciate the ready adaptation of this special design of corset to this need.

It is so constructed that the top line will fall just below the busts, and being short over the hips **will not interfere with easy propulsion** of the wheel.

Do not make the mistake of supposing the garment short waisted because it looks short. It is simply shortened at top and bottom to allow of a greater freedom of motion. Long, graceful waist effects are produced, the same as by the regular corset.

It is made of strongest English coutils, in **White, Drab and Black,** and is **WARRANTED in every particular** to meet the requirements of the most exacting.

Price, $24.00 per dozen.

1894

"C. C. C." Empire Girdle.

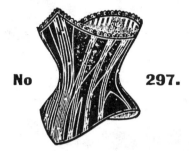

No 297.

HIGH GRADE GOODS.

Similar to, and yet of finer material, than the Columbian Girdle is the Empire Girdle.

All the effects of expensive, hand-made goods are produced in this garment.

Discriminating and fastidious tastes are sure to be pleased with it.

To those who love large freedom of body, and to whom the ordinary corset is a "straight jacket," depriving them of liberty, we earnestly recommend the Girdle as sure to give the desired freedom with proper support.

Stays of "Flexibone."

Materials—Finest Sateens.
Colors—Black and Light Brocade.

Price. $24.00 per Dozen.

"C. C. C." GOODS.

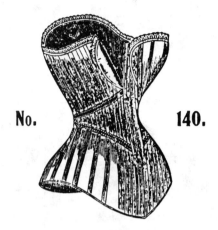

No. 140.

NURSING CORSET.

"Mothers' Comfort."

This illustration shows a simply constructed and convenient nursing corset. Mothers readily appreciate the utility of this garment, as it enables them to keep in the best of form without infringing on the rights of the baby. We sell a good many of them.

Material—Jean and Sateen combination.
Colors—Drab and White.

Price, $10.50 per Dozen.

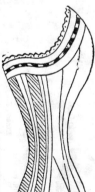

FOREIGN AND DOMESTIC CORSETS.

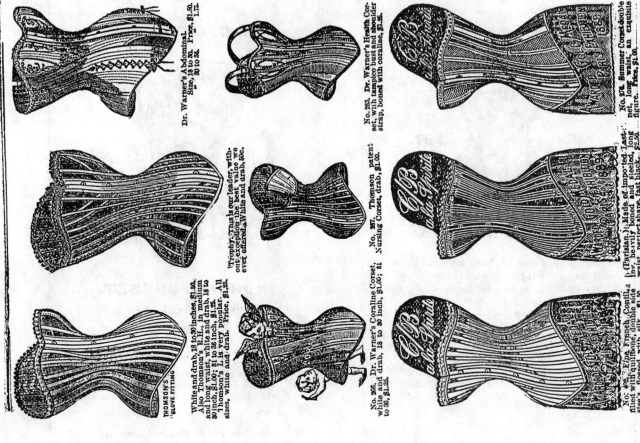

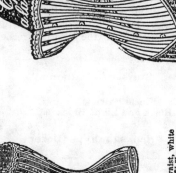

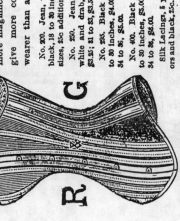

Dr. Warner's Abdominal. Size, 18 to 30. Price, $1.50. 30 to 36. L.H.

No. 253, Dr. Warner's Health Corset, with tampico bust and shoulder strap, boned with coraline, $1.25.

No. 274, Summer Corset—double net, long waist, an exquisite figure. Price, $1.00.

THOMSON'S "GLOVE FITTING."
White and drab, 18 to 30 inches, $1.50. Also Thomson's R.H. in medium and long waist, white and drab, 18 to 30 inch, $1.00; 31 to 36 inch, $1.25. All Thomson's L is very popular. Price, $1.25, white and drab.

Trophy Truss is our leader, without exception the best value we ever offered. White and drab, 50c.

No. 266, Dr. Warner's Coraline Corset, white and drab, 18 to 30 inch, $1.00; 31 to 36, $1.25.

No. 267, Thomson patent Nursing Corset, drab, $1.00.

No. 492, Epe, French, Coutil, filled with quillbone, double side steels, flossed with silk, $1.50.

No. 23, Spoon busk, long waist, high bust, white and drab coutil, 18 to 36 inches, $3.25.

No. 121, Moulded Corset, white and drab Jean, medium length, 75c.

Imported Sateen Corset, long waist, finely shaped. Sizes, 18 to 30. White and drab, $2.00; black, $2.50.

HER MAJESTY'S CORSET.

We are sole agents for this celebrated Corset, and guarantee every pair we sell. It will wear longer, produce a more magnificent figure, and give more comfort to the wearer than any other.

No. 20, Jean, white, drab, and black, 18 to 30 inches, $2.75. Extra sizes, 25c additional.

No. 250, Jean, sateen straps, white and drab, 18 to 30 inches, $3.25; 31 to 33, $3.50; 34 to 36, $3.75.

No. 293, Black Italian Cloth, 18 to 30 inches, $4.00; 31 to 33, $4.50; 34 to 36, $5.00.

No. 400, Black Italian cloth, 18 to 30 inches, $5.00; 31 to 33, $5.50; 34 to 36, $6.00.

Silk Lacings, 5 yards length, colors and black, 25c.

Linen Lacings, white and black, 5 yards length, 8c.

Elastic Lacings, 5c.

Cotton Lacings, 3 cents.

Coronet, Extra long waist, white and drab, 18 to 30 inches, $1.75. P. D. and C. P., inch clasps, kid covered, 25c. C. P., Spoon Clasps, cloth covered, 30c. XL Clasp, cloth for front of corset, &c. Celluloid Protector, to use on side of corset to avoid breaking, 25c.

No. 104, Fast black sateen, extra long waist, $1.50. Imported Side Steels, cloth covered, per pair, 10c; kid covered, 15c. Imported P. D. and C. P., front clasps, cloth covered, per pair, 12½c.

No. 262, Bridal, white only, 18 to 30 inches, $1.00.

1894

"Her Majesty's Corset."

FRENCH CORSETS.

The "Fleur de Lis" Corset.

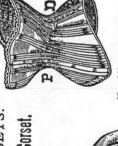

No. 97. Sateen, white and black, very popular, 18 to 30 inches. Price, $3.25.

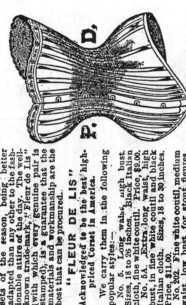

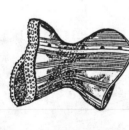

No. 263. Sateen, medium length, white, drab, and black. Sizes, 18 to 26 inches. Price, $2.50.

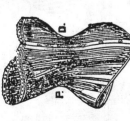

No. 248. Sateen, medium and short lengths. Sizes, 18 to 26 inches. Price, $2.50.

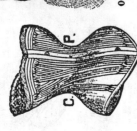

No. 530. P.D. Corset, French coutil, white and drab. Price, $1.75.

No. 152. The Perfect Shape, white and drab coutil, with sateen stripe, 18 to 30 inches. Price, $2.75.

Owned and controlled exclusively in Europe and America by JORDAN, MARSH & CO. For a fine corset it has no equal.

These elegant long-waisted styles hold the first place among the corsets of the season, being better adapted than any other to the fashionable attire of the day. The well-known trade-mark, "Fleur de Lis" (with which every genuine pair is stamped), is a guarantee that the materials and workmanship are the best that can be procured.

"FLEUR DE LIS"

Acknowledged to be the best high-priced Corset in America.

We carry them in the following popular styles:—

No. 5. Long waist, high bust. Sizes, 18 to 26 inches. Black Italian cloth, fine white coutil. Price, $9.00.

No. 5A. Extra-long waist, high bust, in fine white coutil and black Italian cloth. Sizes, 18 to 30 inches. Price, $11.00.

No. 202. Fine white coutil, medium waist, low bust, for stout figures. Sizes, 19 to 30 inches. Price, $6.00.

No. 302. Medium waist, high bust. Sizes, 18 to 30 inches. In black Italian cloth and fine white coutil. Price, $8.00.

Superior, long waist, finely shaped, suitable for a plump figure, white and drab. Sizes, 18 to 30 inches. Price, $3.50.

French Bosom Pads, the correct thing, white only. Price, 45c. Imported Silk Lacings, any length, popular colors. Price, 50c. Corsets fitted, laundered, and repaired a specialty

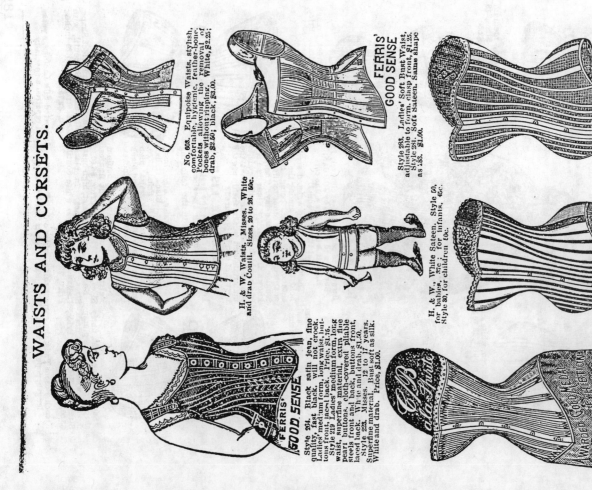

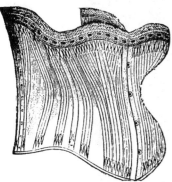

The Viscountess. French hand-made, double side-steels, silk-stitched, white, gray, and black sateen, 13 inches long; sizes, 18 to 28, $3.50.

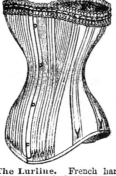

The Lurline. French hand-made, silk-stitched, double side-steels, 13 inches long, white and gray sateen; sizes, 18 to 30, $2.50.

The Ostende. Ventilating, French hand-made, double side-steels, 13 inches long; sizes, 18 to 32, $2.50. Same style, 12 ins. long, $2.50.

The Sadie. French hand-made, 13 inches long, double side-steels, white, gray, blue and black sateen; sizes, 18 to 26, $2.25.

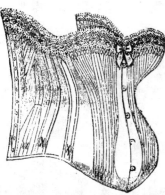

The Linda. French hand-made, 3 side-steels, 16 inches long, low bust, long waist, desirable for stout figures, in white and drab coutil; sizes, 20 to 32, $5.75. Black wool, $6.75.

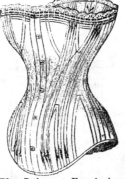

The Lakme. French hand-made, 15 inches long, high bust, extra long waist, very desirable for slender figures, white and gray coutil; sizes, 18 to 26, $4.50. Black wool, $6.50.
Same style, white coutil, 13½ inches long, $4.25.

The Wanda. Ventilating, French hand-made, double side-steels, long waist, 13½ inches long; sizes, 18 to 32, $2.50.
Same style, 12 inches long, $2.50. Similar to above, $1.75.

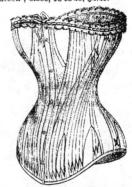

The Donita. French hand-made, 14 inches long, extra long waist and high bust, very desirable for slender figures, in fine white coutil; sizes, 18 to 26, $8.00. Black Wool, $9.00.

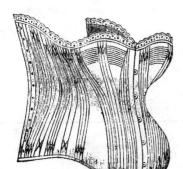

The Exhibition, French hand-made, 14 inches long, low bust and very long over hips, white and gray coutil; sizes, 18 to 28, $3.75.

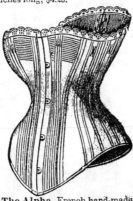

The Alpha. French hand-made, low, corded bust, desirable for stout or medium figures, white and gray coutil; sizes, 18 to 30, $2.25.
Same style, Nursing, $2.75

The Lucille. French hand-made, 13 ins. long, well boned, white and gray coutil; sizes, 18 to 30, $1.75. Similar to above, $1.50.

The Elysee. French hand-made, heavily boned, double side-steels, 14½ inches long, low bust, long waist, white and gray coutil; sizes, 18 to 36, $2.75.

The Marie. French hand-made, extra long waist, high bust, well boned, black, $3.75. White and gray, $3.25. Sizes, 18 to 26.

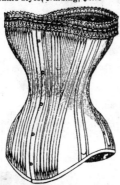

The Camille. French hand-made, 14 inches long, well boned, double side-steels, white, gray, blue and pink sateen; sizes, 18 to 26, $3.25. Black sateen, $3.50.

The Marguerite. French hand-made, well boned, double side-steels, 14 inches long, white and gray coutil; sizes, 18 to 28, $1.50.

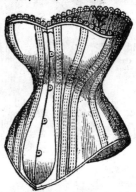

Rival. French hand-made, 12 inches long, low bust, double side-steels, desirable for short, stout figures, white coutil; sizes, 20 to 32, $1.90.

Corsets—

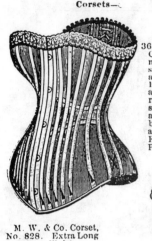

36828 M. W. & Co.'s Corset, No. 828, is made of fine English sateen, shaped exactly like the P. D. French Corset, fits and wears well. We recommend this corset as being comfortable and very durable. Colors: Ecru and drab.
Each $0.85
Per dozen...... 9.00

M. W. & Co. Corset, No. 828. Extra Long Waist.

36829 The Columbian *Dress Reform Waist*, extra length, fluted bust, adjustable to any required size. Made of fine satin finished jean, drab only, shoulder straps. Sizes 20 to 30; style of 36830.
Each $0.75
Per dozen. ... 8.00

36830 M. W. & Co.'s Extra Long Waist, made expressly for us and guaranteed by us. It is the most original, best fitting, easiest and durable waist in the market. Once try a pair you will never wear any other kind. The busts are so designed they can be made any size. Colors: White, drab or black sateen; also made in summer net; are made with clasps or buttoned front. Sizes, 20 to 30....................$0.95
Per dozen 10.00
Extra sizes, 31 to 36. Each... 1.25

M. W. & Co.'s Extra long Waist. No. 36829-30.

36831 M. W. & Co.'s French Strip Corset, No. 831, made expressly for us. This corset is equal in fit, material and durability to any French corset now in the market at double its price. Try one. Colors: Drab, ecru or fast black.
Each.............$ 0.99
Per dozen....... 10.50

M. W. & Co.'s French Strip Corset No. 831.
Please give your size.

36832 M. W. & Co.'s High Bust Dress Form Health Corset has an extra long waist. The bust pads are flexible but always retain the shape. White or drab. Sizes 18 to 30.
Each...........$ 0.99
Per dozen.... 10.50
Absolutely fast black.
Each ..... $ 1.19
Per dozen 12.00
Extra Quality, All English Sateen and French Staying, white, black or drab. Sizes, 18 to 30.
Each ..... $ 1.35
Per dozen. ... 15.00

High bust, extra long waist.

INSURE MAIL PACKAGES.

Corsets—

36833 M.W.&Co.'s Nursing Corset, (No. 833), made expressly for us, is the most convenient ever introduced. The bust pieces have patent clasp fasteners and can be removed or replaced without any trouble, the front is softly corded and the back is regular French strip style. Colors: Fast black or drab only.
Each ....$ 1.25
Per dozen 13.75

M. W. & Co.'s Nursing, style 833.

36834 M. W. & Co.'s Corset No. 834 is the longest waist corset made; suitable only for tall, slim figures. It is made to measure. It has a 14½ inch unbreakable steel, is made of the best English sateen elaborately flossed; comes in black, white or drab; the same sold everywhere for $3.50. Our price.
Each ....$ 2 19
Per dozen.... 24.00

36835 M. W. & Co.'s 6-Hook Columbia Corset No. 835 (Same style as 36834), made of fine jeans with sateen covered strips. Colors, drab only.
Sizes, 18 to 30, Each........................$1.00
Per dozen......................................11.00
Black is all sateen. Each......................1.39
Per dozen......................................15.00

Madam Foy's Improved Corset.

36836 These are the only skirt supporting corsets with shoulder brace and side lacing, and are without exception the best of their kind in the market. White or drab only. Sizes, 18 to 30. Improved.
Per dozen $12.00
Each, including extra sizes...............$1.25

Madam Foy Corset.

36837 Is a Perf[...]ch Form and N[...] set thorou[...] soft and pl[...]ts: made of fine [...]n, with French [...]v-ered strips, [...]or drab; sizes, 1[...]
Each........ [...]0
Per dozne..... [...]0

Nursing.

Corsets—

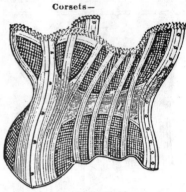

36838-39-40

36838 Ladies' Summer Corset, made of open-work material, very light and cool. White only; sizes, 18 to 30. Each....$0.40 Per dozen....$4.50
36839 Our M. W. & Co.'s Guaranteed Summer Corset, made of extra quality openwork material. Guaranteed not to rip or tear, or money refunded. White or drab; sizes, 18 to 30. Each.. .50
Per dozen..................... 5.50
Extra sizes, 31 to 36. Each................ .75
36840 French Form Long Waist Ventilating summer corset. Made of extra fine open work material, thoroughly boned and stayed; guaranteed not to rip or tear or money refunded. White only. Sizes 18 to 30
Each $0.95
Per dozen... 10.50
Extra sizes, 31 to 36.
Each.... $1.25
36841 Our "Jersey" Corset, made of good serviceable jean. The best in the market at the price. White or drab. Sizes, 18 to 30. Each.....$0.35
Per dozen.... 3.75
36842 Corset is Perfect Fitting French Strip Corset. Colors: White, drab, ecru.
Each..........$0.45
Per dozen...... 5.00

NOTE—We cannot ship corsets if you neglect to give your size.

36843 This finely finished 5-hook corset is made of good sateen, double steel. It has a double section lined with two series of buttons giving extra strength, where it is most needed. White drab or black. Sizes 18 to 30.
Each.............$0.50
Per dozen......... 5.00

36843

36844 Corset, made of extra heavy coutile, long waist, double side steels, guaranteed to outwear any corset in the market at the price, or the money refunded. Sizes, 18 to 30. Colors; White or gray, Each..... $ 0.[...]
Per dozen.... 10.[...]

36844

Bortree's Duple[...] Corset.

36847 Bortree's Perfect F[...]ting Duplex Corset, doub[...] bone, double seam, w[...]ranted not to rip. It ca[...] be adjusted to fit any fo[...] by means of the adjust[...] straps; sizes, 18 to 30.
Each..............$0[...]
Per dozen........ 9[...]
Extra sizes, 31 to 36.
Each.............. 1[...]
Colors: White or drab.

Corsets

36808 Dress Form Corset, is just the thing for any lady wishing a high bust corset, especially any lady of slender form. The busts are self sustaining and no bosom pads need be worn with them. They also have all the essentials of a perfect health corset. They always improve the form. Colors, white and drab. Sizes, 18 to 30.
Each............$0.85
Per dozen........9.00
Same in fast black, without shoulder straps.
Each............$1.00

36809 Extra Quality French Shaped Corset, made of the best quality sateen henrietta cloth, thoroughly boned, richly embroidered, black only. Sizes, 18 to 30. Each......$2.85
Per dozen.........29.50

36810 French Strip Corset, made of fine fast black Italian wool cloth, absolutely unbreakable, a most complete and durable corset, extra long waist, black only. Sizes, 19 to 30. Each..$3.00
Per dozen.........30.00

36811 Bust Supporter is gotten up for ladies who lead an active life, especially those who engage in out door exercise, as it permits of the freest action of every part of the body; made in white, drab or black sateen or white summer net. Sizes, 18 to 30 waist measure. Order one size larger than regular corset size. Each..$0.95
Per dozen............10.50

36812 M. W. & Co.'s Young Ladies Waist, for growing girls 12 to 17 years. Made of white gray or black sateen with soft expanding busts. Sizes, 19 to 28.
Each................$0.79
Per dozen...........8.75

Dr. Strong's Celebrated Tricora Corsets.

One-half dozen assorted sizes at dozen rates. We guarantee every pair to give satisfaction or return the money. Don't forget to give your size.

36814 Doctor Strong's Health Supporter, has perfectly formed self-sustaining Tricora busts, which obviate the use of bust pads. It gives every lady wearing it the outline of perfect development and graceful figure. It remedies defects in ordinary figures, making it a most desirable corset to wear jersey over and enable dressmakers to measure and fit perfectly. The best health corset made. Any lady once wearing it will not be without it. Extra long waists. Sizes, 18 to 30. White or drab.
Each $0.90
Per dozen 9.00

Windsor Cook Stoves
ARE EQUAL TO ANY. PRICES LOW.

Corsets
Remember to give size when ordering Corsets.

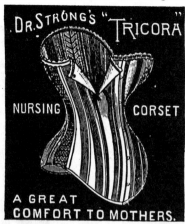

DR. STRONG'S "TRICORA" NURSING CORSET
A GREAT COMFORT TO MOTHERS.

36815 "Tricora" Nursing. Dr. Strong's Tricora Nursing Corset has proved a great comfort to mothers, as it affords perfect freedom of action in every position which the body can assume. It is boned with (waterproof) Tricora stays, which will not be affected by moisture, and being tough, pliable and supporting are absolutely unbreakable. Size, 18 to 30. White or drab.
Each $0.90
Per dozen 9.00

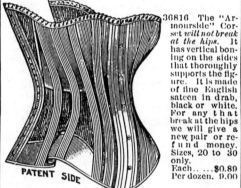

PATENT SIDE

36816 The "Armourside" Corset *will not break at the hips*. It has vertical boning on the sides that thoroughly supports the figure. It is made of fine English sateen in drab, black or white. For any that break at the hips we will give a new pair or refund money. Sizes, 20 to 30 only.
Each.....$0.89
Per dozen. 9.00

Armourside Unbreakable Hip. Long Waist.

36817 Dr. Strong's "Tricora" Relief Corset. The most durable, comfortable and healthful corset ever sold for its price. Adapts itself to the various positions of the body in stooping, gives perfect ease in all positions; affords great relief and comfort to the many who find ordinary corsets oppressive. The "Tricora" stays used for boning are pliable, supporting and absolutely unbreakable. Sizes, 18 to 30. White or drab.
Each.................$0.90
Per dozen 9.00

Ask for it.

36818 Madam Strong's "Health Bodice." A soft, pliable and delightfully comfortable bodice that supports the figure pleasantly but not rigidly, allowing such freedom of action, in any position, as to have the wearer almost unconscious of a bodice. It is supported chiefly by the celebrated (Waterproof) "Tricora" stays that will not absorb or retain moisture and are famous for their durability and comfort giving qualities. It has perfectly formed self-sustaining "Tricora" busts, which will give to every lady wearing it the outlines of perfect development and stylish figure. Sizes, 20 to 30. White, drab or fast black.
Each.................$1.15
Per dozen 12.00

The Yatisi Corsets.

We will take back any of the Yatisi Corsets and return the money after 10 days' wear, if not satisfactory. N. B.—Don't forget to give your size.

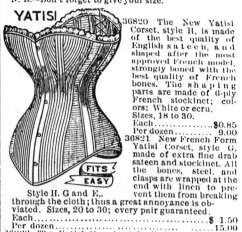

YATISI. Style H. G and E,.

FITS EASY

36820 The New Yatisi Corset, style H, is made of the best quality of English sateen, and shaped after the most approved French model, strongly boned with the best quality of French bones. The shaping parts are made of 6-ply French stockinet; colors: White or ecru. Sizes, 18 to 30.
Each.................$0.85
Per dozen 9.00

36821 New French Form Yatisi Corset, style G, made of extra fine drab sateen and stockinet. All the bones, steel, and clasps are wrapped at the end with linen to prevent them from breaking through the cloth; thus a great annoyance is obviated. Sizes, 20 to 30; every pair guaranteed.
Each.................$1.50
Per dozen...........15.00

36822 The Yatisi Corset, style E, is modeled after the celebrated Fasso Paris made corset, extra long waist, long between the line of the waist and the bust, double side steels, strongly boned; shaping parts are made of 6-ply French stockinet; colors: Ecru or white. Sizes, 18 to 30.$1.15
Per dozen.............12.00

YATISI

FITS EASY

ABDOMINAL

36823 The Abdominal Yatisi Corset was introduced specially for married ladies. It supports the abdomen and prevents the ordinary pressure upon the pelvis organs. It is a most perfect corset for dress purposes, as it has a tendency to increase the length of the waist and lessens the size of the abdomen. Made of a fine quality of English sateen jeans, strongly boned. The shaping parts are made of 6-ply French stockinet; colors: Drab or ecru; sizes, 22 to 30.
Each.............$1.75
Per dozen.........18.00
Extra sizes, 32 to 40.
Each...............2.00

Yatisi Fits Easy NURSING

36824 The Yatisi is the latest and most approved nursing corset. The pivotal bust is its greatest advantage, as it can be removed with ease. It fits perfectly, retains its shape and wears well. It has double front and side steels, and curved shoulder straps; sizes, 18 to 30 only. Each.......$1.00
Per dozen...........10.50

M. W. & Co.'s Corsets.

NOTE.—These corsets are made especially for us and bear our name. The most skillful hands are employed to manufacture them. Every corset bearing our brand is guaranteed by us for wear, fit and quality; if any are found unsatisfactory, return them and we will refund your money or give you a new corset.

Our Absolutely Fast Black Corset.

36827 M. W. & Co.'s Corset, No. 827, is made in fast black only; is modeled after the French C. P. Corset, long waist, full busts, side and double front steels.
Each $0.85
Per dozen.... .. 9.00
Sizes, 18 to 30

M. W. & Co.'s Stainless Black Corset.

FRONT.   BACK.

STYLE 325.

The Globe Bicycle Corset.

This is the only practical Corset for Wheeling, Riding, Golf and Athletics.

Fine Imported Sateens.

Silk Elastic Side Sections.

Only falls enough below waist line to prevent "rolling or wearing" up.

Also just the Corset for the "Marie Antoinette" style of dress.

COLOR: White.

SIZES—18 to 26.

Price, - - - - - - - $1.00

STYLE 200.

LONG LENGTH.

COLORS: White and Drab.

Material: Fine Coutille, with English Sateen Stripping. Heavy Flossing.

Silk Trimmings.

Steels that are warranted not to break in wear.

SIZES—18 to 30.

Price, - - $1.00

STYLE 150.

LONG LENGTH.

Standard Form.

COLORS—White and Drab.

Fine Coutille, finished with English Sateen Stripping, Boned Bust.

This is one of our Best Styles. Beautiful and very Serviceable.

Imported Silk Trimmings. Best Steels.

Sizes—18 to 30.

Price, - - • - $1.00

ca 1895

STYLE 75.

Ventilating Summer Corset.

LONG LENGTH.

COLOR: White.

A Net of beautiful pattern, finished with Coutille Stripping and Girdle.

This Corset has no equal at double the price.

SIZES—18 to 30.

Price, - 50 cents

STYLE 175.

"Globe Nursing."

LONG LENGTH.

COLORS: White and Drab.

Made of Coutille.

Sensible and convenient.

Silk Trimmings.

SIZES—18 to 30.

Price, - - $1.00

STYLE 60.

LONG LENGTH.

COLORS: White, Drab and Black.

Jean Body.

Sateen Strippings.

Boned Bust.

This is something extra, and we make it for a leader and to be able to say that we give the best at all prices. Equal to some One Dollar Corsets.

SIZES—18 to 30.

Price, - - 50 Cents

STYLE 40.

Long Length.

COLORS: White and Drab.

Made out of Coutille.

Corded Bust.

Six-Hook Clasps. Fine Trimmings and Flossings.

Made on one of our best models, and is perfect fitting.

SIZES—18 to 30.

Price, - - 50 Cents

ca 1895

LADIES' ABDOMINAL SUPPORTER.

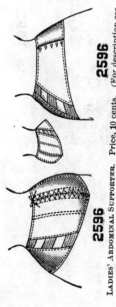

2596

2596

LADIES' ABDOMINAL SUPPORTER. Price, 10 cents. (For description see

1895

No. 2596.—In the accompanying illustrations is shown a very useful piece of wearing apparel for women who are in the least inclined to corpulence. In fact, if it is once adopted, like a well-fitting corset, it will never be omitted from the toilette. White French flannel was the material used in this instance, with an interlining of common canvas. The front portion is shaped with a single centre-seam, but in this instance either side was finished, and eyelets were worked for the lacing. At the sides just above the hips three pieces of elastic are inserted, furnishing sufficient "give" to the belt. The back portions are sloped to be quite narrow, and fastened with buttonholes and small pearl buttons.

The pattern is cut in ten sizes, for ladies from thirty-six to fifty-four inches abdomen measure, and costs 10 cents. To make for a lady of medium size, it will require one and three-eighths yard of material twenty-seven, one and one-eighth yard thirty-six, with three-quarters yard elastic.

Outing flannel, serge, linen, cashmere, etc., may be used in making, and bindings of ribbon may be introduced. If closely stitched throughout by machine it will be additionally supporting.

The Classique Corsets.

Style G.   Style H.   Style D.   Style K.

For descriptions of the above styles, see below.

his celebrated Paris Corset is
ned and controlled exclusively by
-selves in Europe and America,
1 is acknowledged to be the most
fect fitting in the world.

t is used by the modistes who
the fashion in the world of dress,
1 know the correct result is assured
en the gown is fitted over the
ssique.

The Classique.

Only *genuine whalebone* is used,
and they are hand-fashioned by the
most skillful French workers. To
be had in twenty - two different
models, and of the latest and most
desirable materials, including *coutil,
plain and fancy black wool
fabrics, batiste, broché, silk, tulle
and satin.*

Style A.
½ inches long, White Coutil, desirable for short
'cs. Sizes, 18 to 30 inches, $5.50.

Style W.
ȝ inches long, two-side steels, long waist, de-
ʲᵉ for slender or medium figures. Sizes, 18 to
ches.
hite or Gray Coutil, $5.50.

Style BB.
inches long, two side-steels, long waist, me-
1 low bust, desirable for stout or medium fig-
Sizes, 18 to 30 inches.
hite or Gray Coutil, $6.25; Black Wool, $9.75.

Style D.
ȝ inches long, short hips, long, tapering waist,
able for slender figures. (See illustration.)
ȝ, 18 to 24 inches.
hite or Ecru Coutil, $7.50; Black Wool, $9.75;
ι Batiste, $9.50; Embroidered Batiste, $16.50;
ade Silk, $18.50.

Style DD.
inches long, short bust gore, extra long waist,
t hips, desirable for tall, slender figures. Sizes,
· 23 inches.
hite Coutil, $7.75; Black Wool, $10.75.

Style H.
13 inches long, two-side steels, long waist, medium low bust for slender or medium figures. (See
illustration.) Sizes, 18 to 26 inches.
White Coutil, $8.50; Black Wool, $10.50.

Style G.
12 inches long, very low bust, perfect fitting, for
slender or medium figures. (See illustration.) Sizes,
18 to 24 inches.
Striped Batiste, $8.50; Embroidered Batiste,
$16.50.

Style J.
15½ inches long, low bust, long over hips and
abdomen, heavily boned, desirable for stout figures. Sizes, 20 to 32 inches.
In White Coutil, $9.50; Black Wool, $12.50.

Style M.
Same as Style J, with spoon steel. Sizes, 20 to
34 inches.
In White or Ecru Coutil, $9.75; Black Wool, $13.50.

Style T.
16½ inches long, heavily boned, long waist, low
bust, desirable for stout figures. Sizes, 21 to 28
inches.
In Ecru Coutil, $14.50; Black Wool, $16.50.

Style K.
15 inches long, heavily boned, deep bust gore,
.long tapering waist, for stout and medium figures.
(See illustration.) Sizes, 19 to 28 inches.
White or Ecru Coutil, $10.50; Black Wool, $13.50;
Silk or Satin Brocade, $24.50.

Style N.
15 inches long, short bust gore, extra long tapering waists, for slender or medium figures. Sizes,
18 to 24 inches.
White or Ecru, $10.50; Batiste, Silk or Satin,
Broché, $19.50 to $22.50.

Style R.
18 inches long, spoon steels, low bust, very long
over hips and abdomen, desirable for stout figures.
Sizes, 21 to 28 inches.
Ecru Coutil, $14.50; Black Wool, $16.50.
French Empire and Décolleté Corset. Sizes, 18
to 26 inches.
Coutil, $2.50; Black Wool, $2.50; Batiste, $3.85;
Brocade Satin, $5.75.

The Camille. French sateen, 14½ in. long, medium low bust, long waist, double side-steels, white, gray or black; sizes, 18 to 28 in., $3.25.

Hair Cloth Skirts, Bustles, Dress Pads, Ladies' and Children's Stocking Supporters and Steels to match all our Corsets.

The Constant. French coutil, heavily boned, double side-steels, white or gray; sizes, 18 to 26 inches, $2.75.

The Lakme. French coutil, 15 in. long, extra long waist, double side-steels, sizes, 18 to 26 in., white or gray, $4.50. Black sateen, $6.00.

The Lisette. French sateen, 11½ inches long, white, gray or black; sizes, 18 to 30 inches, $2.50.

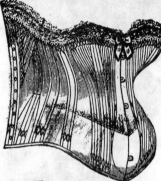

The Lindie. French hand-made, 3 side-steels, 16 inches long, low bust, long waist, desirable for stout figures; sizes, 20 to 34 inches, white or drab coutil, $5.75. Black wool, $6.75.

The Lahore. French hand-made, low bust, very desirable for stout figures, heavily boned, double side-steels, 13 inches long, white or gray coutil; sizes, 22 to 36 in., $5.50.

The Elysee. French hand-made, heavily boned, double side-steels, 14½ inches long, low bust, long waist, white or gray coutil; sizes, 18 to 36 inches, $2.75.

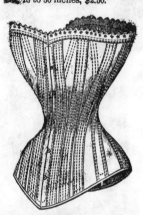

The Marguerite. French hand-made, well boned, double side-steels, 14 inches long, white or gray coutil; sizes, 18 to 26 inches, $1.50.

The Cyclist. Black, white or gray sateen; sizes, 18 to 26 inches, $1.00.

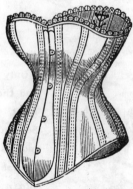

Rival. French hand-made, 12 inches long, low bust, double side-steels, desirable for short, stout figures, white coutil; sizes, 20 to 32 inches, $1.90.

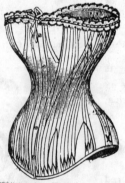

The Donita. French hand-made, 14 in. long, extra long waist and high bust, very desirable for slender figures, fine white coutil; sizes, 18 to 26 in., $8.00. Black wool, $9.00.

The Equestrian. French coutil, 11½ inches long, very short hip, sizes, 18 to 26 inches, white, $2.50. Black sateen, $2.75.

The Lurline. French sateen, 13 in. long, medium low bust, double side-steels, white or gray; sizes, 18 to 28 in., $2.50.

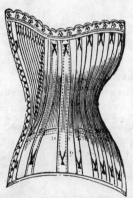

The Venus. French hand-made, long waist, with very high back, sizes, 18 to 26 inches, white or gray sateen, $3.00; black sateen, $3.25.

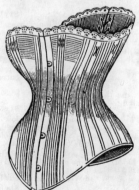

The Alpha. French hand-made, low, corded bust, desirable for stout or medium figures, white or gray coutil; sizes, 18 to 30 in., $2.00. Same style, Nursing, $2.50.

The Lucille. French coutil, 13 inches long, double side-steels, white or gray; sizes, 18 to 30 in., $1.75. Similar to above; sizes, 18 to 26 inches, $1.50.

Creates an
Exquisite Figure.

Produces a
Long Slender Waist.

Her Majesty's Corset

The GREATEST HEALTH-GIVER and BEAUTIFIER of the FIGURE EVER PRODUCED.

Endorsed by the Elite, Profession, and Well-dressed Women of the World.

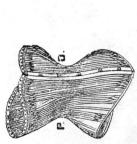

HER MAJESTY'S CORSET

PRICES.

NO. 200.

Jean, White, Drab, and Black.

18 to 30 inches, . . $2.75
Extra sizes, 25c additional.

NO. 250.

Jean, Sateen Straps, White and Drab.

18 to 30 inches,	$3.25
31 to 33 "	3.50
34 to 36 "	3.75

NO. 275.

Fine Sateen, White and Drab.

18 to 30 inches,	$3.75
31 to 33 "	4.25
34 to 36 "	4.75

NO. 295.

Black Italian Cloth.

18 to 30 inches,	$4.00
31 to 33 "	4.50
34 to 36 "	5.00

NO. 400.

Black Italian Cloth.

18 to 30 inches,	$5.00
31 to 33 "	5.50
34 to 36 "	6.00

Satin.

White and black brocade of exquisite designs. Very light weight made to order in any color.

18 to 30 inches,	$15.00
31 to 33 "	16.00
34 to 36	17.00

We sell "Her Majesty's Corset," under the following guarantee:

That it will create a more **exquisite figure**, a **longer** and more **graceful waist**; increase the **size** of the **bust**; reduce the **size** of the **abdomen**; wear **longer** and give **more ease** and **comfort** than any other corset made.

If "Her Majesty's Corset" does not fully accomplish the above within thirty days from the date it is sold, we will refund the money.

TO OUR CUSTOMERS: We have, for many years past, been the **Sole Agents** of Her Majesty's Corset. It is without doubt the most perfectly constructed corset that has ever been produced; and we also feel that we are offering for sale an article of rare merit, and one that will give the most complete satisfaction.

JORDAN, MARSH & CO., Boston, Sole Agents.

BOSTON, MASS.

FRENCH CORSETS.

Dernier Modele de la Maison
LEOTY.

No. 152. The perfect shape, white and drab coutil, with sateen stripe, 18 to 30 inches Price, $2.75

No. 50. P. D. Corset, French coutil, white and drab. Price, $1.75

No. 97. Sateen, white and black, very popular. 18 to 30 inches Price, $3.25

No. 248. Sateen, medium waist, 4-hook clasp, heavily boned, flossed with silk, excellent shape. Price, $2.50.

No. 157. French sateen, bust corded venus back, hip gores, 4-hook clasp, double side steel, silk flossing. Price, $2.50.

No. 28. Spoon steel, long waist, high bust. Suitable for stout figures. White and drab. Price, $3.25.

LEOTY, the world's greatest Corset; the very latest fashion, perfectly modelled, hygienic, and of the most unique design. For sale only by Jordan, Marsh & Co. White, $15; black, $16.

"Fleur de Lis" Corset.

Owned and controlled exclusively in Europe and America by

Jordan, Marsh & Co.

For a fine corset it has no equal.

These elegant long-waisted styles hold the first place among the corsets of the season, being better adapted than any other to the fashionable attire of the day. The well-known trade mark, "Fleur de Lis" (with which every genuine pair is stamped), is a guarantee that the materials and workmanship are the best that can be procured.

We carry them in the following popular styles:

No. 5. Long waist, high bust. Sizes, 18 to 26 inches. black Italian cloth, fine white coutil. Price, $9.

No 5A. Extra-long waist, high bust, in fine white coutil and black Italian cloth. Sizes, 18 to 30 inches. Price, $11.

No. 292. Fine white coutil, medium waist, low bust, for stout figures. Sizes, 19 to 30 inches. Price. $6.

No. 292. Medium waist, high bust. Sizes, 18 to 30 inches. In black Italian cloth and fine white coutil. Price, $8.

BOSTON, MASS.

JORDAN, MARSH AND COMPANY,

Without an Equal.
The No. 41
F. P. Corset.

AN ALL-COUTIL FRENCH GORED Corset, Long Waist, Low Under Arms, Heavily Flossed, and Lace Trimmed.

EASY AND PERFECT FITTING.

WHITE AND DRAB. Sizes, 18 to 30.

$1 per pair.

Once tried, always worn.

F. P. Corsets. Prices from 75c to $2 pair.

SOMETHING NEW

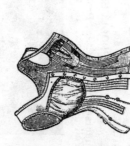

FERRIS' GOOD SENSE

Ladies', Long Waist.
No. 230. Sateen, $1.25. White, drab, or black.
" 219. Superfine, $1.50.
" 264. Fine black, $1.75.
Misses'. 12 to 17 years.
Buttons front, laced back. White and drab.
No. 227. Sateen, 75c.
" 223. Superfine, $1.
" 215. White only, 75c.

No. 603, Equipoise Waist, stylish, comfortable, hygienic. Whalebone pockets, allowing the removal of bones without ripping. White, $2.25; drab, $2.50; black, $3.

Silk Laces, 5-yard lengths, white, black, and colors, 25, 37, and 50c, according to width and quality.
Warner's Tampeco Bosom Pads, 25, and 50c each.
Imported Spiral Bosom Pads. Price, 50c.

No. 540. French Corset, beautiful shape, long waist, short hip, heavily boned, silk flossed. Black, $3.25; white, $3.
I. C. Bicycle or Riding Corset. Particularly adapted to all kinds of gymnastic exercises. Very popular. White and black. Price, $2.50.

BOSTON, MASS.

JORDAN, MARSH AND COMPANY,

1896

W. B.
America's Popular Corset.

With an Impenetrable Protection Added.

No. 428. White only, heavily boned, extra length, flossed with silk. Price, $1.50.

No. 363. Made of extra-fine material, six-hook front, extra length, three side steels. White, drab and black. Price, $2.75.

EXTRA LONG WAIST.
No. 453. Summer corset, beautifully made of imported net of special pattern, white only. Price, $1.

EXTRA LONG WAIST.
No. 425. Fast black Sateen, only two side steels, tastefully trimmed, perfect fitting Price, 75c.

No. 410. Extra-long waist, high bust, made of coutil, with sateen strips, silk flossed, white or drab. Price, $1.

No. 134. Extra-long waist, made of French sateen, with Venus back, beautiful shape, handsomely flossed with silk, white and drab. Price, $1.75.

No. 411. Imperial Jean, white and drab, sateen strips, French waist, whalebone bust, finely fitting. Price, 75c.

BOSTON, MASS.

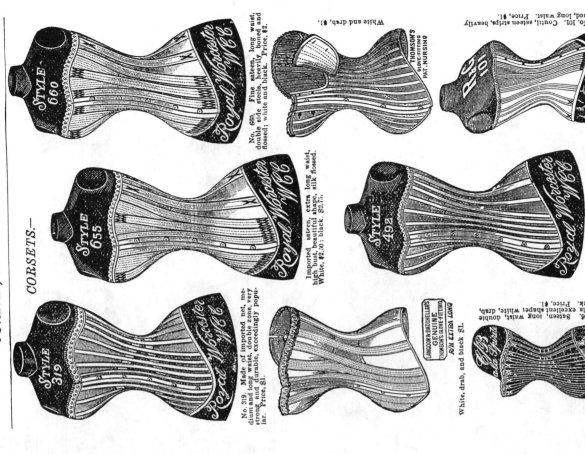

Style 418. French coutil, 12½ in. long, short hips, long waist, white only; sizes, 18 to 24 inches, $5.50.

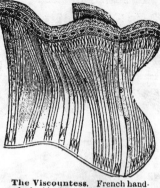

The Viscountess. French hand-made, double side-steels, silk-stitched, white, gray or black sateen, 13 in. long; sizes, 18 to 28 inches, $3.50.

The Marie. French coutil, with sateen strips, long waist, high bust, 14 inches long, white or gray, $6.25; black; sizes, 18 to 26 in., $3.75. Similar to above, white or gray, $2.00.

The Sadie. French sateen, 13 in. long, medium low bust, white, gray, blue and black; sizes, 18 to 26 inches, $2.25.

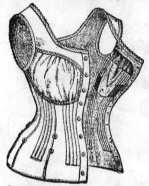

Style 603. Equipoise. For ladies, boned front and back, medium or long waist, at $2.00; finer quality, in white twill or black sateen, $3.00; sizes, 20 to 34 in. No. 611. Misses, 12 to 17 years; sizes, 22 to 28 in., $1.75.

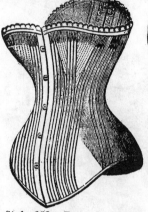

Style 259. Extra long waist, well boned, white, gray or black sateen; sizes, 18 to 26 inches, $1.25.

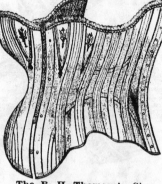

The R. H. Thomson's Glove-Fitting, 18 to 32 in., $1.00; G, $1.50; E, white or black, $1.75; sizes over 32, 25c extra. Young ladies', white or gray, 18 to 28 inches. 75c.

Dr. Warner's Health, white or gray; sizes, 18 to 30 in., $1.25. Abdominal, white or gray; sizes, 20 to 30 inches, $1.50; extra sizes, $1.75.

H. & W. Boys' Waists. 2 to 12 yrs., 48c. Child's and Misses' Corded Waists; sizes, 20 to 30 in., 25c and 39c.

The Eclipse. Nursing, white or gray coutil; sizes, 18 to 30 in., $1.00.

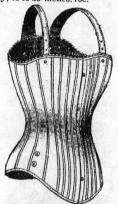

The Pearl. Misses' first corset; 18 to 26 in., white or gray sateen, 45c.

Young Ladies' Long Waist, well boned, white or gray sateen; sizes, 18 to 26 in., 95c. Black sateen; $1.25.

Good Sense. Waist Style 215, 7 to 12 years, white, 75c.

Style 219. Good Sense. Ladies' Long Waist, buttons front, laced back and over hips, extra fine material, pearl buttons, in white, $1.50; sizes, over 30 inches, $1.75.

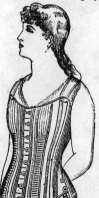

Style 223. Good Sense. Misses', 12 to 17 yrs., buttons front, laced back, soft bust, $1.00.

Style 229. Good Sense. Boys' or Girls', 1 to 4 years, in white, 50c.

Style 204. Good Sense. Boys' or Girls', 4 to 6 years, white, 50c.

CORSET DEPARTMENT

In ordering give number **worn** or the waist measure. For Misses and Children give size of the waist **instead of age.**

No. 738. Madame Warren's Dress Form Corset, perfect shape, long waisted, unbreakable over the hips, long high bust, 18 to 30 inches, white or drab, $1.25; white ventilated corset, $1.25.

No. 149 EXTRA LONG WAIST.

No. 740. S. C. Alexandria Cloth Corset, long waist, heavily boned, white, black or drab, 18 to 30 inches, $1.00; also in summer corset, $1.00.

The Cleopatra.
OUR OWN EXCLUSIVE IMPORTATION.

Cleopatra

Made of the best quality sateen, high back, extra long waist, heavily boned, sizes 18 to 26 ins., white or drab, $4.25; black, $5.00. Made of Coutil, extra heavily boned, long waist, high back, in drab and white, $4.50; in black, $6.00, sizes, 19 to 30 inches.

No. 742. Young Ladies' Alexandria Cloth Corset, heavily boned, high back. length of front steels 12½ inches, 18 to 26 inches, suitable for misses from 13 to 15 years old, in drab or white, $1.00.

No 225. IMPROVED

No. 744. Alexandria Cloth Corset, long waist, double front steel, white or drab, 18 to 28 inches, 75c.

No. 746. Abdominal Corset, 18 to 30 inches. $1.50; 33 to 36 inches, $1.75. Thompson's G. French Coutil Corset, drab or white, 18 to 32 inches. $1.50; 30 to 36 inches, $1.75.

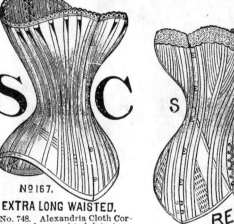

No 167. EXTRA LONG WAISTED.

No. 748. Alexandria Cloth Corset, extra long waisted, latest approved French shape, double bones all through, double front steels, in white or drab, 18 to 30 inches, $1.25; in black, $1.50.

RELIEF.

No. 750. S. C. Abdominal Corset, well boned, long waist, elastic sides, white or drab, 21 to 36 inches, $1.50.

No. 752. Thompson's E Sateen Corset, long and medium waist, drab, black or white, 18 to 30 inches, $1.75.
Thompson's Ventilating short or medium waist, 18 to 32 inches. $1.00; 33 to 36, $1.25.

CORSETS—

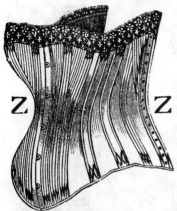

No. 754. Coutil Corset, extra long waist, well boned, sizes, 18 to 30 inches, white or drab, $2.98; in black, $3.65.

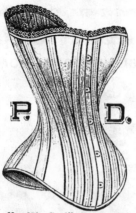

No. 756. Coutil Corset, long waisted, in white or gray, 18 to 30 inches, $1.75; with boned bust $2.25; extra long, sateen, $3.25; also ventilating corset, $1.75.

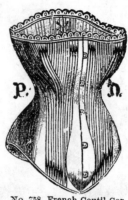

No. 758. French Coutil Corset, spoon steel, long waist, gray or white, 20 to 30 inches, $3.25.

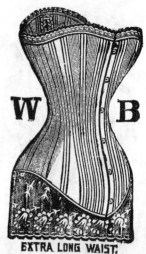

EXTRA LONG WAIST.

No. 760. Extra Long Waist, white and drab, 18 to 26 inches, $1.00; black, $1.25. Same style, sateen strips, white, drab, black, $1.50.

No. 762. Patent Shoulder Brace, in white or drab, sizes 1, 2, 3, 4, according to length of waist, 75c. Postage, 10c.
Little Beauty Waists for childrens' sizes, from 22 to 27 inches waist measure, white only, 40c
Thompson's R.H. Short Jean Corset, length 11 inches, in white or drab, 18 to 32 inches, $1.00; 33 to 36 inches, $1.25.

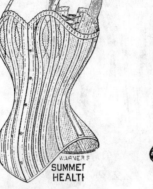

SUMMER HEALTH

No. 764. Dr. Warner's Health Corset, with Coraline, white or drab, 18 to 30 inches, $1.25; in black, long, $1.50; also in a summer corset waist, $1.25.

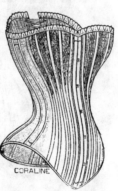

CORALINE

No. 766. Dr. Warner's French Model Coraline Corset, boned bust, white or drab, 18 to 30 inches, $1.00; black, $1.25.

No. 768. Misses' Corset, well boned, 19 to 26 inches, white or drab, 60c.
C. P. Sateen Corset, length, 11 inches, in drab and white, $2.25; black, 2.50; 18 to 30 inches.
Dr. Warner's Young Ladies' French Sateen Corset, suitable for a miss from 15 to 18 years or a slight lady, white or drab, sizes, 18 to 25 inches, $1.00.

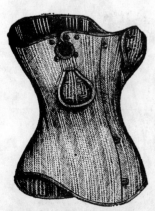

No. 770. Nursing Corset, reversible flap, white or drab, 19 to 30 inches, $1.00.

No. 772. Young Ladies' Waist, plaited bust, extra superfine cloth, 13 to 17 years, sizes 20 to 27 inch, $1.00.
Misses' Waist, waist measure, 22 to 27 inches, 75c.

FERRIS' GOOD SENSE

No. 774. Ladies' medium form, sateen cloth, button front and laced back, 20 to 30 inches, $1.00, white and drab. Fine sateen, white and drab, lace hips, $1.50.
No. 776. Equipoise waist, made of heavy twill, all whale bone, 8 and 9 inches under arm, white only, $2.25.

FERRIS' GOOD SENSE

No. 778. Good Sense Sateen Corset Waist, Sizes 19 to 30 inches, fast black, $1.25.

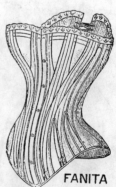

FANITA

No. 780. The Fanita French Coutil, pure whale bone, white or drab, 18 to 30 inches, $4.50; in black imported sateen, $6.00.

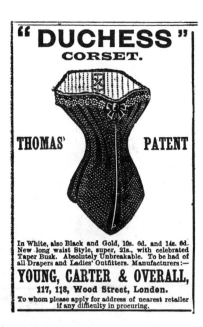
The H. & W. Underwaists
and Hose Supporters,

Made of best quality, soft, durable materials, superior in fit, finish and workmanship. Buttons firmly and correctly put on. Patent re-enforced
armholes and belts. Clothing thoroughly supported
from the shoulders.

STYLE No. 100.
Sizes, 22 to 28 inches, heavy imported piqué, 55c; with pearl buttons, 69c.

STYLE No. 60.
Children, 1 to 6 years, fine, soft
imported piqué, 22 to 26 inches, 48c;
with pearl buttons, 65c.

**H & W WAIST.
STYLE No. 25.**
Boys' Skeleton Waist. Made of
fine, soft jean striped with sateen,
cut low and open front, suspender
attachment on back, H. & W. hose
supporters at the side. Sizes, 2 to 10
years, 50c.

STYLE No. 400.
Ladies' Bicycle Waist (superior
shape). Made of fine English sateen,
boned with French horn, buttoned or
clasp front. Adapted to all kinds of
gymnastic or out-of-door exercises.
Sizes, 18 to 26 inches, waist measure. White or drab, $1.00.

HOSE SUPPORTERS.

**Fine Nickel-Plated Button Clasps,
Superior quality Webbing.**

Ladies,' with belt, cotton		19c.
" without belt, "		12c.
Misses,' " " "		12c.
Children's, " " "		10c.
White or black.		

Ladies' satin belt		65c.
" silk, without belt		30c.
Misses' " " "		23c.
Children's silk " "		23c.
White, black, pink or blue.		

**H & W WAIST.
STYLE No. 245.**
For Misses, 10 to 16 years of age,
sizes, 20 to 28 inches. Fine sateen,
corded strips, superior shape, especially adapted for growing girls,
buttoned in front, laced in back, 50c.

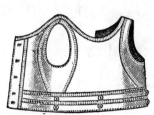

STYLE No. 50 S.
Children's Waist, 1 to 6 years,
sizes, 22 to 26 inches, light-weight
twill, 35c; also in fine cambric with
pearl buttons. 40c.

STYLE No. 310.
Fine Corded Waist for Girls from
4 to 12 years of age, with slight bust
and hip fullness, sizes, 21 to 28 inches,
39c.

STYLE No. 220.
Suspender Waist for Boys from 3
to 10 years of age, open front, with
extra buttons for trousers, white
only, made of fine, soft coutil.
Sizes, 3 to 10 years, 50c.

Address all orders to Stern Brothers.

There are beautiful lines here that tell of a fortune in health.

1896

Its Wonderful How

the news spreads—the excellencies of the

Genuine Jackson Corset - Waist

are being spread far and near.

Such Healthful Lines, are developed by their wear that one
Such Graceful Lines, tells another and our sales are jumping.
Such Comforts   Send us your waist measure, together
with **$1.25** for a pair—stating whether you want white, drab,
black, ecru, gold, blue or pink.   Agents wanted.

THE GENUINE JACKSON CORSET-WAIST—the American-
made success of the day.

Sole Mfrs.—Jackson Corset Co., Jackson, Mich.

LOOMER'S

It's Solid Comfort   At all Times

YCLING~RECREATION CORSET.

Comfortable, Graceful and Healthful.

All these are combined in the

L.L. Cycling-Recreation Corset

No more distressing long steels, only

Ease and Comfort at All Times

endorsed by leading physicians   Price $1.25.
postpaid.   At your dealer's or write

L. L. LOOMER'S SONS, Sole Mfrs,
OGEPORT, CONN,   and   CHICAGO, ILL.

As Graceful as the New Woman

all the time—at work, a-wheel,
in negligee—is she who wears a

G-D Bicycle Waist

Wear a Bicycle Waist and get
perfect comfort—a sound pair
of lungs—a graceful figure and
rosy cheeks. Price $1.00, at
dealers or by mail—postpaid.
SIZES 18 to 30,
Waist Measure.

Booklet Free

Gives Such Comfort

G-D Chicago Waist

Price - - $1.00.

Allows perfect freedom of
motion and perfect development of the body. Wear one
and discover what real comfort
is.

Fitted to Living Models.

Graceful; comfortable. Popular price. Made of sateen
—Black, White Drab, or Summer Netting. SIZES—
18 to 30, waist measure. Ask your dealer for the
"G.-D." Waist. If he hasn't it, send us $1.00, together
with size and color desired, and we will send you one
prepaid. Take no other—None as good.

Gage-Downs Co., 268 Fifth Avenue, Chicago.

1897
NEW JERSEY'S CORSET STORE

THE best "adv." the NEWARK BEE-HIVE has is its reputation for keeping in stock all the good and stylish CORSETS—250 kinds to select from, all at reasonable prices. You get exactly what you ask for—Long, Medium, Short, Bicycle, Nursing, Abdominal or Cutaway Hips. Expect things different when you come here—larger department, freshness, fit, comfort, satisfaction—expect your dollars to do their very best. Nothing sells Corsets so well as genuine goodness and polite attention—both here; expert fitters always in our department, and here is a list of some of the Corsets we sell. Read and keep it for reference:

HER MAJESTY—White, Black and Colors, **$2.75 to $4.**

P. N.—White, Drab and Black, including Abdominal and Nursing, **75c. to $1.75.**

Ball's Corsets—White and Drab, **$1.**

LA VIDA—White, Drab and Black, **$3.50, $4.50 and $7;** or Grass Linen Embroidered, **$9.**

W & B—White and Drab, **50c. to $1.50;** Black, **$1 to $2.**

H & S—White and Drab, **50c. to $1.50;** Black, **75c. to $2.50;** or *ELITE* in White and Drab, **$1.25 to $2.75;** or in Black, **$3.25.**

R & G—White and Drab, **50c. to $2;** or Black, **$1 to $2.**

H & H—White and Drab, leather tips included, **50c. to $1.**

P. D.—White and Drab, **$1.75.**

McGRAW'S—Abdominal in White and Drab, **$1.50;** extra sizes, **$1.75.**

FRENCH GIRDLE in White, **$1.50.**

J. B.—White and Drab, **$1.**

Dr. Warner's CORALINE, NURSING and HEALTH, **$1 to $1.35.**

Thomson's GLOVE-FITTING, Young Ladies, **75c.;** or Ladies, **$1 to $1.50.**

TRICORA—Armorside, Misses in White, **75c.;** Ladies, in White and Drab, **$1;** extra sizes, **$1.25.**

Mme. Foy's Celebrated Corsets, **$1.25.**

C. B., a la spirite—White, Drab and Black, **$1 to $1.75.**

Loomer's Cutaway and Mode Bust, Black and Drab, **$1.25.**

SONNETTE—White, Drab and Black, **75c. to $2.**

NEMO—tipped top and bottom, **$1.**

C. P.—White or Drab, **$1.50 to $3;** or Black, **$2.50.**

PRIMA DONNA—White and Drab, **$1 to $1.50.**

B B Corset Waists—**25c.**

LITTLE BEAUTY Waists—Childs to Misses, **32c. to 50c.**

Z Z—White, Drab and Black, **$1.75 to $4.75.**

FASSO—in White, extra fine, **$5 to $7.25.**

ROYAL WORCESTER—White, Drab and Black, **$1 to $1.50.**

Ferris' GOOD SENSE Corset Waists—Ladies and Children, **25c. to $1.50.**

H & W Waists—1 to 12 years, **34c. to 65c.**

FLEXIBONE—White and Drab, **$1.50 to $3.**

FRENCH WOVEN Corset—**75c. to $1.95.**

V V Corst Waists—Infants to Ladies—**40c. to $1.**

THE BEE-HIVE also carries a complete line of all kinds of SUMMER CORSETS—can fit any figure. Newest clasps and laces in Linen, Elastic and Silk. Every desirable make of Bustles, Hip Pads and Bosom Forms. Makes no difference what you want in these lines—YOU CAN FIND IT HERE.

L. S. PLAUT & CO.

4-15

707 to 721 Broad Street, Newark, N. J.

Mail Orders Quickly Filled.
Close Saturdays 10 P. M.
Other Days 6 P. M.

CORSET.

DIRECTIONS FOR THE FRONT.

Use same measures as for basque, subtracting ½ inch from bust, waist and hip measures. The ½ inch is gained on the bust, by the overlapping of front dart, which makes it necessary to cut the front piece of the front separately. The Base Line at top of diagram is represented by the bust line, the darts are marked 2½ and 3 inches below as in ordinary dress waist, while the waist line is placed at distance of underarm from Base Line, or 9¼ inches in diagram and drawn straight across. The Base line extends 6 inches below waist line in order to obtain the correct hip measure, but the corset proper is only 5 inches below waist line, tapering gradually to a length of 3 inches over the hip. This length may be regulated and curved, however, to suit taste of the wearer. It must also be left to the individual judgment as to placing the stays, usually casings on each seam and between each seam will be sufficient. For large forms both darts may be made to overlap the same as front one.

DIRECTIONS FOR THE BACK.

Use ordinary measures, subtracting ½ inch from bust, waist and hip measures. You will observe that the center back line extends beyond the Base line ¼ inch at bottom of diagram and corset is same length over hip and in center of back as the front. In this diagram the back is divided into two equal parts; for larger forms divide into three sections.

1897

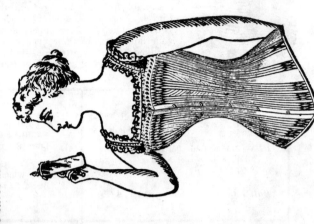

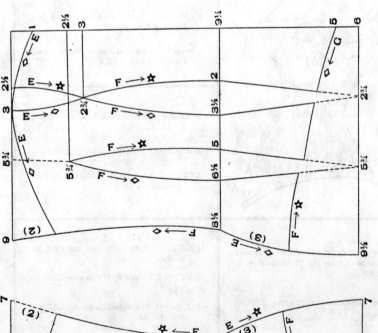

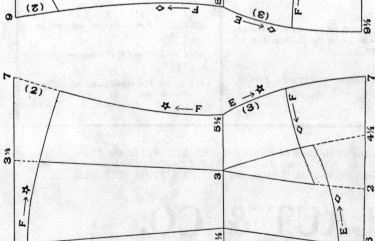

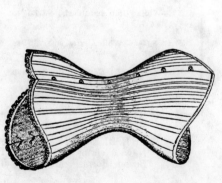

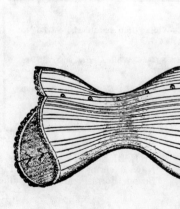

P.N. CORSETS.

ALL HAVE CORK PROTECTED CLASPS.

1897

Highest Unsolicited Testimonials Received Daily for

SCALES' Patent 'GEM CORSET,'

With Elastic Abdominal Belt Combined. The belt attached to a Hygienic Corset (recommended by the Faculty) cannot be displaced or wrinkled. It entirely avoids a high figure, marvellously improving the same, and never fails to reduce corpulency. It affords permanent support, and is most comfortable in every position of the body.

SATISFACTION GUARANTEED.

Should our stock sizes not fit we exchange and make to order, with any alterations 1/3 extra. White or Dove, 18/6; Black, 21/-; Satin (colours), 31/6. Sent post free to any lady on receipt of waist size and P.O. Name and patent number stamped on each corset.

R. SCALES & Co.,
Corset Manufacturers,
Newark-on-Trent, England.

Sole Agents for N.S.W.:
DAVID JONES & CO., Sydney.

1897

S & W 'Princess' Corsets.

In Black, Dove, White, &c.,
Prices, 2/11½, 3/11, 4/11, 5/11, and upwards.
For Style & Value Unsurpassed.
To be obtained from principal Drapers and Outfitters.
WHOLESALE AND EXPORT—
STRUGNELL & WATKINS,
50, Aldermanbury, London, E.C.

1898

1898

CORSETS.

200. Sizes 19 to 23. "KARA" FRENCH COUTIL, 12 inches long, 4 hooks, white only...........$1.50

201. Sizes 20 to 26. "KARA NURSING" FRENCH COUTIL, 13½ in. long, 5 hooks, white only ...$1.90

N. B.—Any style corset can be altered for nursing, to lace at top, 50 cents extra; or with laps as per cut, 75 cents extra.

202. Sizes 18 to 24. "KARA" FRENCH COUTIL, 11½ inches long, two side steels, extra short over hips, suitable for riding, cycling, etc., in white Coutil, $1.65; black Sateen $2.10

203. Sizes 20 to 28. "KARA" FRENCH COUTIL, 15 inches long, 5 hooks, spoon steels, medium low corded bust, white or gray...............$2.90

203½. Sizes 21 to 30. "KARA" FRENCH COUTIL, similar in style to No. 203, low bust, not corded, long over hips, white or gray. $3.85; black Sateen..$4.50

204. Sizes 18 to 30. "KARA" FRENCH COUTIL, 13½ inches long, 5 hooks, medium waist, white or gray, $1.50; black Sateen $2.10

204½. SAME SHAPE AS ILLUSTRATION, 4 hooks, in Linen, sizes 18 to 26...............$1.95

205. Sizes 18 to 24. "KARA BODICE," FOR CYCLING, FRENCH COUTIL, 11½ inches long in front, 5 hooks, white only..............$1.50

206. Sizes 18 to 24. "KARA" FRENCH COUTIL, strapped with Sateen; 14½ inches long, 5 hooks, patented double side steel; white or gray, $2.25; black Sateen, sizes 18 to 26 ....$2.75

207. Sizes 18 to 26. "GRECIA" FRENCH COUTIL, 12½ inches long, 4 hooks, short hips, lace trimmed top and bottom; in white, $2 95; black Sateen, $3.45

208. Sizes 18 to 26. "GRECIA" FRENCH COUTIL, 12½ inches long, 5 hooks, straight fr nt, low bust, real whalebone, plush around bottom, desirable for medium figures $4.75

209. Sizes 18 to 24. "KARA" FRENCH COUTIL, 15 inches long, 5 hooks, long waist and high bust, white or gray, $2.50; black Sateen $3.00

210. Sizes 18 to 26. "GRECIA" FRENCH COUTIL, 15 inches long, 5 hooks, two side steels, straight front effect, deep bust gores, long waist; white Coutil, $3.75; black Sateen...............$4.50

211. Sizes 18 to 26. "GRECIA" FRENCH COUTIL, 13½ inches long, 5 hooks, medium waist; sizes 24 to 26 have two side steels; in white, $3.00; black Sateen, 3.50; white Cotton Batiste........$2.85

212. Sizes 18 to 26. "GRECIA" FRENCH COUTIL, 13 inches long, 5 hooks, straight front, deep bust gores, in white, $3.75; black Sateen......$4.25

213. Sizes 18 to 26. "GRECIA" FRENCH COUTIL, 15 inches long, 5 hooks, extra long waist, two side steels; in white Coutil, $4.25; black Sateen..$4.90

In ordering Corsets, please state definitely the size desired, or mention exact waist measurement, taken over dress.

JOHN WANAMAKER

CORSETS DRESS IMPROVERS BUSTLES

No. 183. Lillian corsets made of fine coutil, medium waist, corded bust, two side steels, trimmed with lace and ribbon insertion, 2.00. Same style, without corded bust, made of coutil, 1.25.

No. 184. Ferris bicycle waists, distended bust, shoulder straps, rubber strips on side, which add comfort to the wearer, 1.00

No. 185. L. R. nursing corsets, long waist, made of jean, two side steels, 1.00. Same style, in fine coutil, 1.75

No. 186. Equipoise waists for absolute comfort, made of double muslin, buttoned front, boned back and front, 8 inches under arm, 2.25. Equipoise waists in finer muslin, single material, 3.00

No. 187. L. R. corsets, extra long waist, made of jean, sateen strips, two side steels, boned bust, fan back, white and drab, 1.50

No. 188. H. & S. corsets, extra long waist, made of jean, sateen strips, two side steels, boned bust, white and drab, 1.00.

No. 189. Thompson's glove-fitting corsets, medium waist, low bust, short hip, trimmed with lace top and bottom, white and drab, 1.00.

No. 190. L. R. abdominal corsets, made of coutil with spoon clasp, three side steels, boned bust, gored on hips, fan back, suitable for stout figure, 2.75; sizes, 32 to 36 inches, 3.00. Same style in black sateen, 3.25; sizes, 32 to 36 inches, 3.50.

No. 191. Lillian corsets, extra long waist made of fine coutil, boned bust, fan back, two side steels, white and drab, 3.50.

Same style in black sateen, 4.00

No. 192. French hair cloth bustles, 50c

No. 193. Tampico forms, 50c; small size, 25c

No. 194. French hair cloth hip bustles, 75c

P. D. corsets, medium length, made of fine coutil, sateen strips, boned bust, 2.50

L. R. corsets, long waist, made of jean, sateen strips, three side steels, boned bust, white and drab, 75c

L. R. corsets, medium waist, heavily boned, 1.00; 32 to 36 inches, 1.25

Warner's Coraline misses' corsets, with shoulder straps, 68c

FALL and WINTER, 1898-99

CORSETS.

In ordering, give number worn or the waist measure.   For Misses and Children, give size of the waist instead of age.

No. 100. La Vida, new short corset, all whalebone, embroidered in pink, blue and lavender, trimmed with lace and ribbons, $5.98; also long waist, $5.98; same corset in plain materials, plain white, drab and black, $4.50.

No. 116. Dr. Warner's French Model Coraline Corset, boned bust, white or drab, 18 to 30 inches, $1.00; black, $1.25; fine sateen, white and drab, $1.75; black, $2.00. Warner's Health Corset, white, drab and black, $1.25.

No. 104. La Vida, extra long waist, white and drab coutil, all whalebone, $3.50; black sateen, $4.00.

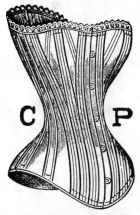

No. 106. C. P. French Coutil, long waist, white and drab, $1.75; white and drab, corded bust, $2.25; spoon steel, white and drab, $3.25; black sateen, $4.75.

No. 102. La Vida, new straight front model, all whalebone, white and drab, $5.98; black, $6.98.

No. 110. P. N. Corset of coutil, extra long waist, sateen strips, white, drab and black, 18 to 26 inches, $1.50; sateen, $1.25; medium length, $1.00.

No. 112. Abdominal Corset, 18 to 30 inches, $1.50; 33 to 36 inches, $1.75; Thomson's G. French Coutil Corset, drab or white, 18 to 32 inches, $1.50; 33 to 36 inches, $1.75; Thomson's E, white, drab and black sateen, 18 to 30 inches, $1.75.

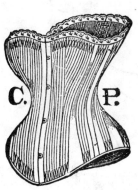

No. 114. C. P. Corset, fine French sateen, silk fanned, drab, white and black, 18 to 30 inches, $2.75; C. P. Venus, white and drab, $3.50; black, $3.75.

No. 108. P. D. Coutil Corset, long waist, white or drab, 18 to 30 inches, $1.75; boned bust $2.50; extra long sateen, $3.50; ventilating corset, $2.50.

CORSETS.

No. 165. C. B. Corset, extra long waist, white and drab, 18 to 28 inches, 75c; fine sateen, white, drab, and black..............................$1.25

No. 167. Her Majesty's Corset, jean, white or drab, also black sateen, 19 to 30 inches, $2.75; 31 to 33 inches, $3.00; 34 to 36 inches, $3.25. Black, heavy sateen, 19 to 30 inches, $4.00; 31 to 33 inches, $4.50; 34 to 36 inches, $5.00. Take measure tightly around the waist, and order corset two inches smaller than this measurement.

No. 183. The Nemo Nursing Corset, white and drab, 19 to 30 inches, $1.00.

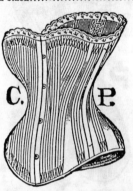

No. 171. C. P. Fine French Sateen, 18 to 30 inches, white, drab and black, $2.75; extra long waist, white and drab coutil, 18 to 26 inches, $1.75; spoon steel, $3.25; black sateen, $4.75.

No. 173. Abdominal Supporter, made of best material, with strong elastic bands, $1.75. When ordering, give measure from curve of back around abdomen.

No. 175. Patent Shoulder Brace, in white or drab, sizes 1, 2, 3, 4, according to the length of waist, 75c.

No. 177. Little Beauty Waists for Children, sizes from 22 to 27 inches waist measure, white only, 40c.

No. 179. Thomson's R. H. Short Jean Corset, length 11 inches, in white or drab, 18 to 32 inches, $1.00; 33 to 36 inches, $1.25.

No. 169. All Whalebone, low bust, long over the hips and abdomen, suitable for stout figures, white, drab and black, $4.50.

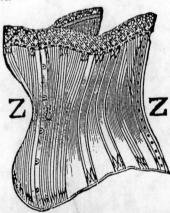

No. 185. Coutil Corset, extra long waist, well boned, white or drab, 18 to 30 inches, $3.25; in black, $4.00; long waist, white and drab coutil, 18 to 26 inches, $1.98.

No. 187. Ladies' Medium Form Sateen Cloth, button front and laced back, white and drab, 20 to 30 inches, $1.00; fine sateen, white and drab, lace hips. $1.50.

No. 189. Equipoise Waist, made of heavy twill, all whalebone, 8 and 9 inches under arm, white only, $2.25.

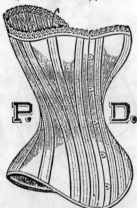

No. 181. P. D. Coutil Corset, long waist, white or drab, 18 to 30 inches. $1.75; boned bust, $2.50; extra long sateen, $3.50; ventilating corset, $2.00.

CORSETS.

No. 143. La Vida, extra long waist, white and drab coutil, all whalebone, $3.50; black sateen, $4.00.

No. 145. Short Hip Corset, white and drab, coutil and black sateen, $1.00; white batiste, $1.00.

No. 147. French Coutil Corset, with sateen strips, heavy boned bust, long waist, sizes 18 to 27 inches, white, drab or black, $1.50; well boned medium, in drab or white, 18 to 30 inches, $1.25; ventilating, medium, long waist, $1.00.

No. 149. Short Hip Corset, all whalebone, white and black, $4.50; same in embroidered cloth, white, ecru and black, $5.98.

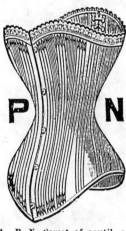

No. 151. P. N. Corset of coutil, extra long waist, sateen strips, white, drab and black, 18 to 26 inches, $1.50; sateen, $1.25; medium length, $1.00.

No. 153. La Vida, new straight front model, all whalebone, white, drab and black, $6.98.

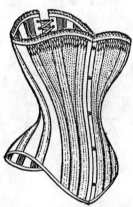

No. 155. Dr. Warner's French Model Coraline Corset, boned bust, white or drab, 18 to 30 inches, $1.00; black, $1.25. Warner's Health Corset, white, drab and black, $1.25.

No. 157. Extra long waist, white and drab coutil, sateen strips, also black sateen, $1.50; white and drab jean, $1.00.

No. 159. Sonnette Corset, medium waist, white, drab and black sateen, $1.50; long waist, $1.00, $1.25.

No 161. Abdominal Corset, 18 to 30 inches, $1.50; 33 to 36 inches, $1.75; Thomson's G. French Coutil Corset, drab or white, 18 to 32 inches, $1.50; 33 to 36 inches, $1.75; Thomson's E. white, drab and black sateen, 18 to 30 inches, $1.75.

No. 163. W. B. Short Corset, white, drab and black sateen, 18 to 26 inches, $1.00.

R & G CORSETS

R & G Corsets are the best for the following reasons:
They fit. They wear. They hold their shape.

They are made in a sufficient variety of styles to fit any figure. They are the same size from the day you first put them on until you discard them forever.

They are modeled on a perfect, natural human form, and their shape is made absolutely permanent by stretching over our steam iron form.

By this process, which we control exclusively, every atom of stretch is taken out of the goods. The corsets are dampened and clamped down on the hollow, iron form, with a pressure of six hundred pounds. Then the steam is turned into the form and the corset dries.

The material used in R & G Corsets is good. We don't say much about the materials because any manufacturer can buy good material. It isn't material that makes a corset good.—it is brains, and skill and careful work.

We put the same brains and skill into our dollar corsets that we do into our four-dollar ones.

So far as style, fit, comfort and wear are concerned our dollar corsets are as good as the more expensive ones—and better than expensive ones of any other make.

Our new number, 397, is perhaps, the most wholly satisfactory corset we ever made. It is a short corset, but has length enough in the bust and over the hips to bring out all the good points in the figure.

It can be had in 10,000 stores. If you have any trouble getting it, send us your dollar, tell us your size, and your dealer's name, and we will see that you get the corsets.

Send for our free booklet, "CHOOSING A CORSET." It will give you corset facts that you should know.

R & G CORSET CO., 355 Broadway, N. Y.

1899

1900s

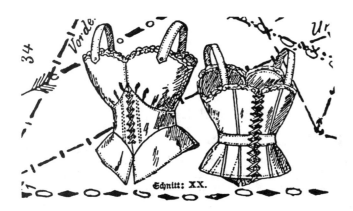

281. Unterleibchen für junge
Mütter.
Ueber das Arbeiten von Unter-
leibchen s. Seite VIII, von Hemden
Seite II.

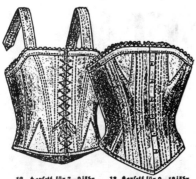

12. Korsett für 7—9 jähr.
Mädchen. Schnitt: XII auf
der Rückf. des Schnittbl. I.
Erforderl.: 35 cm Drell.

13. Korsett für 9—13 jähr.
Mädchen. Schnitt: XIII auf
der Rückf. des Schnittbl. I.
Erforderl.: 40 cm Drell.

10. Leibchen für 3—4 jährige
Mädchen. Schnitt: X auf der
Rückseite des Schnittblattes I.
Erf.: 30 cm Drell.

11. Leibchen für 4—6 jährige
Mädchen. Schnitt: XI auf der
Rückseite des Schnittblattes I.
Erf.: 35 cm Drell.

1900

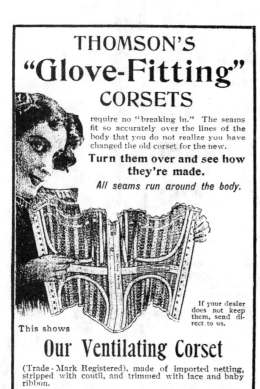

1900

1900 La Vida CORSETS

are without question superior to **any imported** corset sold in this country to-day. La Vidas are .all strictly hand-made, of the best and newest French materials, full gored, all whalebone and beautifully finished.

We recommend them strongly to every woman who has been wearing French corsets and paying an exorbitant price for them.

La Vidas are fitted to American models when manufactured, and they fit the American figure without alteration. This cannot be said of any imported corset.

La Vida Corsets are made in styles to suit all figures. We have. them in short, medium, long and extra long waist styles, and different shape bust and hips.

No. 609. For short waisted stout figures, very low bust, long over hips, made of imported satin finished diamond cloth, in white, drab and black, sizes 19 to 36 inches.. .... $4.50

THE LATEST FRENCH MODELS OF
LA VIDA CORSETS WITH

STRAIGHT FRONT EFFECT.

No. 648. For slender, long waisted figures, long over hip, made of French white coutil and black diamond cloth, sizes 18 to 26 inches. $6.98

No. 680. Same as style No. 648 in mohair batiste, sizes 18 to 26 inches.............. $5.98

No. 681. For well developed figures, medium, low, full bust, long over hip, made of French white coutil and black diamond cloth, sizes 20 to 28 inches................................... $6.98

No. 686. For medium and slender figures, made of French white coutil and black diamond cloth, sizes 18 to 26 inches................ $4.98

No. 509. **Extra Long Waist**, high bust, made of imported satin finished diamond cloth, in white, drab and black, sizes 18 to 30 inches................................. ......$4.50

No. 672. For long waisted figures, made of diamond sateen, in white and drab, sizes 19 to 30 inches, $2.75; black sateen............. $3.00

No. 631. For medium waisted figures, short full hip, made of diamond cloth, white and black, handsome lace trimming, sizes 18 to 26 inches, $4.50; same in embroidered cloth......$5.98

No. 670. **Short Hip**, white and drab coutil sizes 18 to 26 inches, $2.50; black sateen. $2.75

CORSETS.

"SONNETTE"

No. 344. Sonnette Corset, medium waist, white and drab coutil, sateen strips in black sateen..................................$1.25

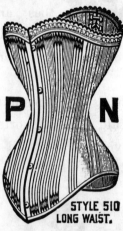

STYLE 510
LONG WAIST.

No. 346. P. N. Corset of coutil, extra long waist, sateen strips, white, drab and black, 18 to 26 inches, $1.50; sateen, $1.25; medium length..................................$1.00

SONNETTE

No. 348. Sonnette Corset, white, drab and black sateen........................$1.98

No. 352. Abdominal Supporter, made of best material, with strong elastic bands, $1.75. When ordering, give measure from curve of back around abdomen.

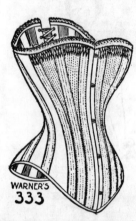

WARNER'S
333

No. 358. Dr. Warner's French Model Coraline Corset, boned bust, white or drab, 18 to 30 inches, $1.00; black, $1.25. Warner's Health Corset, white, drab and black....$1.25

THOMSON'S "GLOVE-FITTING" CORSET
PARIS SHAPE (SHORT HIP)

No. 362. Thomson's Short Hip Corset, white, drab and black..............$1.50

No. 356. Thomson's R. H. Short Jean Corset, length 11 inches, in white or drab, 18 to 32 inches, $1.00; 33 to 36 inches...$1.25

No. 360. Patent Shoulder Brace, in white and drab, sizes 1, 2, 3, 4, according to the length of waist..................................75c

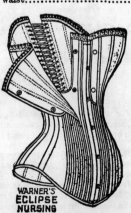

WARNER'S
ECLIPSE
NURSING

No. 364. Warner's Nursing Corset, white and drab................$1.00

W.B.

No. 366. Extra long waist, white and drab coutil, sateen strips, also black sateen, $1.50; white and drab jean........................$1.00

No. 354. Little Beauty Waists for Children, sizes from 22 to 27 inches waist measure, white only..................................40c

Silk Corset Laces, 5 yards long, white, drab, black, pink, blue, orange, heliotrope, 35c. each. Hoop Skirt Tape Front with elastic, hoops all the way up, $1.50; Tape Front without elastic, $1.25; Round Hoop Skirt, 85c.; Tape Front, hoops half-way up, $1.00.

CORSETS.

No. 324. W. B. Short Corset, white, drab and black sateen, 18 to 26 inches....$1.00

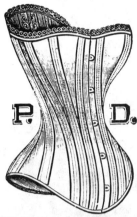

No. 326. P. D. Coutil Corset, long waist, white or drab, 18 to 30 inches, $1.75; boned bust, $2.50; extra long sateen, $3.50; ventilating corset... ....$2.00

No. 328. Abdominal Corset, 18 to inches, $1.50; 33 to 36 inches, $1.75; Thomson's G. French Coutil Corset, drab white, 18 to 32 inches, $1.50; 33 to 36 inches $1.75; Thomson's E. white, drab and black sateen, 18 to 30 inches. $1.75

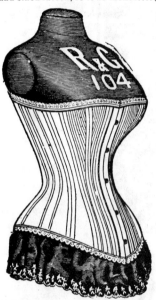

No. 330. French Coutil Corset, with sateen strips, heavy boned bust, long waist, sizes 18 to 27 inches, white, drab or black, $1.50; well boned medium, in drab or white. 18 to 30 inches, $1.25; ventilating, medium, long waist $1.00

No. 332. Her Majesty's Corset, jean, white or drab, also black sateen, 19 to 30 inches, $2.75; 31 to 33 inches, $3.00; 34 to 36 inches, $3.25. Black, heavy sateen, 19 to 30 inches, $4.00; 31 to 33 inches, $4.50; 34 to 36 inches, $5.00. Take measure tightly around the waist, and order corset two inches smaller than this measurement.

No. 334. Short Hip Corset, white and drab coutil and black sateen, $1.00; white batiste........................$1.00

No. 336. Ladies' Medium Form Sateen Cloth, button front and laced back, white and drab, 20 to 30 inches, $1.00; fine sateen, white and drab, lace hips........$1.50

No. 338. Equipoise Waist, made of heavy twill, all whalebone, 8 and 9 inches under arm, white only........................$2.25

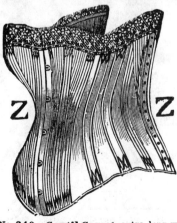

No. 340. Coutil Corset, extra long waist, well boned, white or drab, 18 to 30 inches, $3.25; in black, $4.00; long waist, white or drab coutil, 18 to 26 inches........................$1.98

No. 342. C. B. Corset, extra long waist, white and drab, 18 to 28 inches, 75c; fine sateen, white, drab and black. $1.25

1901

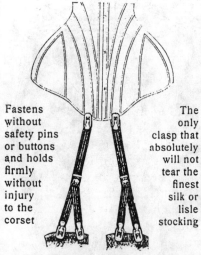
1902

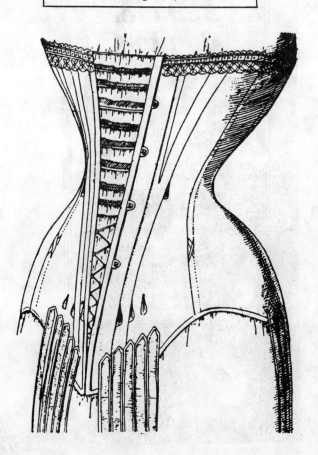

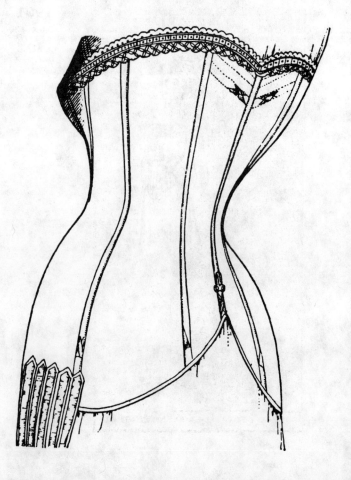

Sahlin Perfection=Lace Stay

A FLAT=LACING CORSET

Notice the triangular cloth eyelet; no metal eyes to corrode, rust or pull out. The lacer lies perfectly flat, does not twist, but draws easily, will not wear out, does not make painful ridges in the flesh nor show through the outer garments. This Perfection-Lace Stay is used solely on the **Sahlin Corsets**

THE SAHLIN CORSET

is a Model of Elegant Form designed on such artistic lines as to fit and give grace and erect carriage to every figure. In every latest fabric, the line of corsets are unequalled for excellence and beauty of manufacture. Sahlin Corsets have merits not found in any other corset on the market, either in the United States or Europe. If you wish to be satisfied, accept no substitute. The name **Sahlin** is stamped on every garment. Ask your dealer. If he cannot supply you, order direct. Popular prices.

$1.00 to $5.00
Postpaid

In ordering, state size and color wanted. Write for **FREE** catalogue containing interesting literature,

"How to Wear a Corset."

SAHLIN CORSET CO., 41 FULTON ST., CHICAGO, ILL.

1902

WB ERECT FORM CORSETS

THE W. B. Erect Form is the original "Long Hip" Corset. It is the most perfect model of this vogue. The Long Hip Erect Form not only gives the figure a graceful erect form poise but rounds off the figure and reaches well down over the hips, absolutely insuring a perfect set to the new habit skirts.

Ask for the following styles

Erect Form 989 at $1.00
Erect Form 992 at $1.50
Erect Form 711 at $2.00
Erect Form 713 at $4.00

If your dealer cannot supply you, write direct to us and mention his name, state size and number desired, enclose post-office money order or check and the corset will be sent to you.

WEINGARTEN BROS., Makers
Dept. E, 377-379 Broadway, New York

Largest Manufacturers of Corsets in the World.

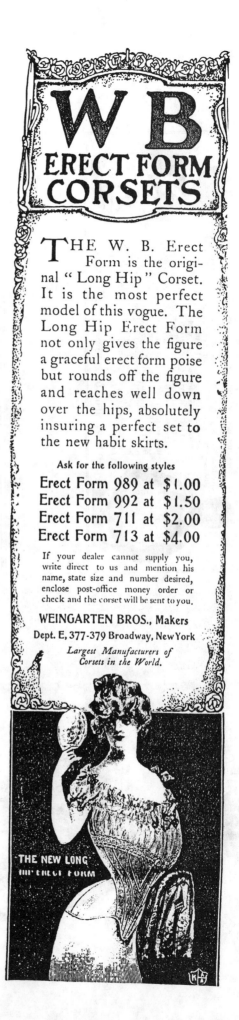

THE NEW LONG HIP ERECT FORM

Corsets and Dress Improvers

No. 2601.—L. R. corsets, bias gored, dip hip, long waist, sizes 18 to 30, $1.50.

No. 2602.—L. R. corsets, bias gored, straight front, extremely long over abdomen and hips, a good model for stout figures, sizes 22 to 30, $2.50.

No. 2603.—Dainty girdles of white tape for young ladies, sizes 18 to 24, $1.00.

No. 2604.—Lea corsets, made expressly for us, bias gored, long dip hips, front garters attached, sizes 19 to 30, $2.50.

No. 2605.—Warner's Lorena corsets of batiste, bias gored, medium length, made of rust-proof steels, sizes 18 to 24, $1.00.

No. 2606.—Warner's Irene, of fine batiste, bias gored, dainty corset for short, slender figures, sizes 18 to 24, $1.50.

No. 2607.—Ferris waists, of jean, laced on hips, sizes 19 to 30, $1.25.

No. 2608.—Equipoise waists, fine twill, low neck, inches under arm, sizes 22 to 30, $3.00.

No. 2609.—Nemo self-reducing corsets, long hips, low bust, supports and reduces abdomen, sizes 21 to 30, $2.50.

No. 2610.—Ruffs of net, made extra full for bust of corsets, $1.25.

No. 2611.—Small pad bustles, 25c.

No. 2612.—Hygeia wire forms, light and cool, 50c.

No. 2613.—Fairy bust forms of fine net, 50c.

No. 2614.—Empire wire bustles, 25c.

In ordering corsets do not omit size. Measure waist tight over dress, and order corset two inches less than measure

FALL and WINTER, 1903-1904

Corsets

No. 2501.—L. R. corsets of sateen, low bust, medium length, heavily boned, sizes 19 to 30, $1.00.

No. 2502.—L. R. corsets, low bust, short hip, for slender figures, sizes 18 to 23, $1.00.

No. 2503.—L. R. corsets of fine coutil, bias gores, for medium figure, sizes 18 to 30, $1.50.

No. 2504.—L. R. corsets of fine coutil, medium long waist, bias gores, prettily trimmed with lace top and bottom, sizes 18 to 30, $2.00.

No. 2505.—L. R. corsets, made especially for stout figures, of heavy coutil, bias gores, long over abdomen and hips, sizes 21 to 33, $3.75.

No. 2506.—L. R. girdles of batiste, prettily trimmed with lace top and bottom. These girdles are for slight forms or for growing girls, sizes 18 to 24, $1.00.

No. 2507.—L. R. girdles, for slender figures, fine batiste, a nice shirtwaist corset, sizes 18 to 23, $1.50.

No. 2508.—L. R. nursing corsets, medium long waist, strongly boned, sizes 19 to 30, $1.00.

No. 2509.—L. R. corsets, medium long waist, dip hip, bias gored, low bust, sizes 18 to 30, $1.00.

In ordering corset do not omit size. Measure waist tight over dress, and order corset two inches less than measure

FALL and WINTER, 1903-1904

Lillian Corsets

No. 2401.—Lillian corsets of fine coutil, bias gored, medium long waist, sizes 19 to 30, $2.50.

No. 2402.—Lillian corsets of coutil, low bust, long over abdomen and hips, garters attached, sizes 19 to 30, $3.50.

No. 2403.—Lillian corsets, extreme straight front, low bust, long hips, front garters, sizes 19 to 25, $6.50.

No. 2404.—Lillian corsets, extreme straight front, long dip hip, low bust, front and side garters attached, sizes 19 to 26, $7.00.

No. 2405.—Lillian corsets of strong coutil, bias gored, strongly boned, medium long waist for full figures, sizes 19 to 36, $9.50.

No. 2406.—Lillian corsets of coutil, extremely strongly boned, front and side garters, a good for stout figures, sizes 20 to 32, $10.00.

No. 2407.—Lillian corsets of white dotted silk tiste, medium long waist, front and side garters, 19 to 27, $12.50.

No. 2408.—Lillian corsets of fine coutil, low bust, long hips, for full figures, sizes 20 to 29, $12.50.

No. 2409.—Lillian girdles of white satin ribbon, desirable for evening wear, sizes 18 to 23, $5.50.

In ordering corsets do not omit size. Measure waist tight over dress, and order corset two inches less than measure

FALL and WINTER, 1903-

BE TRIM

The narrow-hipped, slender appearance with attractively
defined waist line is acquired by wearing the

"Dip Hip" G-D *Justrite* Corset

The correct corset for women desirous of having a smart appearance. Have one
fitted to you at your dealers. A variety of styles for every type of figure.

Sold by leading dealers everywhere. Write for our "Corset Guide;"
shows latest models; helps you select the right one for your figure. **FREE**

GAGE-DOWNS COMPANY, 268 Fifth Avenue, CHICAGO

Photograph of Style No. 204

1904

The Shoulder Pull

The Ferris Waist puts the weight and pull of the child's clothing in the right place—evenly on both shoulders—relieving the tightness and strain at the waist line, and giving the back proper poise and support.

FERRIS
GOOD SENSE WAISTS

hold skirts and hose in the best way. They are made for women and children of every age and size, and are sold by leading dealers. The name is sewed in red on every waist.

Illustrated Ferris Book mailed free.

THE FERRIS BROS. COMPANY,
341 Broadway, New York.

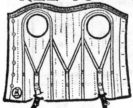

THREE J. C. C. GRACES

The perfect contour of these splendid models denotes the *style* standard for all **J. C. C. Corsets.** In beauty of fabric, embellishment of lace, and in strength virtue, a **J. C. C.** is fully up to all that is expected of a *good* corset.

You will find these worthy models at first-class stores. An order by mail will be promptly filled, either by your dealer or by us. The styles here listed are up to fashion's need, and are an assured *fit* for the types of figure designated.

"1905," Long Skirt		$1.00 per pair 1.75 extra fine material
"Fashion Hip"......	average figures	1.00 per pair
"Peerless"......		1.00 per pair
"Royales"..........		1.50 per pair
"Gold Medal"........	slender figures	1.00 per pair
"Allright"..........		1.00 per pair
"Superb Form"......	medium full figures	1.50 per pair
"New Grand"........	stout figures	1.50 per pair

THE JACKSON CORSET CO., Jackson, Mich.

The **"R.S."**
PATENT REDUCING
CORSET.
With Elastic Abdominal Belt
Entirely avoids a high figure, and reduces corpulency. Gives a flat front effect and strong binding support with absolute comfort.

BLACK, WHITE, OR DOVE,
Real **10 6** *Whalebone.*
Sizes stocked, 19 to 36 inches: over 30-inch waist, 4d. per inch extra. Should stock sizes not fit, we exchange and make with any alterations, 1 6 extra. Sample sent to any lady, post free, upon receipt of waist size and P.O. Abroad Orders, 1/6 extra.

R. SCALES & CO.,
Corset Specialists,
Newark-on-Trent, Eng.

10/6

1905

The CINOPI
(REGD.)
The Best Belted Corset
Ever Introduced.

Straight Fronted. 15-ins. deep.
This Corset has a buckle attached to each side of the belt, which allows the front to be made tight or loose as desired.

To be had in French Grey, White, or Black, **8/11**; also in Black Broché, **14/6.**

Of all Drapers, or on receipt of Postal Order and size of Waist to—

KIRBY BROS. (Dept. 10), Commercial Rd., PECKHAM, S.E.
Illustrated Price List Free.

The Vogue of the Girdle

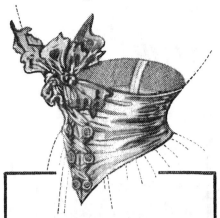

Every fashion paper illustrates it
Every fashion leader advocates it
Every fashion article preaches it

Our Girdle Foundations are time-savers. They're of crinoline with Featherbone supports—and may be quickly and easily covered to suit any fancy.

The Featherbone's as readily sewn through as is the crinoline. And it's supple, pliable and thin, fitting in to the waistline snugly and in graceful curves. There are styles of Girdle Foundations for every figure and every taste.

Phyllis Girdle Foundation No. 2   Retails at 20 Cents

No. 0 Phyllis, for short-waisted figures, blunt point front and back, **12c. No. 2 Phyllis**, wide and unbound, to cut what shape you please, **20c. No. 4 Phyllis**, pointed in front and above and below waistline in back, **15c. No. 5 Phyllis**, extreme corselet shape, fastens in back, **18c. No. 6 Phyllis**, pointed below waist in front and above in back, fastens in back, **15c. No. 12 Phyllis**, fastens in back, **12c.**

All girdles made in black and white, waist sizes 20 to 34.

No. 6 Girdle Foundation   Retails at 15 Cents

Make your collars over **Warren's Featherbone Stock Foundations.** Of mousseline de soie, with supports of fine collarbone; perfect fitting, comfortable, durable; in black and white; round and pointed; heights 1½ to 2½; sizes 12 to 16. Retail at 10c. and 20c.

Warren's Featherbone and Featherbone Specialties are carried by reliable dealers everywhere. If yours can't supply you send to us direct, with price. **Write for catalogue.**

Look for the Warren Featherbone trademarks, the turkey, the feather and the red letter tag—they're your surety of quality.

The Warren Featherbone Co.

Maple Street, Three Oaks, Mich.

BRANCHES IN:
NEW YORK: 44 East 23d Street, Corner Fourth Avenue.
BOSTON: 7 Temple Place.
CHICAGO: 706 Marshall Field Annex Building.
SAN FRANCISCO: 6-8 Sutter Street.
MONTREAL & TORONTO: The Featherbone Novelty Co.

1905

W.H.B. "DIMINUENT" CORSETS.

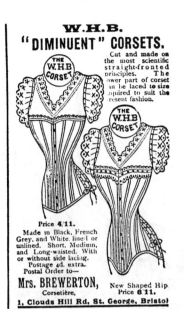

Cut and made on the most scientific straight-fronted principles. The lower part of corset can be laced to size required to suit the present fashion.

Price **4/11.**
Made in Black, French Grey, and White, lined or unlined. Short, Medium, and Long-waisted. With or without side lacing.
Postage 4d. extra.
Postal Order to—

Mrs. BREWERTON,
Corsetière,
1, Clouds Hill Rd, St. George, Bristol

New Shaped Hip
Price **6/11.**

IZOD'S CORSETS.

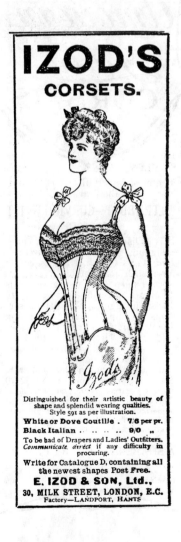

Distinguished for their artistic beauty of shape and splendid wearing qualities.
Style 591 as per illustration.

White or Dove Coutille . **7/6** per pr.
Black Italian . .. . **9/0** „

To be had of Drapers and Ladies' Outfitters. *Communicate direct* if any difficulty in procuring.

Write for Catalogue D, containing all the newest shapes Post Free.

E. IZOD & SON, Ltd.,
30, MILK STREET, LONDON, E.C.
Factory—LANDPORT, HANTS

American Lady CORSETS

1905

150 STYLES — $5.00 to $1.00

The most important corset creation of the year is our

"ULTRA BUST—CURVING WAIST"
Model 750

It is a distinct innovation in corset designing. Like all *American Lady* Corsets it has the essentials for stylish form building, but the special purpose of this garment is to give a sweeping curve effect to the entire figure. The lateral sections accomplish this by training the flesh from the front to the sides and back. They produce the ideal contour upon which to fit the fashionable fall gown.

Made of fine coutil in white and drab. Sizes 18 to 30. The price, $2.00

Sent prepaid if not procurable at your dealers. There are many other new styles of *American Lady* Corsets now on sale at the stores. All are perfect fitting and the great variety of designs insures

A SHAPE FOR EVERY FIGURE

American Lady Corset Co.
New York   Detroit   Chicago
Write for new booklet.

American Lady CORSETS

FORM-TRAINING SERIES

For women of full development for figures where there is an abundance of flesh or physiques exhibiting a tendency toward corpulency, these models are earnestly prescribed. They are the first and only ready-made, medium-priced corsets to successfully accomplish the task of TRAINING large forms into lines of symmetry and fashion. The horizontal lower section eradicates all abdominal prominence. There is no forcing or unnatural manipulation—these designs TRAIN the form so that the results may be permanent and without ill effects.

Model 590
For large Figures. Fine Coutil material. Supporters front and side. White only $5.00

Model 585
For medium large figures. Made of Coutil. Supporters front and side. White and Drab $3.50

Model 775
For large Figures. Without gores. Hercule cloth. White and Drab. Sizes 20 to 30. $3.50

150 STYLES
A SHAPE FOR EVERY FIGURE

American Lady Corset Co.
DETROIT. NEW YORK. CHICAGO.

JOHN WANAMAKER, NEW YORK 1905

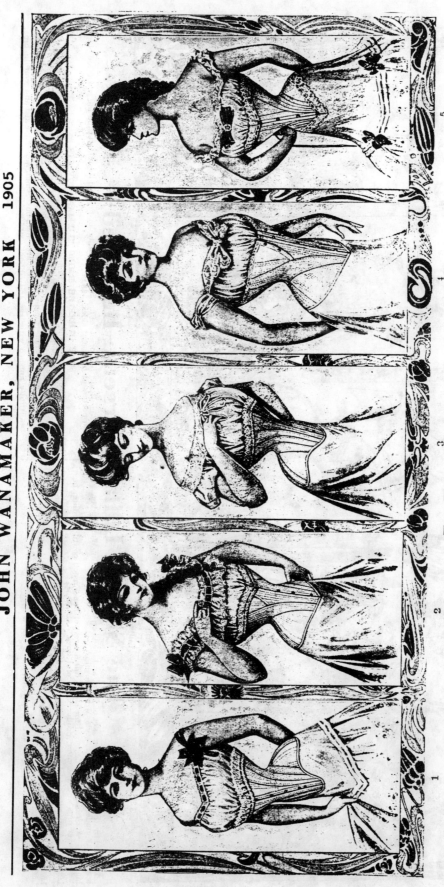

L. R. Corsets

L. R. Corsets are designed from latest Paris models, and made especially for The Wanamaker Store by the best American *corsetier*

DESCRIPTIONS OF OTHER FAVORITE L. R. MODELS

1—For medium figures; straight-front gored Corsets; long over hips and abdomen; $1.00.
2—Medium bust and hips; full gored and bias cut; light and comfortable; $1.00.
3—For slight figures, cut in Empire mode from waist up; long over hips and abdomen; $1.00.
4—Nursing Corsets; convenient; and aiding the figure to regain its normal lines; $1.00.
5—A good model for slender and medium figures; light-weight; medium bust; small waist and short hips; $1.50.

11—Short Corsets, for slight figures; low bust and short hips; $1.00.
12—Empire girdles; for girls and petite figures; fine batiste; lace-trimmed top and bottom; $1.00
13—For medium figures; gives right proportions to figure; is comfortable and graceful; $1.50.
14—For medium and full figures; moderately high bust; small waist; long over hips and abdomen; $1.50.
15—A graceful model, which fits without constraint, and gives the approved rounded contour. Medium bust; short hips; $2.00.

JOHN WANAMAKER, NEW YORK 1905

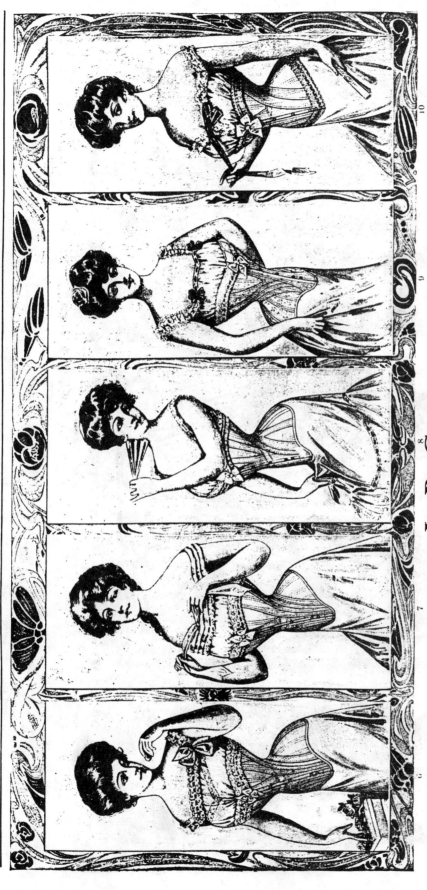

L. R. Corsets

6—High bust; small tapering waist and long hips; a beautiful model for average figures, giving comfort and grace; $2.00.
7—A new model, with high bust; small waist; medium hips; bringing out the most graceful lines of the figure; $2.00.
8—Newest Fall model; for tall figures; gives roundness of waist, curve of hips; long under arm; long back-line; $3.00.
9—A beautiful model, of fancy silk-figured brocade; long, small waist; high bust; moulds the figure into elegant lines; $5.50.
10—A model for full, stout figures; long over hips and abdomen; medium bust; low under arm; heavily boned; made to withstand severe usage; $3.75.

MORE L. R. CORSETS AND OTHER STYLISH WANAMAKER MODELS

16—L. R. Corsets for long-waisted figures; high bust and long hips; $2.50.
17—L. R. Corsets of fancy figured brocade; high bust; small waist; long hips; beautifully finished; $5.00.
18—L. R. Corsets of fancy figured silk batiste, for slender figures, medium high bust; small tapering waist and short hips; $5.50.
19—Wanamaker Special Corsets, No. 162; made of light-weight batiste; medium bust and long hips; $1.00, and worth one-half more than their price.
20—Wanamaker Special Corsets, No. 163; for average figures; of fine quality batiste; beautifully finished with lace and ribbon; medium bust, dip hips; $1.50, worth a dollar more.

More Corsets, Corset Waists and Accessories

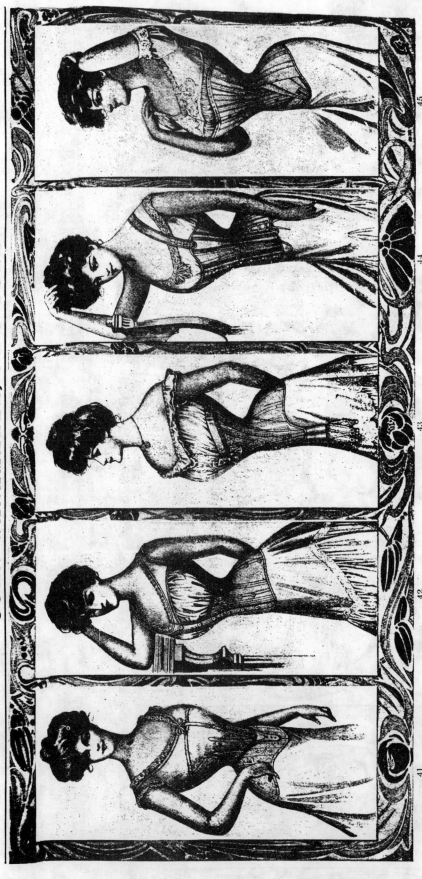

41—Lillian "Brassière" Bust Supporter and Corset Cover combined; lightly boned; of easily laundered batiste; edged with lace and ribbon. Sizes 32 to 46; $1.00.
42—"Equipoise" Waists; white only. Sizes: 20 to 34 in.: 8 inches under arm; $3.00.
43—Wanamaker Special "Lea" Corsets; latest model; fine coutil; trimmed with lace and ribbon. Moderately high bust; dip hips; supporters attached; in white only; $2.50.
44—Ferris "Good Sense" Waists; sateen cloth; buttoned in front; medium form and length; hip-lacing for adjustment. Sizes 20 to 30, $1.25; sizes 31 to 36, $1.50.
45—Nemo Self-reducing Corsets; for stout figures; long hips; medium bust; low under arm; completely reduces hips and abdomen; heavily boned. Sizes 20 to 36 in.; $2.50.

Wanamaker Special Corsets "R. & G. 1905." Fine batiste, medium bust; supporters front and sides. Sizes 18 to 26 only; $1.00.
Wanamaker Special Corsets "P. N. 1201." Light-weight coutil; for medium and full figure. Long over hips and abdomen; low under arm; supporters front and sides. Sizes 18 to 30; $1.3
"Wanamaker Special" extra wide Tape Girdles; for slight figures; with supporters; $1.0

CORSET ACCESSORIES

Net Ruffs, to fill in corsets, for slender figures; $1.00.
"Fairy" Bust Forms; white net; 50c. Ferris Bust Forms; cover can be removed to be washed; $
"Empire" Wire Bustles; light and cool. 25c. Small hair pad Bustles; 25c.
"Century" Side Shields; prevent side-steels of corsets from breaking; 20c. pair.

No. 1 is a ribbon or tape girdle, especially favored for golf, tennis and other outdoor sports; No. 2 is a novelty corset of brocaded satin, lacing at each side of the front; No. 3 combines a bust supporter of white satin ribbon and a hip reducing corset of sateen; No. 4 is a slightly boned silk jersey model for a medium figure, giving the high bust effect.

1905

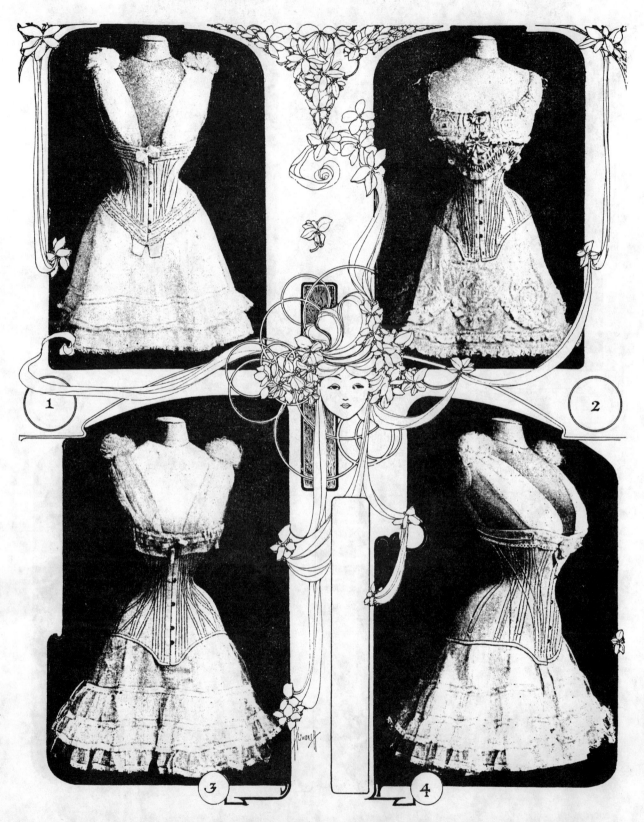

No. 1 is a plain little corset designed especially to soften the angles of an extremely slight figure; No. 2, made of fancy sateen with ribbon decoration, shows the natural hip and high bust effect; No. 3, illustrated in white coutil, is for larger hips and high bust; No. 4, of white satin, is designed to reduce the too pronounced curves below the waist.

1905

The Corset that lengthens the waist

To secure a long waist, yet a small one without increasing abdomen and hips, requires the finest art of the corsetiere. The genius of the artist is shown in the effects produced by the new spring

G-D Justrite CORSET.

No two figures are exactly alike. The G-D Justrite Corsets are made in such a wide variety of models and sizes that every woman may find the one exactly suited to herself.

Ask at the shops for the G-D Justrite Corset and don't be persuaded to purchase any other. If not easily obtainable, write us and we will see that you are supplied.

Made in plain and fancy materials from $1 to $5 according to quality of fabric.

Our free book, "JUST THE RIGHT CORSET," is valuable to women who give thought to their appearance. Write for it.

Gage-Downs Company   268 Fifth Avenue   Chicago

1906

1906

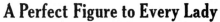

IN SUPPORT

of well tried rules for health and comfort notice the straps of the Ferris Waist. The weight of heavy skirts, damaging to the strongest woman's constitution is transferred from waist to shoulders, leaving the body free and untrammelled.

FERRIS' GOOD SENSE
Corset Waist

is made to suit all tastes in high or low bust, long or short waist. Children's, 25c. to 50c. Misses', 50c. to $1. Ladies', $1 to $2. For sale by all retailers.

1906

FOR FIFTY YEARS
THOMSON'S "GLOVE-FITTING" CORSETS

have been famous throughout the world for models of excellency and graceful effect. This season we are introducing our latest invention, the

NEW GRAND DUCHESS

The patented feature (illustrated) consists of a separate transverse and horizontal section. By this device the proper support is given where most needed, carrying all excess flesh from front to back, preserving the flat line at the abdomen, and *permanently* creating in the figure a rounded waist and long flowing lines.

Price $1.50 to $5 the pair.

GEORGE C. BATCHELLER & CO.
New York   Chicago   San Francisco

They are called "Glove-Fitting" because they fit as well and feel as comfortable as a fine kid glove.

1906

A Faultless Figure

has the long lines, well accentuated round waist, modified hips and a graceful waist line. All these and from two to four inches longer waist are given by the

G-D *Justrite* CORSET.

In the variety of models offered by this scientifically designed corset, every fault is corrected, every good line and graceful curve brought out.

Ask at the corset department for G-D Justrite. Have several styles fitted to you until you find *your corset*. If a store does not keep the G-D Justrite *don't buy* an inferior corset. Write us and we will see that you are supplied *at once*. The extreme comfort and the attractiveness of your figure in a G-D Justrite make it *pay you to insist upon getting this corset.*

Our "Corset Book" is the latest authority on the correct lines of the figure. We send it *free*.

Gage-Downs Co., 265 Fifth Ave., Chicago

WARNER'S
Rust=Proof
CORSETS

Our Spring Styles Are Made on
LOUIS XV

"SECURITY"
Rubber Button
Hose Supporters
Attached

Prices from One to
Five Dollars

THE WARNER
BROS CO

New York, Chicago
San Francisco

Straight-Front Lines
With the Added Beauty of Curves at Waist, Back and Sides

Every Pair Guaranteed

1906

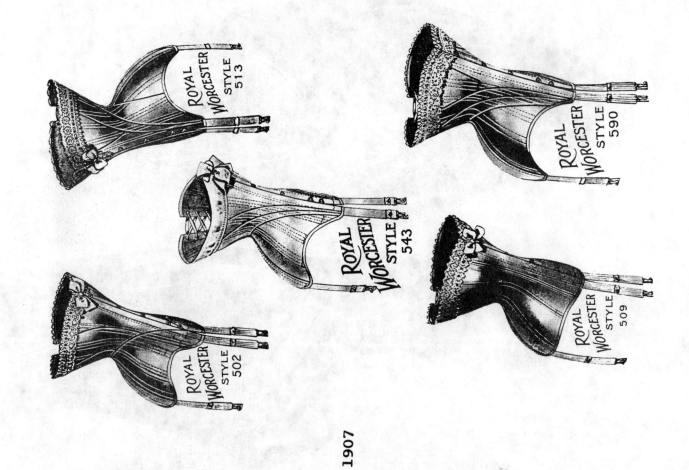

ROYAL WORCESTER STYLE 513

ROYAL WORCESTER STYLE 590

ROYAL WORCESTER STYLE 543

ROYAL WORCESTER STYLE 509

ROYAL WORCESTER STYLE 502

1907

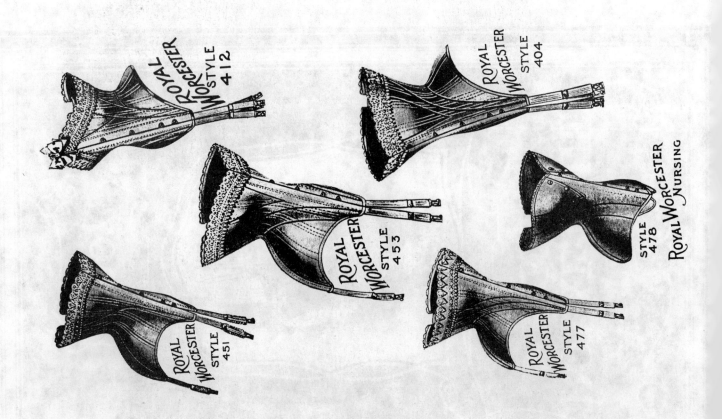

ROYAL WORCESTER STYLE 412

ROYAL WORCESTER STYLE 404

ROYAL WORCESTER STYLE 453

ROYAL WORCESTER NURSING STYLE 478

ROYAL WORCESTER STYLE 451

ROYAL WORCESTER STYLE 477

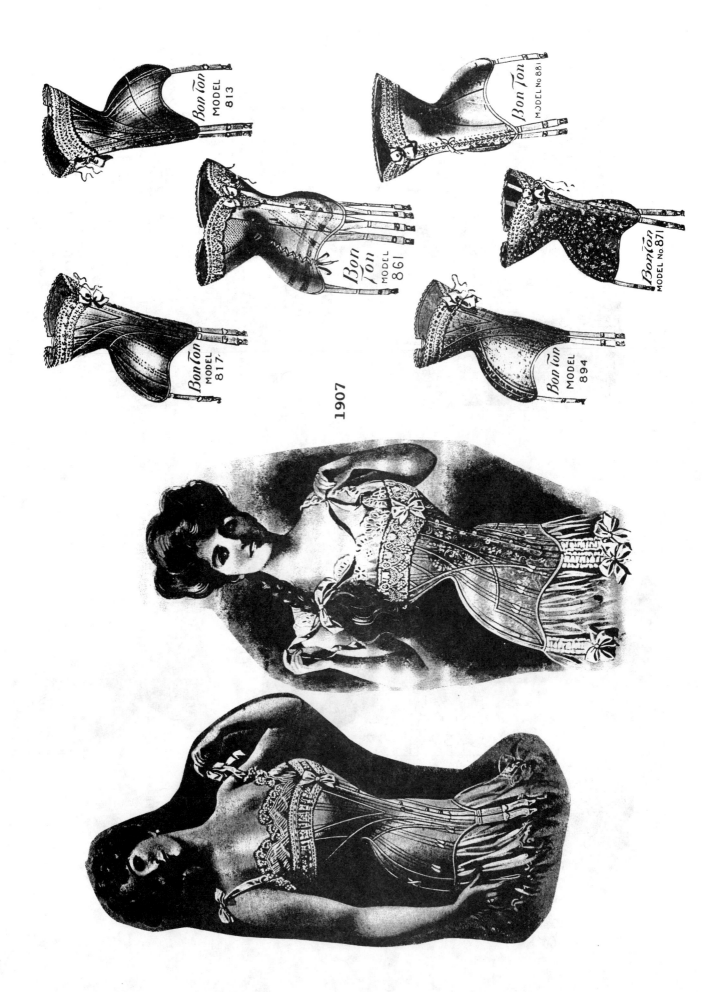

Bon Ton MODEL 813

Bon Ton MODEL No 881

Bon Ton MODEL 861

Bon Ton MODEL No 871

Bon Ton MODEL 817.

Bon Ton MODEL 894

1907

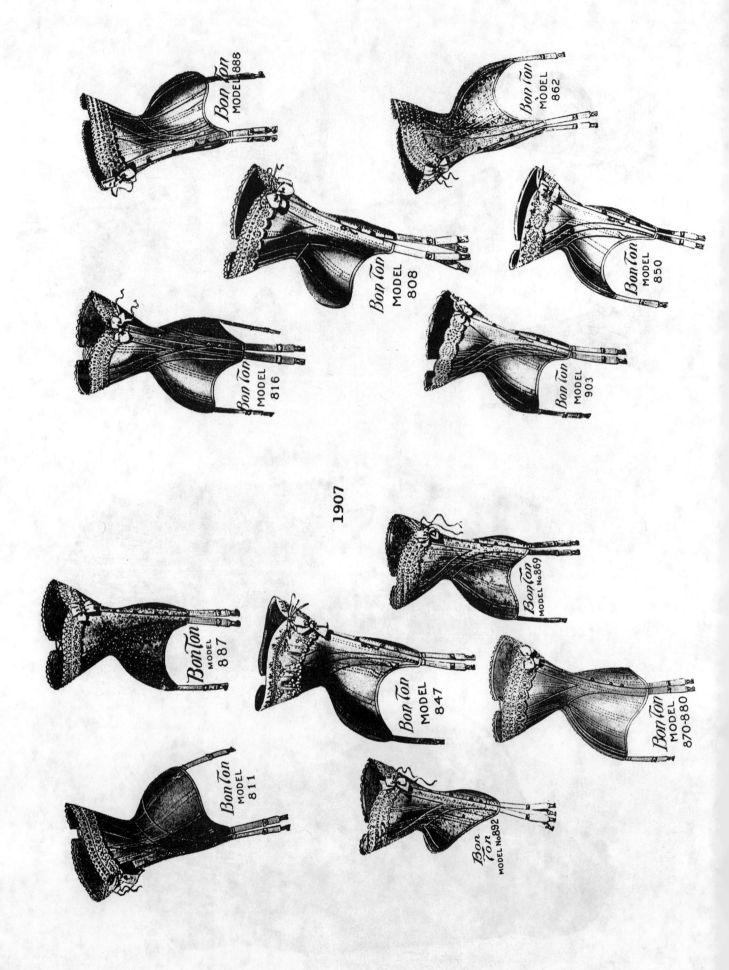

1907

Bon Ton MODEL 888

Bon Ton MODEL 862

Bon Ton MODEL 808

Bon Ton MODEL 850

Bon Ton MODEL 816

Bon Ton MODEL 903

Bon Ton MODEL No 869

Bon Ton MODEL 887

Bon Ton MODEL 847

Bon Ton MODEL 870-880

Bon Ton MODEL 811

Bon Ton MODEL No 892

1907

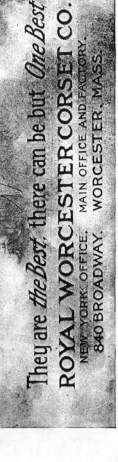

Your Modiste WILL SUCCEED AS NEVER BEFORE IF YOU WEAR A

BON TON CORSET

SUPPLYING THE MAXIMUM OF COMFORT, STYLE AND VALUE

Sold by the leading Dealers. If yours cannot supply you write us for information where to buy.

They are *the Best,* there can be but *One Best*

ROYAL WORCESTER CORSET CO.

NEW YORK OFFICE, 840 BROADWAY.

MAIN OFFICE AND FACTORY, WORCESTER, MASS.

1907

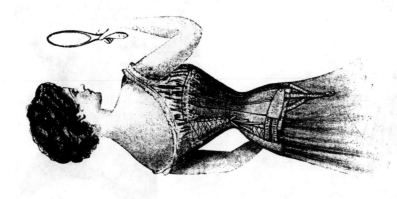

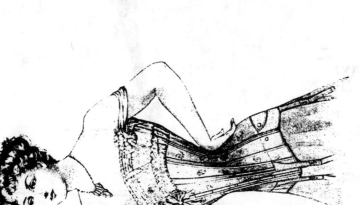

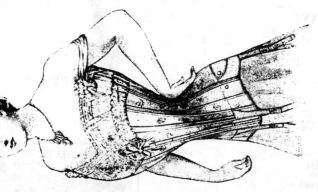

1908

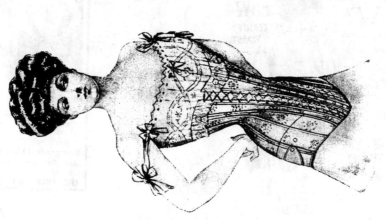

THE HEATH
MATERNITY CORSET

Does away with all need of abdominal belt, as corset and belt are one, and a perfect support after confinement. As flexible and well fitting as a good glove, and will keep the figure in perfect proportion.

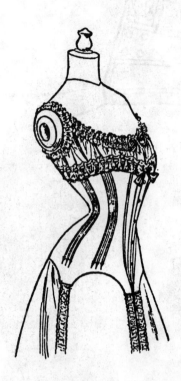

1908

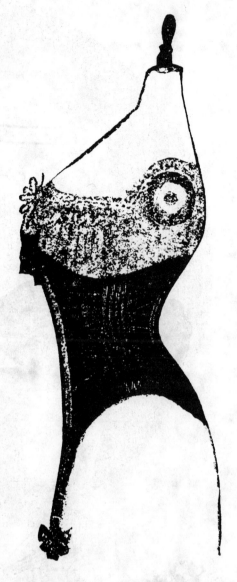

1908

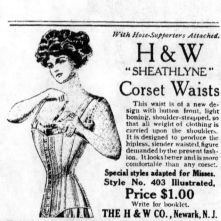

1909

1909

1909

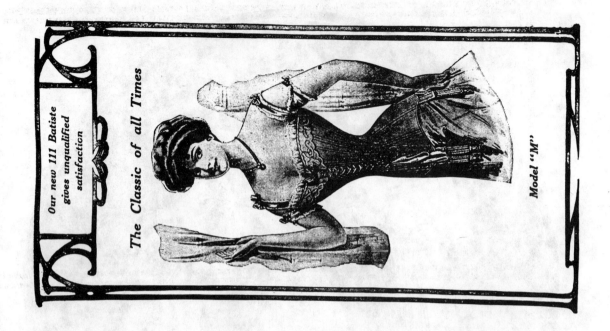

Our new 111 Batiste gives unqualified satisfaction

The Classic of all Times

Model "M"

Gossard Corsets are Rust Proof

The Hipless Model

Model "F"

Concerning
The
Gossard
Corset

"They Lace
In Front"

1909

1909

The Gossard is the only Hygienic Corset

L'Irresistible

Model "L"
L'Irresistible

It is worth the price
to have a beautiful
figure

Model "F"

New Grand Duchess Model D

THOMSON'S "GLOVE-FITTING" CORSETS

WITHOUT strapping or tightly lacing the figure in an uncomfortable manner, these famous corsets have always stood foremost as the best with which to follow latest fashion. Our

New Grand Duchess

spring models are of the very stylish "sheath" effect, and will equalize the bust, waist and hip lines, whether the figure is slender or stout. The graceful flowing lines thus produced, as shown in the spring fashion plates, are obtained in every figure if the proper model is selected.

These corsets are called "Glove-Fitting" because they fit as well and feel as comfortable as a fine kid glove.

For sale at corset department all stores

George C. Batcheller & Co.,
Fifth Avenue, Cor. 18th Street
NEW YORK

A LA C/B SPIRITE

THE EXPERT DESIGNING and the unusually careful tailoring of the C/B A LA SPIRITE CORSET keep the waist line slim and graceful.   It feels better, looks better and wears better than any other corset made.

1909

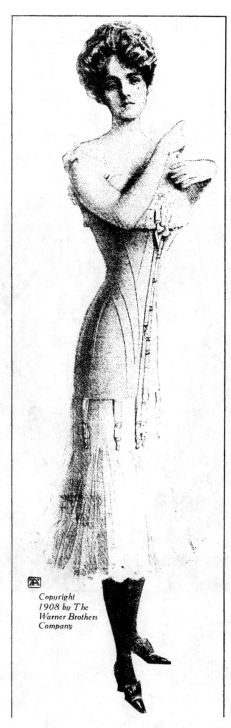

Copyright
1908 by The
Warner Brothers
Company

1909

WOMEN'S CORSETS

No. 211—D/A made of fine french coutil, strongly gored, rust proof filling, lace and ribbon trimmed, medium bust, long hip, 18 to 30. . . . . $1.75

464—D. & A. made of imported french coutil, long over abdomen and hip, webbing hose supporters, lace and ribbon trimmed, white, Sizes, 18 to 30. . . . . . . $2.25

492—D. & A. Rust proof filling, new long back and hip, well gored, strong hose supporters, 18 to 30 . . . $1.00

B60—R. & G. Imported coutil, rust proof filling, medium bust, skirt effect over abdomen and hip, white, Sizes, 18 to 30. . . . . $2.00

32—Waist Extender of hamburg, four ruffles, with ribbon and beading top trimmed $1.00

A70—R. & G. Low bust, Medium bust, long skirt effect over hip and abdomen, rust proof filling, white, Sizes, 18 to 30. . . . . $1.50

C—Blouse Distender, lawn covered, sterilized hair filled, lace trimmed; color white, ... 40c

BB—Blouse Distender, silk covered back and front, hair filled galloon frill; color white, ... 85c

424—Blouse Distender, plaited washable twill with removable hair cloth, making a good form, durable and washable, white, ... 75c

C60—R. & G. Imported french coutil, rust proof filling, medium bust, new long skirt effect over abdomen and hip, lace and ribbon trimmed, Sizes, 18 to 30. . . $2.50

FERRIS WAISTS 1909

No. 720—Ladies', long hip and medium bust, hose supporters attached or No. 220, without in white. Sizes, 19 to 30.
.. .. $1.50

No. 724—Ladies', long hip and long waist, hose supporters attached, pearl buttons, white. Sizes, 19 to 30. $2.50

No. 730—Ladies', medium hip and waist, pearl buttons, hose supporters side and front, white. Sizes, 18 to 30.
.. .. $2.00

No. 250—Ferris baby waist, superfine cloth, white, two rows pearl buttons, at waist, 6 months to 1½ years 60c

No. 339—Young ladies', 7 to 12 years, laced back, button front. Sizes, 21 to 27, white, ...
No. 212—Fine double ply, corded linen waist, for children, 5 to 9 years. Sizes, 21 to 28 inches, ... $
No. 229—Double ply linen childs' waist, two rows of buttons, 2 to 4 yrs. also.
141—corded waists, white twill, 4 to 8 years .. .. ..
No. 204—Heavy corded waist, 4 to 6 years .. .. ..
No. 223—Young ladies', 12 to 17 years, fine quality sateen, button front, laced back. Sizes, 19 to 28, wh $
Style 227 exact model, not so good a quality .. .. $

1909

NEMO "Kosmo" Corset No. 160
Unbreakable Hip
$2.50 Value at $1.50

No. 29X5. The best corset made for everyday wear, is neat and shapely. Has the patented Nemo "unbreakable hip" device, a crossed boning over the hips, which keeps the side steels from breaking. Made with the Nemo "triple-strip" re-enforcement bones and steels and cannot cut through; is of stout coutil; has a medium low bust, low under arm, long

back and hip; easy and comfortable for all day wear. A corset that is needed by every woman of medium or stout figure. An economical corset because it lasts so long. Nemo "Kosmo," No. 160, sizes 19 to 30, price $1.50; sizes 31 to 36, price...$1.75

CORSETS

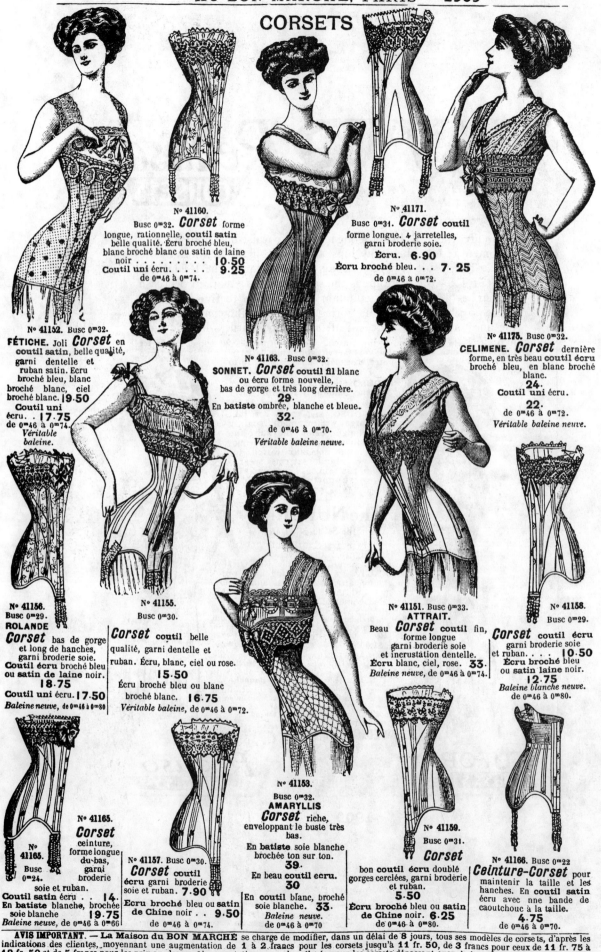

Nᵒ 41160.
Busc 0ᵐ32. *Corset* forme longue, rationnelle, **coutil satin** belle qualité. Écru broché bleu, blanc broché blanc ou satin de laine noir **10.50**
Coutil uni écru. **9.25**
de 0ᵐ46 à 0ᵐ74.

Nᵒ 41171.
Busc 0ᵐ31. *Corset* coutil forme longue. 4 jarretelles, garni broderie soie.
Écru. **6.90**
Écru broché bleu. . . **7.25**
de 0ᵐ46 à 0ᵐ72.

Nᵒ 41152. Busc 0ᵐ32.
FÉTICHE. Joli *Corset* en **coutil satin**, belle qualité, garni dentelle et ruban satin. Écru broché bleu, blanc broché blanc, ciel broché blanc. **19.50**
Coutil uni écru. . **17.75**
de 0ᵐ46 à 0ᵐ74.
Véritable baleine.

Nᵒ 41163. Busc 0ᵐ32.
SONNET. *Corset* coutil fil blanc ou écru forme nouvelle, bas de gorge et très long derrière.
29.
En batiste ombrée, blanche et bleue.
32.
de 0ᵐ46 à 0ᵐ70.
Véritable baleine neuve.

Nᵒ 41175. Busc 0ᵐ32.
CELIMENE. *Corset* dernière forme, en très beau **coutil écru** broché bleu, en blanc broché blanc.
24.
Coutil uni écru.
22.
de 0ᵐ46 à 0ᵐ72.
Véritable baleine neuve.

Nᵒ 41156.
Busc 0ᵐ29.
ROLANDE
Corset bas de gorge et long de hanches, garni broderie soie.
Coutil écru broché bleu ou satin de laine noir. **18.75**
Coutil uni écru. **17.50**
Baleine neuve, de 0ᵐ46 à 0ᵐ80.

Nᵒ 41155.
Busc 0ᵐ30.
Corset coutil belle qualité, garni dentelle et ruban. Écru, blanc, ciel ou rose.
15.50
Écru broché bleu ou blanc broché blanc. **16.75**
Véritable baleine, de 0ᵐ46 à 0ᵐ72.

Nᵒ 41151. Busc 0ᵐ33.
ATTRAIT.
Beau *Corset* coutil fin, forme longue garni broderie soie et incrustation dentelle.
Écru blanc, ciel, rose. **33.**
Baleine neuve, de 0ᵐ46 à 0ᵐ74.

Nᵒ 41158.
Busc 0ᵐ29.
Corset coutil écru garni broderie soie et ruban. **10.50**
Écru broché bleu ou satin laine noir.
12.75
Baleine blanche neuve.
de 0ᵐ46 à 0ᵐ80.

Nᵒ 41165.
Corset ceinture, forme longue du bas, garni broderie soie et ruban.
Nᵒ 41165.
Busc 0ᵐ24.
Coutil satin écru . . **14.**
En batiste blanche, brochée soie blanche **19.75**
Baleine neuve, de 0ᵐ46 à 0ᵐ66.

Nᵒ 41157. Busc 0ᵐ30.
Corset coutil écru garni broderie soie et ruban. **7.90**
Écru broché bleu ou satin de Chine noir . . **9.50**
de 0ᵐ46 à 0ᵐ74.

Nᵒ 41153.
Busc 0ᵐ32.
AMARYLLIS
Corset riche, enveloppant le buste très bas.
En batiste soie blanche brochée ton sur ton.
39.
En beau coutil écru.
30
En coutil blanc, broché soie blanche. **33.**
Baleine neuve.
de 0ᵐ46 à 0ᵐ70

Nᵒ 41159.
Busc 0ᵐ31.
Corset
bon coutil écru doublé gorges cerclées, garni broderie et ruban.
5.50
Écru broché bleu ou satin de Chine noir. **6.25**
de 0ᵐ46 à 0ᵐ80.

Nᵒ 41166. Busc 0ᵐ22
Ceinture-Corset pour maintenir la taille et les hanches. En **coutil satin** écru avec une bande de caoutchouc à la taille.
4.75
de 0ᵐ46 à 0ᵐ70.

AVIS IMPORTANT. — La Maison du BON MARCHÉ se charge de modifier, dans un délai de 8 jours, tous ses modèles de corsets, d'après les indications des clientes, moyennant une augmentation de 1 à 2 francs pour les corsets jusqu'à 11 fr. 50, de 3 francs pour ceux de 11 fr. 75 à 19 fr. 50 et de 5 francs pour les prix au-dessus. L'augmentation sera plus élevée pour les corsets dépassant 0ᵐ35 de busc et 0ᵐ80 de tour de taille.

Avec le numéro du modèle choisi, nous donner la mesure d'une moitié de Corset prise au ruban de taille.

CORSETS

Avec le Numéro du modèle choisi, nous donnons la mesure d'une moitié de Corset prise au ruban de taille.

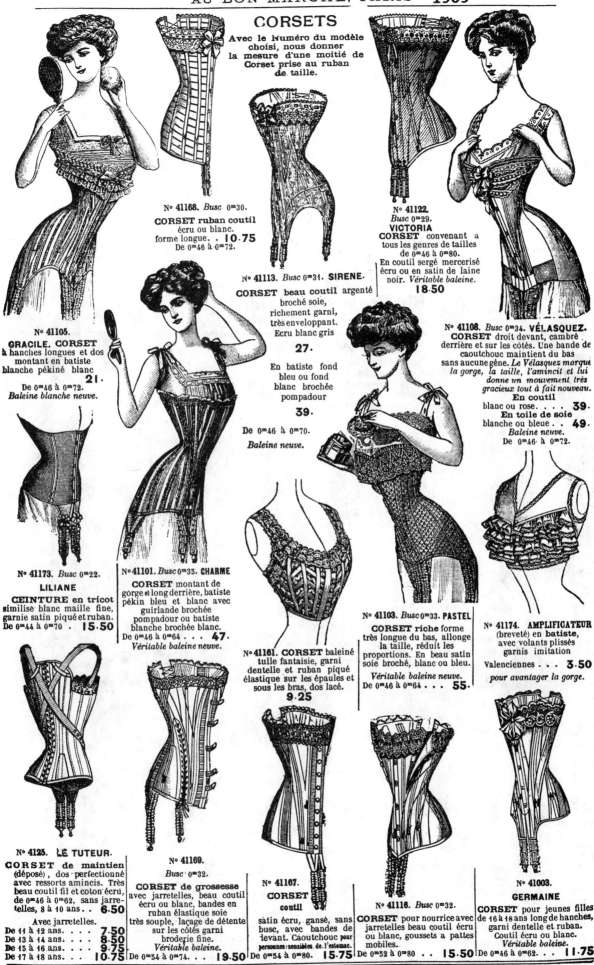

N° 41168. Busc 0m30.
CORSET ruban coutil écru ou blanc. forme longue. . **10.75**
De 0m46 à 0m72.

N° 41113. Busc 0m31. **SIRENE.**
CORSET beau coutil argenté broché soie, richement garni, très enveloppant. Ecru blanc gris
27.
En batiste fond bleu ou fond blanc brochée pompadour
39.
De 0m46 à 0m70.
Baleine neuve.

N° 41122.
Busc 0m29.
VICTORIA CORSET convenant a tous les genres de tailles de 0m46 à 0m80. En coutil sergé mercerisé écru ou en satin de laine noir. *Véritable baleine.*
18.50

N° 41105.
GRACILE. CORSET à hanches longues et dos montant en batiste blanche pékiné blanc
21.
De 0m46 à 0m72.
Baleine blanche neuve.

N° 41108. Busc 0m34. **VÉLASQUEZ.**
CORSET droit devant, cambré derrière et sur les côtés. Une bande de caoutchouc maintient du bas sans aucune gêne. *Le Vélasquez marque la gorge, la taille, l'amincit et lui donne un mouvement très gracieux tout à fait nouveau.*
En coutil
blanc ou rose. . . . **39.**
En toile de soie
blanche ou bleue . . **49.**
Baleine neuve.
De 0m46 à 0m72.

N° 41173. Busc 0m22.
LILIANE
CEINTURE en tricot similisé blanc maille fine, garnie satin piqué et ruban.
De 0m44 à 0m70 . **15.50**

N° 41101. Busc 0m35. **CHARME**
CORSET montant de gorge et long derrière, batiste pékin bleu et blanc avec guirlande brochée pompadour ou batiste blanche brochée blanc.
De 0m46 à 0m64 . . . . **47.**
Véritable baleine neuve.

N° 41161. CORSET baleiné tulle fantaisie, garni dentelle et ruban piqué élastique sur les épaules et sous les bras, dos lacé.
9.25

N° 41103. Busc 0m33. **PASTEL**
CORSET riche forme très longue du bas, allonge la taille, réduit les proportions. En beau satin soie broché, blanc ou bleu.
Véritable baleine neuve.
De 0m46 à 0m64 . . . **55.**

N° 41174. AMPLIFICATEUR (breveté) en **batiste**, avec volants plissés garnis imitation Valenciennes . . . **3.50**
pour avantager la gorge.

N° 4125. LE TUTEUR.
CORSET de maintien (déposé), dos perfectionné avec ressorts amincis. Très beau coutil fil et coton écru, de 0m46 à 0m62, sans jarretelles, 8 à 10 ans. . **6.50**
Avec jarretelles.
De 11 à 12 ans. . . . **7.50**
De 13 à 14 ans. . . . **8.50**
De 15 à 16 ans. . . . **9.75**
De 17 à 18 ans. . . **10.75**

N° 41169.
Busc 0m32.
CORSET de grossesse avec jarretelles, beau coutil écru ou blanc, bandes en ruban élastique soie très souple, laçage de détente sur les côtés garni broderie fine.
Véritable baleine.
De 0m54 à 0m74 . . **19.50**

N° 41167.
CORSET coutil
satin écru, gansé, sans busc, avec bandes de devant. Caoutchouc pour **personnes sensibles de l'estomac.**
De 0m54 à 0m80. **15.75**

N° 41116. Busc 0m32.
CORSET pour nourrice avec jarretelles beau coutil écru ou blanc, goussets à pattes mobiles.
De 0m52 à 0m80 . . **15.50**

N° 41003.
GERMAINE
CORSET pour jeunes filles de 16 à 18 ans long de hanches, garni dentelle et ruban. Coutil écru ou blanc.
Véritable baleine.
De 0m46 à 0m62 . . . **11.75**

Envoi sur demande de notre Catalogue spécial des CORSETS et d'ORTHOPÉDIE.

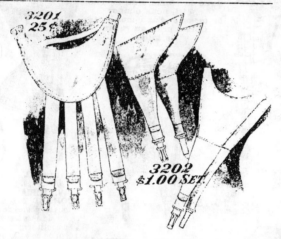

3201 25¢

3202 $1.00 SET.

Good Reliable Corsets at Big Price Reductions

POSTAGE, IF MAILED, CORSETS, WITH BOX, 22c; WITHOUT BOX, 17c. COR-SET WAISTS, 5c. SUPPORTERS, 5c.

The Gimbel Corset Section brings to the "Great Annual Sale of White" Corsets priced so low one might fear the quality, if not as-sured they possessed the regular Gimbel standard of merit—they do.

3205 45¢

No. 3201. PAD ABDOMINAL BELT SUPPORTERS. Help to reduce the abdomen. All colors. Special. 25c.

No. 3202. THE RIPROOF HOSE SUPPORTERS. Will outwear any corset; webbing non elastic in white only; can be sewed on any corset without weakening the elastic strands. For front and side. 50c pair; $1.00 set.

No. 3204. WOMAN'S G. B. CORSETS, STYLE, 707. Coutil; especially adapted for the present fashion; double hose supporters. Sizes, 18 to 30 inches. $1.00 value. Special, 75c.

No. 3205. WOMAN'S G. B. CORSETS, STYLE 600. Directoire hips, reducing the entire lower part of the figure to give the slim effect; double supporters. Sizes, 18 to 28 inches. Value, 75c. **Special, 45c.**

No. 3206. CHILD'S CORSET WAIST. Puffed back and front, lace-trimmed neck and arm-holes; eyelets for hose supporters; taped buttons. Sizes, 2 to 14 years. Value, 35c. Special, 25c.

No. 3207. CHILD'S CORSET WAIST. Good quality material; puffed front; taped buttons; worked button-holes. Ages, 2 to 10 years. Value, 20c. Special, 10c.

3204 75¢

3206 25¢

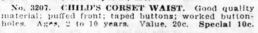

3207 10¢

1910s

1910s

FERRIS WAISTS

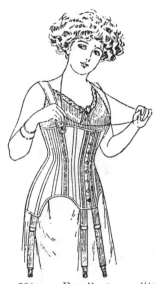

No. 721 — Medium high bust, long over hips and back; hose supporters front and sides. Price $1.50

No. 724 — Excellent quality Coutil. Pearl buttons, medium high bust, extreme length at back and hips, lightly boned, hose supporters at front and sides. Sizes: 19 to 28 .. .. Price $2.50

No. 223 — Young ladies, 12 to 17 years, fine quality Sateen, button front, laced back. Sizes: 19 to 28 .. .. Price $1.50

No. 339 — Young ladies, 7 to 12 years, laced back, button front. Sizes: 21 to 27 .. .. Price $0.75

No. 181 — Fine finish and quality trimmed with edging, made in defferent lengths to fit ages from 6 months to 14 years .. .. .. Price $0.75

No. 279 — Made of strong Coutil, removable elastic; boys' waist suspenders; hose supporters with each waist; ages: 3 to 10 years. Price $0.80

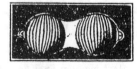

Style C. — Blouse Distender, Lawn covered, sterilized hair filled, lace trimmed, color White. Price $0.40

Style 424 — Blouse Distender, plaited washable twill with removable hair cloth, making a good form, durable and washable, White .. .. Price $0.75

Style 32 — Waist Extender of Hamburg, four ruffles, with ribbon and beading top trimmed. Price $1.00

WOMEN'S CORSETS — *Continued*

D. & A. CORSET MODEL 623

No. 623 — Reflects new idea of corset designing art, medium low bust, long French Directoire, sloping hips and back, with newest front idea, giving great freedom of movements, made of English Coutil, three pair of suspenders; for average, also stout figures; White only. Sizes: 18 to 30 . . . . Price $1.90

D. & A. MODEL 598

598

No. 598 — A special value for the money; low bust, very long skirt, made of English Coutil, trimmed with lace and ribbon, four hose supporters; for slim and medium figures; White only. Sizes: 18 to 30 . . . . Price $1.00

NUFORM 499

No. 499—A model for tall, well-proportioned figures; the bust is just the correct height, though not extreme; the hip, back and abdomen lines are long, and so constructed as to give a slight "incurve" at the waist line. The material is an excellently finished Batiste, trimmed with edging; hose supporters attached. Sizes: 18 to 30 . . . . Price $3.00

NUFORM 780

No. 780 — A Reduso model in every detail, like Reduso 776; ideal for tall, well-proportioned figures, requiring the added length above and below the waist; lace trimmed; made of a wear-defying quality of Batiste, with three pair of hose supporters attached. Sizes: 19 to 36 . . . . Price $4.00

NUFORM 496

No. 496—An excellent model for average and well-developed figures; has the latest medium bust height, is long over hips, back and abdomen, with just a suspicion of an "incurve" at the waist line; made of an excellent Batiste, trimmed with pretty embroidered edging; hose supporters attached. Sizes: 18 to 30. For this model in Coutil see style 485 . . . . . Price $2.00

NUFORM 495

No. 495—A straight-line model almost identical in construction with the famous W. B. Nuform Style 478; style 495 is slightly higher in the bust, however, with same length over hips, back and abdomen; constructed to insure perfect comfort for any average figure; made of durable Batiste, lace trimmed; supporters attached. Sizes: 18 to 30 . . . . . . Price $1.50

TERMS NET, NO CASH DISCOUNT.

WOMEN'S CORSETS — *Continued*

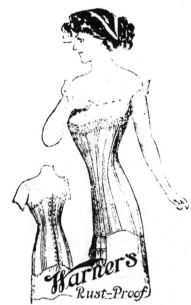

No. 155—Suitable for tall, medium figures; the waist is long, the bust medium, the hips, front and back very long, conforming to the requirements of the new gowns; White Coutil; 12½ inch clasp, 6 hooks. Sizes: 18 to 30 inches. . . . . Price $2.00

No. 601 — Warner's — A remarkable corset at the price; tall and medium well-proportioned figures will find it admirable; medium bust, very long hip and back; White Batiste; 13 inch clasp, 6 hooks. Sizes: 18 to 30 inches. . . . . Price $1.50

No. 180—For tall, stout figures, medium waist, medium low bust; a model of very new and very handsome lines; it will noticeably improve the figure; White Coutil; 13 inch clasp, 6 hooks. Sizes: 20 to 36 inches . . . . Price $2.50

D. & A. MODEL 620

No. 7070—For tall, medium and average figures, long waist, medium bust and very long skirt; a corset of unusually beautiful lines, giving slightly defined waist and long easy curves; White Batiste; 13½ inch clasp, 6 hooks. Sizes: 18 to 30 inches . . . . Price $6.50

No. 278—A full gored model for average figures; a deservedly popular model of very new lines and great comfort; it is of medium height above the waist, though very long below, and is intended for medium figures; White Batiste; 12½ inch clasp, 6 hooks. Sizes: 18 to 30 inches. Price $3.00

No. 620 — Is the very newest pattern for average and slim figures, low bust and long Directoire skirt, made of English Coutil, trimmed with lace and ribbon, four hose supporters of super lisle; White only. Sizes: 18 to 30 . . . . Price $1.50

WRITE FOR OUR SEWING MACHINE CATALOGUE.

FERRIS WAISTS

No. 721 — Medium high bust, long over hips and back; hose supporters front and sides. Price $1.50

No. 724 — Excellent quality Coutil, Pearl buttons, medium high bust, extreme length at back and hips, lightly boned, hose supporters at front and sides. Sizes: 19 to 28 . . . . Price $2.50

No. 223 — Young ladies, 12 to 17 years, fine quality Sateen, button front, laced back. Sizes: 19 to 28 . . . . Price $1.50

No. 339 — Young ladies, 7 to 12 years, laced back, button front. Sizes: 21 to 27 . . . . . . Price $0.75

No. 181 — Fine finish and quality trimmed with edging, made in defferent lengths to fit ages from 6 months to 14 years . . . . . Price $0.75

No. 279 — Made of strong Coutil, removable elastic; boys' waist suspenders; hose supporters with each waist; ages: 3 to 10 years. Price $0.80

No. 452 — Brassière. — Good quality Batiste, trimmed with lace, closed front. Sizes: 32 to 44. Price $0.75

Style C. — Blouse Distender, Lawn covered, sterilized hair filled, lace trimmed, color White. Price. $0.40

Style 424 — Blouse Distender, plaited washable twill with removable hair cloth, making a good form, durable and washable, White . . . . Price $0.75

Style 32 — Waist Extender of Hamburg, four ruffles, with ribbon and beading top trimmed. Price. $1.00

ADDRESS ALL CORRESPONDENCE TO THE COMPANY TO INSURE PROMPT ATTENTION.

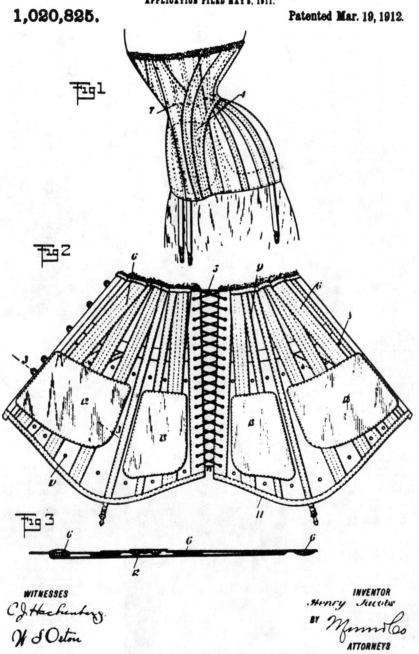

Fig 1

Fig 2

Fig 3

1^{50} 2741 2742

2734 1^{50}

2747 3^{00}

2750 2763 1^{00}

Maternity Corset

2761 2762 5^{00}

2734—"NATIONAL" Bust-Forming Guaranteed Corset, especially designed for women of slight form who desire a perfect figure. It is firmly boned and fitted with an adjustable strap in the back as shown in the small picture, which holds the corset firmly at the waist-line, giving the fashionable hip effect and also the well outlined bust. Trimmed with lace and ribbon; four hose supporters attached. WHITE Batiste only. SIZES: 18 to 30. Worth $2.00.
OUR PRICE, Two for $2.90; each $1.50
—*and we pay expressage.*

2741—"NATIONAL" Guaranteed Corset, with medium low bust, for *short, medium or stout figures*. This model is especially designed for figures requiring extra abdominal support. The bias reverse abdominal straps, with hose supporters attached, hold the figure erect and shapely. It is cut long over the hips, is firmly boned and very flexible. Lace- and ribbon-trimmed. WHITE Coutil only. SIZES: 18 to 30. Remarkable value.
OUR PRICE, Two for $2.90; each $1.50
—*and we pay expressage.*

2742—Same as No. 2741, but with medium high bust for *average tall, medium or stout figures*. WHITE Coutil only. SIZES: 18 to 30.
OUR PRICE, Two for $2.90; each $1.50
—*and we pay expressage.*

2747—This specially designed "NATIONAL" Guaranteed Maternity Corset is scientifically constructed to give just the support necessary, and is absolutely healthful and comfortable. The elastic panels at each side of the center-front and the side lacings make the corset adjustable and give perfect support to the abdomen. The boning and front steels are just the right length, and four durable hose supporters are attached. The corset is ideal also for wear during convalescence. Firm, soft Coutil, handsomely trimmed with lace and ribbon. WHITE ONLY. SIZES: 19 to 36. Order the size corset you usually wear and we will send correct size. No other measurements are necessary. Would cost $4.00 elsewhere.
OUR PRICE, Two for $5.75; each $3.00
—*and we pay expressage.*

2761 2762 5^{00}

2767—Silk Corset Laces, 4 yards long, in white, pink or light blue— Two for 39 cents.

2750—A decided bargain—"NATIONAL" Guaranteed Corset, made with medium low bust, for *average figures*. Long over the hips, reinforced at the waist-line and has four hose supporters attached. Daintily trimmed with lace and ribbon. WHITE Coutil only. SIZES: 18 to 30. Well made, exceptionally serviceable, and very low in price.
OUR PRICE, Two for $1.95; each $1.00
—*and we pay expressage.*

2763—"NATIONAL" Guaranteed Corset, same style as No. 2750, but made with medium high bust, for *average figures*. WHITE Coutil only.
OUR PRICE, Two for $1.95; each $1.00
—*and we pay expressage.*

2761—You save $2.00 on this "NATIONAL" Guaranteed Corset. It is made with elastic bands for reducing the figure; with medium low bust, suitable for *short, medium figures*, or for *average medium figures* requiring a strong corset. The reducing appliance with hose supporters attached is further reinforced by broad bands of elastic webbing—see where arrow points in illustration—which makes the corset cling to the figure, and gently, but firmly supports the abdomen in its natural position. It is strongly boned with Duplex steels, has extra hooks below the front steels and six hose supporters are attached. French Coutil, trimmed with ribbon-run lace and ribbon bow. WHITE ONLY. SIZES: 19 to 36. This corset gives to the wearer the graceful lines that are usually found only in a made-to-order corset, and would cost you $7.00 if bought elsewhere.
OUR PRICE, Two for $9.75; each $5.00
—*and we pay expressage.*

2762—"NATIONAL" Guaranteed Corset, same as No. 2761, but with medium high bust, for *average or tall figures, medium or stout*. WHITE Coutil only. SIZES: 19 to 36.
OUR PRICE, Two for $9.75; each $5.00
—*and we pay expressage.*

1912

2706
2707
$3.00

$2.00 2753
2754

2764
79¢

2755
$1.00

2739
2740
$2.00

Maternity
& Nursing
Corset

Read "How to Order Corsets" on Page 164.

2706—A regular $4.00 value. This "NATIONAL" Guaranteed Reinforced Corset is especially designed for reducing the figure. Medium low bust, suitable for *short figures, medium or stout.* Splendidly made, boned with Duplex steels and fitted with broad front steels. The hip portion is cut long and six reliable hose supporters are attached, while a reinforced bias strap, fastening with a strong, easily adjusted clasp fastener, extends entirely over the abdomen, reducing it without uncomfortable pressure. French Coutil, handsomely trimmed with ribbon-run lace and bow. WHITE ONLY. SIZES: 19 to 36. This model is splendidly made in every detail and is guaranteed to give you satisfactory service. Excellent value. *OUR PRICE,* **Two for $5.75; each $3.00** —and we pay expressage.

2707—"NATIONAL" Guaranteed Reinforced Corset, same as No. 2706, but made with medium high bust for *tall figures, medium or stout.* WHITE Coutil only. SIZES: 19 to 36. *OUR PRICE,* **Two for $5.75; each $3.00** —and we pay expressage.

2739—"NATIONAL" Guaranteed Corset, special Maternity Model, designed with unusual and improved features. The boning is firm and flexible, the front steels end at just the right depth, and the lacings at each side conform this scientifically built corset to the figure, giving perfect support to the abdomen. Four hose supporters attached. This corset is also ideal for wear during convalescence, and the nursing feature is entirely new, and very convenient and practical. WHITE Coutil only. SIZES: 19 to 36. Order size corset you usually wear and we will send correct size. No other measurements are necessary. Worth $3.00. *OUR PRICE,* **Two for $3.88; each $2.00** —and we pay expressage.

2740—"NATIONAL" Guaranteed Maternity Corset, same as No. 2739, but without nursing feature. SIZES: 19 to 36. *OUR PRICE,* **Two for $3.88; each $2.00** —and we pay expressage.

2767—Silk Corset Laces, 4 yards long, in white, pink or light blue— Two for 39 cents.

2753—Stylish "NATIONAL" Guaranteed Corset with medium low bust, for *average medium figures.* The hips are cut very long, and are carefully proportioned to give absolute freedom of movement. Reliably boned and fitted with strong front steels. The vents in the front of the corset give exceptional comfort to the wearer. Four hose supporters are attached, the two in front being arranged so as to hold the figure in the correct position. Handsomely trimmed with dainty lace and ribbon. WHITE Coutil only. SIZES: 18 to 30. This very fashionable model is priced very low. *OUR PRICE,* **Two for $3.88; each $2.00** —and we pay expressage.

2754—"NATIONAL" Guaranteed Corset, same as No. 2753, but made with medium high bust, for *average tall medium figures.* WHITE Coutil only. SIZES: 18 to 30. *OUR PRICE,* **Two for $3.88; each $2.00** —and we pay expressage.

2755—"NATIONAL" Guaranteed Corset made with medium bust and long hips, light weight and flexible, suitable for women or misses. Prettily trimmed with embroidery edge, and four hose supporters are attached. WHITE Coutil only. SIZES: 18 to 28. A very comfortable corset, especially suitable for house wear, outing or general wear and will give exceptionally good service. Worth $1.50. *OUR PRICE,* **Two for $1.95; each $1.00** —and we pay expressage.

2764—"NATIONAL" Guaranteed Corset Waist for misses and growing girls. The boning is light and flexible, the front closes with strong taped buttons, and the back laces like a corset. Four elastic hose supporters are attached. WHITE Coutil only. SIZES: 19 to 28. This Corset Waist should be ordered *two inches* smaller than waist measure taken over your dress. Splendid value. *OUR PRICE,* **Two for $1.55; each .79** —and we pay expressage.

National Cloak and Suit Company.

2717—"NATIONAL" Guaranteed Corset, with girdle-top and long hip, light weight and flexible, for *slender or medium figures*, and especially suitable for misses and small women. Four reliable hose supporters attached. WHITE Coutil only. Daintily trimmed with lace and ribbon. SIZES: 18 to 26. Guaranteed to give satisfactory wear.
OUR PRICE, Two for $2.90; each $1.50
—*and we pay expressage.*

2703—"NATIONAL" Guaranteed Corset with girdle-top, for *slender or medium figures*. Same style as No. 2717, but cut shorter below the waist-line. WHITE Coutil, prettily trimmed with lace and ribbon. SIZES: 18 to 26. A splendid corset at a remarkably low price.
OUR PRICE, Two for $1.95; each $1.00
—*and we pay expressage.*

2745—"NATIONAL" Guaranteed Corset with medium low bust, for *average, short or medium figures*; long over hips and strongly boned. The specially designed abdominal reducing front is reinforced by bias tailored gores. Six hose supporters are attached and a convenient skirt hook is provided. Fine quality French Coutil, trimmed with ribbon-run Swiss embroidery and ribbon bow. WHITE ONLY. SIZES: 18 to 30. This corset is exceptionally effective in reducing the abdomen and is very comfortable...*OUR PRICE*, Two for $5.75; each $3.00
—*and we pay expressage.*

2746—"NATIONAL" Guaranteed Corset, same as No. 2745, but made with medium high bust for *tall, average figures*. Fine quality French Coutil. WHITE ONLY. SIZES: 18 to 30.
OUR PRICE, Two for $5.75; each $3.00
—*and we pay expressage.*

2720—A decided bargain—"NATIONAL" Guaranteed Corset, front lacing model, with medium low bust, for *average figures*. The Duplex boning is firm and very flexible, giving strength and splendid wearing qualities. Four reliable hose supporters. WHITE Coutil only, attractively trimmed with dainty lace and ribbon. SIZES: 19 to 30. A very stylish model. This corset should be ordered *one inch smaller than waist measure taken over your dress.*
OUR PRICE, Two for $3.88; each $2.00
—*and we pay expressage.*

2765—"NATIONAL" Guaranteed Corset, front lacing model, same as No. 2720, but made with medium high bust, for *tall, average figures*. French Coutil. WHITE ONLY. SIZES: 19 to 30. This corset should be ordered *one inch smaller than waist measure taken over your dress.*
OUR PRICE, Two for $3.88; each $2.00
—*and we pay expressage.*

2756—You save $1.00 on this "NATIONAL" Guaranteed Corset made for reducing the figure, with adjustable abdominal straps. This medium low bust model is especially suited to *short figures, medium or stout*, or to *slight figures requiring a strong corset*. It is strongly boned with Duplex steels, is fitted with broad front steels, and has six durable hose supporters. It is trimmed with lace and ribbon, and a convenient skirt hook is provided. French Coutil. WHITE ONLY. SIZES: 19 to 36. This corset is guaranteed to give satisfactory wear. Value $3.00.
OUR PRICE, Two for $3.88; each $2.00
—*and we pay expressage.*

2757—"NATIONAL" Guaranteed Corset, same as No. 2756, but with medium high bust, for *tall figures, medium or stout, or tall slight figures requiring a strong corset*. WHITE Coutil only. SIZES: 19 to 36.
OUR PRICE, Two for $3.88; each $2.00
—*and we pay expressage.*

2767—Silk Corset Laces, 4 yards long, in white, pink or light blue—Two for 39 cents.

203 to 217 West 24th Street, New York City

A Gift of Grace with Every "NATIONAL" Corset

WITH EVERY "NATIONAL" Corset goes a gift of grace and charm, a changed and more fascinating figure and always added personal beauty.

So true is this that we wish it were possible to give one "NATIONAL" Corset with every "NATIONAL" Suit or Dress. Of course, this is entirely impossible, but if it could be done we would supply the corset simply to have you know this greater delight and to learn how much better a dress or suit can look.

"NATIONAL" Corsets were made wholly because of our wish to have "NATIONAL" Suits and Dresses look their best—to bring out the beautiful lines we so carefully design in our garments. They were made, not primarily for profit—but for your pleasure, your delight your greater beauty.

So well, so perfectly are "NATIONAL" Corsets made, that we actually place our signed guarantee tag, shown on this page, on each corset.

One word more—a word of frank advice. Never economize on a corset. Save, if you must, on other things, but buy the best, the most expensive corset you can afford. You will be amply repaid for every cent spent on a "NATIONAL" Corset. The better the corset, the better the figure.

So, how important it is, that every woman—that you—select correctly designed, carefully made corsets! How urgent it is—how necessary to your own stylish appearance—that you learn the greater beauty and gracefulness of "NATIONAL" Corsets!

2758—This "NATIONAL" Guaranteed Reinforced Corset has been especially designed for reducing the figure, and to effect the graceful, smooth lines which are so much favored in the present styles. It is medium low bust, suitable for *average figures, medium or stout*, is heavily boned with Duplex steels and fitted with broad front steels. The hip portion is cut long and six durable hose supporters are attached, while the reinforced bias straps, fastening with a strong flat clasp, extend entirely over the abdomen, reducing it without uncomfortable pressure. Made of fine French Coutil, handsomely trimmed with ribbon-run lace, and finished with a dainty ribbon bow. WHITE ONLY. SIZES: 19 to 36. The right poise of body, becoming gracefulness and stylishness cannot be obtained without the right corset. Because this is a "NATIONAL" Corset, it will give you the desired effect. It is built to give a graceful figure, and it is guaranteed to give you satisfactory service.
OUR PRICE, **Two for $3.88; each $2.00**
—*and we pay expressage.*

2759—"NATIONAL" Guaranteed Reinforced Corset, same as No. 2758, but made with medium high bust, for *tall figures, medium or stout.* WHITE Coutil only. SIZES: 19 to 36.
OUR PRICE, **Two for $3.88; each $2.00**
—*and we pay expressage.*

2760—"NATIONAL" Guaranteed Reinforced Corset, same as No. 2758, but especially designed for *short stout figures*, and made with medium low bust. WHITE Coutil only. SIZES: 19 to 36.
OUR PRICE, **Two for $3.88; each $2.00**
—*and we pay expressage.*

HOW TO ORDER CORSETS

If you know what size corset you wear, and it is the right size for you, order your "NATIONAL" Corset by that size. If you do not know, or are not quite sure, you will find it a very simple matter to get a perfect-fitting corset at the "NATIONAL"

Order by size, not by waist measure. The correct size of your corset is three inches smaller than your waist measure taken over your dress. If your waist measure is 23 inches, order a corset Size 20; if your waist measure is 28 inches, order Size 25; and so on. Front Lacing Corsets, No. 2720 and No. 2765, shown on Page 166, should be ordered Size one inch smaller than your waist measure. Corset Waist No. 2764, shown on Page 166, should be ordered Size two inches smaller than your waist measure. In ordering, use the Ready-Made Order Blank, Page 213 or 215 of this Style Book.

2758 $200
2759

"NATIONAL"
CORSET
GUARANTEE TAG

This "NATIONAL" Corset is made of the very best material, especially selected for its service-giving qualities. It gives the proper support and is comfortable because it is constructed on the most scientific and healthful lines.

We guarantee it to give satisfactory wear or replace it with another corset free of charge.

National Cloak & Suit Co.
New York City

"NATIONAL" Reducing Corset

National Cloak and Suit Company.

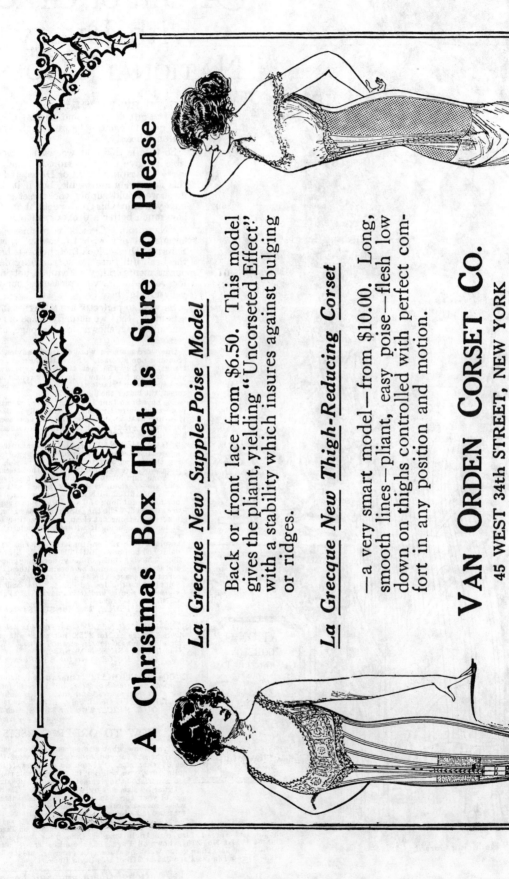

Everlastik

Trade Mark Reg. U. S. Pat. Off.

"The Garter Web That Out-lasts the Corset"

Woven by an exclusive process (patent applied for) that prevents the rubber strands from slipping back after being cut by a needle and leaving the web lifeless. Retains its elasticity under all conditions. The name EVERLASTIK is stamped on the back of the genuine.

Corset makers who are thoughtful of your satisfaction equip their corsets with hose supporters of EVERLASTIK, which saves you the bother of renewing them. Buy these corsets or demand hose supporters of EVERLASTIK on the corsets you do buy.

The following corset and hose supporter makers use EVERLASTIK:

**Benjamin & Johnes, Newark, N. J.
Dominion Corset Co., Quebec
Van Orden Corset Co., Newark, N. J.
Ottenheimer & Weil Co., New Haven
George Frost Company, Boston
C. J. Haley & Co., New York City**

Hose supporters of EVERLASTIK are sold by progressive dealers. If yours hasn't them, send us his name and 25c for a trial pair. Good dealers also sell EVERLASTIK by the yard.

EVERLASTIK in wide widths is used by leading corset makers as gores, insets, bands, etc. It lengthens the life of the corset and adds to its comfort.

We also manufacture Hub Brand Lisle Web, which comes in all widths and sizes. It is adapted to practically every purpose for which lisle elastics are used.

HUB GORE
Boston
(Est. .

Makers of

1913

Splendid Corsets, Forms and Sanitary Goods

After thorough and long-continued comparison and tests we have found Gimbel Corsets the best in style, fabric and workmanship at the various prices. Even the 50c models are on the latest fashionable lines, and they will give the good service expected.

C-6900 G. B. Special Corsets. Made especially for our trade of fancy corded madras. Medium low bust, extreme long hip. Daintily trimmed with embroidery. Hooks and eyes below steels in front. Two pairs hose supporters. Sizes, 18 to 30. Very fine quality at an exceedingly low price. 50c. Weight, wrapped, 22 ounces.

C-6901 Sanitary Belt. State waist measure. Very serviceable and useful. Sizes, 24 to 36. 25c. Weight, wrapped, 3 ounces.

C-6902 G. B. Special Corsets. Splendid model for average figures. Double hooks. Cable elastic hose supporters attached. Embroidery at top. Elastic band inserted at bottom of back skirt prevents bones from sticking out in back. Excellent value. Sizes, 18 to 30. 75c. Weight, wrapped, 24 ounces.

C-6903 American Lady Corset. New low bust model. Cleared hip bone style preventing the discomfort of a steel pressing on the hip bone. Embroidery top. Three pair hose supporters. Splendid corset for all-around use and is splendid value. Sizes, 18 to 30. $1.50. Weight, wrapped, 23 ounces.

1913

C-6901 25¢

C-6900 50¢

C-6905 50¢

C-6902 75¢

C-6903 $1.50

C-6907 $1.50

C-6908 $2.00

C-6906 50¢

C-6909 50¢

C-6904 $3.00

C-6904 Maternity Waist. Made with elastic insets down front of waist. Embroidery on top. Laced back and side to adjust to comfort of wearer. Soft clasp down front. Splendid convalescent waist. $3.00. Weight, wrapped, 26 ounces.

C-6905 Perfect Bust Form. For slender figures. Boned throughout. Sizes, 34 to 38. 50c. Weight, wrapped, 9 ounces.

C-6906 Sanitary Dress Protector. Cambric yoke around hips. Rubber sheeting below. Practical for wear with summer dresses and skirts. 50c. Extra size, 75c. Weight, wrapped, 7 ounces.

C-6907 Athletic Waist. Short clasp front. Elastic sections at bust in front to permit freedom of action. Medium hip. Three pairs removable hose supporters. Sizes, 19 to 28 inches. Fine for sports. $1.50. Weight, wrapped, 17 ounces.

C-6908 Dr. Gertrude Rosenthal's "Prudent" Belt, Absorber and Sanitary Protector. A great scientific, practical garment, perfected in conformity with the laws of nature. An indispensable necessity and great economy to the woman using it. Removable sponge can be cleaned and dried in a moment. Waterproof shield prevents chafing of the limbs or soiling of clothing. There are no safety pins to be bothered with, no hooks and eyes, no annoyances of any kind attached to this invention. It is explicitly described in the directions which accompany each outfit. The price is very reasonable considering its high-grade qualities. The outfit consists of a fitted belt, a sanitary protector and two net-covered sponge absorbers. Size 2 for hip measure 32 inches or less, $2.00; size 3 for hip measure 33 to 39 inches, $2.25; size 4 for hip measure 40 to 47 inches, $2.50; size 5 for hip measure 48 to 55 inches, $2.75.

C-6909 Tourists' Comfort Sanitary Napkins. Seamless. Comfortable and antiseptic. Done up in a neat box. Half dozen in a box, 25c. Weight, 13 ounces. One dozen in box, 50c. Weight, 16 ounces.

"La Markette" and the "Eugenie" we can especially recommend for correctness of outline and wonderful wearing qualities, although no popular or worth-while make is debarred from our Corset Salons. Our Pink Shops are the fashionable corset-fitting parlors of the East. The "Eugenie" is a fine French corset with adaptations of American ideas.

C-6700 "La Markette" Corset. Made of fine batiste. Free from bones over hips. Commonly known as the cleared hip bone corset. Discomfort arising from pressure of corset bone over hip is here done away with. Two hooks and eyes are under front steels. Broad silk ribbon with bow at front is a pretty ornamental finish at the top edge. These corsets are models of comfort and stylish lines. Sizes, 19 to 28. $3.00. Weight, wrapped, 25 ounces.

C-6701 "La Markette" Hip Confiner. Splendid corset for medium and small figures. Bones are light but firm. Extra long skirt below waist. Several eyelets in front below steels help the idea of confining width of hip. A strong broad elastic band through waist-line accomplishes the object of this garment without interfering with the ease of the wearer. $3.50. Sizes, 19 to 26. Weight, wrapped, 22 ounces.

C-6700 $3.00

C-6701 $3.50

C-6702 $5.00

C-6702 "La Markette" Corset. A model designed to meet the latest decree of fashion. This corset will fit the average figure, giving grace and desired outline without loss of comfort. Made of brocade with a pretty trimming of lace and ribbon as a finish. Dainty bow in front. Back and sides are very long below waist-line. Front has the circular cut in front, affording comfort when in a sitting position. $5.00. Sizes, 19 to 30. Weight, wrapped, 30 ounces.

C-6703 "La Markette" Model. Splendid model, new for 1914. Bust is extremely low, graduating to medium high in back. Draw string at top. Very long over hips. Wonderfully good outlines. Hose supporters at front and sides of heavy suspender webbing and strong elastic. Unusually dainty finish at top, of lace and ribbon. Good wearing and good style with the straight lines demanded by gowns of today. Really an expensive model at low price. $2.50. Weight, wrapped, 29 ounces.

C-6704 "La Markette" Corset. Bust is exceedingly low. The extreme straight style giving the large waist line and reducing size of hip. Made in dainty pink brocade. A perfect fitting and perfect wearing corset, and every necessary detail has been given proper attention. Pretty lace and ribbon trimming. Hose supporters of French webbing. Corset bones are arranged to come each side of the hip bone, affording comfort. $7.50. Sizes, 19 to 28. Weight, wrapped, 31 ounces.

C-6705 "Eugenie" Dancing Corset. Gives the corsetless figure with correct "slouch." Low bust, with silk elastic top. Closed back. Hooks and eyes are below steels in front. Very deep elastic band at waist. Three pairs of frilled elastic hose supporters. Medium length, curves up slightly at bottom edge in front. Extremely pliable yet affording sufficient support. Sizes, 19 to 26. $6.00. Same model, laced in back $8.00. Weight, wrapped, 22 ounces.

C-6703 $2.50

C-6704 $7.50

C-6705 $6.00

The Acme of Corseting. Proper Cuts for Fashion's Demands

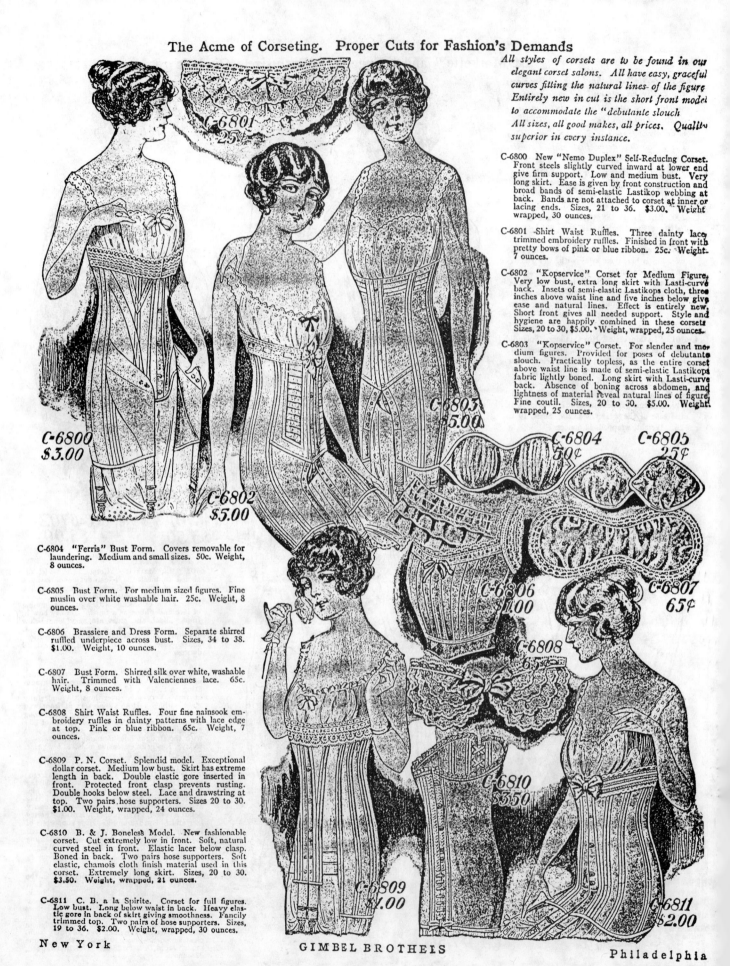

All styles of corsets are to be found in our elegant corset salons. All have easy, graceful curves fitting the natural lines of the figure. Entirely new in cut is the short front model to accommodate the "debutante slouch" All sizes, all good makes, all prices. Quality superior in every instance.

C-6800 New "Nemo Duplex" Self-Reducing Corset. Front steels slightly curved inward at lower end give firm support. Low and medium bust. Very long skirt. Ease is given by front construction and broad bands of semi-elastic Lastikop webbing at back. Bands are not attached to corset at inner or lacing ends. Sizes, 21 to 36. $3.00. Weight wrapped, 30 ounces.

C-6801 Shirt Waist Ruffles. Three dainty lace trimmed embroidery ruffles. Finished in front with pretty bows of pink or blue ribbon. 25c. Weight, 7 ounces.

C-6802 "Kopservice" Corset for Medium Figure. Very low bust, extra long skirt with Lasti-curve back. Insets of semi-elastic Lastikops cloth, three inches above waist line and five inches below give ease and natural lines. Effect is entirely new. Short front gives all needed support. Style and hygiene are happily combined in these corsets Sizes, 20 to 30, $5.00. Weight, wrapped, 25 ounces.

C-6803 "Kopservice" Corset. For slender and medium figures. Provided for poses of debutante slouch. Practically topless, as the entire corset above waist line is made of semi-elastic Lastikops fabric lightly boned. Long skirt with Lasti-curve back. Absence of boning across abdomen, and lightness of material reveal natural lines of figure. Fine coutil. Sizes, 20 to 30. $5.00. Weight, wrapped, 25 ounces.

C-6804 "Ferris" Bust Form. Covers removable for laundering. Medium and small sizes. 50c. Weight, 8 ounces.

C-6805 Bust Form. For medium sized figures. Fine muslin over white washable hair. 25c. Weight, 8 ounces.

C-6806 Brassiere and Dress Form. Separate shirred ruffled underpiece across bust. Sizes, 34 to 38. $1.00. Weight, 10 ounces.

C-6807 Bust Form. Shirred silk over white, washable hair. Trimmed with Valenciennes lace. 65c. Weight, 8 ounces.

C-6808 Shirt Waist Ruffles. Four fine nainsook embroidery ruffles in dainty patterns with lace edge at top. Pink or blue ribbon. 65c. Weight, 7 ounces.

C-6809 P. N. Corset. Splendid model. Exceptional dollar corset. Medium low bust. Skirt has extreme length in back. Double elastic gore inserted in front. Protected front clasp prevents rusting. Double hooks below steel. Lace and drawstring at top. Two pairs hose supporters. Sizes 20 to 30. $1.00. Weight, wrapped, 24 ounces.

C-6810 B. & J. Boneless Model. New fashionable corset. Cut extremely low in front. Soft, natural curved steel in front. Elastic lacer below clasp. Boned in back. Two pairs hose supporters. Soft elastic, chamois cloth finish material used in this corset. Extremely long skirt. Sizes, 20 to 30. $3.50. Weight, wrapped, 21 ounces.

C-6811 C. B. a la Spirite. Corset for full figures. Low bust. Long below waist in back. Heavy elastic gore in back of skirt giving smoothness. Fancily trimmed top. Two pairs of hose supporters. Sizes, 19 to 36. $2.00. Weight, wrapped, 30 ounces.

C-6800 $3.00

C-6801 25¢

C-6802 $5.00

C-6803 $5.00

C-6804 50¢

C-6805 25¢

C-6806 $1.00

C-6807 65¢

C-6808 65¢

C-6809 $1.00

C-6810 $3.50

C-6811 $2.00

A STYLE FOR EVERY FIGURE | STRONGSMYTH | SATISFACTION GUARANTEED

CORSETS

ANY STYLE ON THIS PAGE 98¢

DON'T FORGET SIZE
The size of corset you wear is two inches less than your waist measure taken over your corset.

LIGHT WEIGHT BATISTE
FOR AVERAGE FIGURES
IIF5602 PRICE EACH **98c**

SIZES 18 to 30. State Size

Very long in back and over hips. Medium low bust, light weight batiste. Non-rustable boning, four supporters, silk embroidery trimming, bust draw strings. Length of back, 18 inches. Over hips from waist down, 15 in. Front clasps, 12½ inches. Shipping wt., 1 lb. 8 oz.

FRONT LACING CORSET
IIF5604 PRICE EACH **98c**

SIZES 18 to 30. State Size

The corset of the present. Snug fitting back, comfortable for all figures. Latest low bust. Very long in back and over hips. Strong coutil, rust-proof boning. Four strong supporters, embroidery trimming. Length in back 18 inches; over hips from waist down, 15 inches; front clasps, 11 inches. Shipping wt., 1 lb. 8 oz.

"STRONGSMYTH" REDUCER
IIF5615 SIZES 19 to 30 **98c**
IIF5616 SIZES 32 to 36 **$1.19**

Guaranteed to prove as satisfactory in wear and reducing accomplishments as any reducing corset double our price. Material is strong coutil and rust-proof boning. Six supporters, graduated front clasp. Good medium length. Back, 17 inches; over hips from waist down, 11½ inches. Front clasp 13 inches. Shipping wt., 1 lb. 10 oz.

FREE HIP CORSET
VERY LOW BUST
IIF5620 PRICE EACH **98c**

SIZES 18 to 25. State Size

The newest corset for slender figures. Lightly boned, giving the wearer the stylish uncorseted effect. Material is strong coutil and rustproof boning. Very long in back and over hips. Back, 19 inches. Over hips from waist down, 15 inches. Front clasp, 11 inches. Shipping weight, 1 lb. 6 oz.

NEW "TANGO" CORSET
NATURAL FIGURE EFFECT
IIF5605 PRICE EACH **98c**

SIZES 18 to 25. State Size

This season's newest corset. Restores the natural figure, producing the new corsetless effect. Very low in bust, and long in back, and over hips. Very few steels, making this a very comfortable garment. Material is strong coutil and rust-proof boning. Length of back 18 inches, over hips, 16 inches. Front clasp is 9¾ inches long. Shipping wt., 1 lb. 6 oz.

FOR FULL FIGURES
IIF5610 PRICE EACH **98c**

SIZES 18 to 36. State Size

For well proportioned figures. Good medium length but not extreme. Has graduated front clasp which flattens abdomen. Strong coutil and rust-proof boning. Six supporters, lace trimming and bust drawstrings. Length of back, 16½ inches; over hips from waist down, 11½ inches; front clasp, 13 inches. Shipping weight, 1 lb. 10 oz.

NEW "STRONGSMYTH SPECIAL"
THE PRIDE OF OUR CORSET SHOP
IIF5612 PRICE EACH **98c**

SIZES 18 to 30. State Size

No pains or expense have been spared to make this, our new "STRONGSMYTH SPECIAL," the best corset in the world for the price. Material is good quality, strong coutil and guaranteed rust-proof double boning. Six suspender web supporters, lace trimming, ribbon bow and draw strings to control the bust. Will fit average figures being long in back and over hips and medium low in bust. Length of back, 17 inches; over hips from waist down, 14 inches; front clasp, 12½ inches. Shipping weight, 1 lb. 7 oz.

VERY SHORT CORSET
IIF5622 PRICE EACH **98c**

SIZES 18 to 36. State Size

An old favorite for those who cannot wear the long corsets. Material is doubled over the abdomen, making this corset especially desirable for full figures. Material is strong coutil and non-rustable boning. Back is 13 inches long, over hips from waist down, 8½ inches; front clasp, 11 inches. Shpg. wt., 1 lb. 6 oz.

VERY HIGH BUST
IIF5624 PRICE EACH **98c**

SIZE 18 to 30. State Size

Especially suitable for tall, slender figures, but preferred by many women who desire a high bust. Material is good coutil and non-rustable boning. Long in back and over hips. Length of back, 16½ inches; over hips from waist down, 10 in.; front clasp, 12 in.; height of bust from waist up, 8 in. Shipping wt., 1 lb. 7 oz.

PERFECT in STYLE, FIT and WEAR
De Luxe Corsets

VERY LONG CORSET
PERFECT IN STYLE, FIT AND WEAR
GOOD $3.00 VALUE
11F5628 PRICE EACH **$1.69**
SIZES, 18 TO 30
Be Sure to Mention Size

All that can be desired in a corset, regardless of price, is embodied in this model. Strictly up to date in style, being very long in back and over hips, and medium low in bust. Material is fine quality strong coutil and rust-proof double boning. Six strong suspender web hose supporters and handsome silk stitching below steels to prevent them from breaking through the material. Two hooks and eyes and rubber lacing below front clasp keep the long skirt snug and comfortable to the figure. Is exquisitely trimmed with satin and wide lace. Length of back, 16 inches; over hips from waist down, 15 inches; front clasp, 11¾ inches long. Shpg. wt., 1 lb. 10 oz.

"DE LUXE SPECIAL"
GENUINE WABONE
ACTUAL $5.00 VALUE
11F5632 PRICE EACH **$2.89**
SIZES, 18 to 30
Be Sure to State Size

The WABONE stays in this corset give the wearer complete comfort and at the same time properly support the figure. Very latest model. Very low in bust and very long in back, front and over hips. Material is finest quality imported coutil. Has six strong suspender web hose supporters and rubber lacing below front clasp, which holds the long skirt snug and smooth to the figure. Length of back, 19½ in. Front steel, 11½ in.; over hips from waist down, 15 in. Shpg. wt., 1 lb. 12 oz.

SILK BROCADED
DRESS CORSET
REGULAR $4.00 VALUE
11F5634 PRICE EACH **$2.48**
SIZES, 18 to 30
Be Sure to State Size

A corset for women of refinement. Especially worn on dress occasions. Up-to-date model. Medium low in bust, very long in back, front, and over hips. Guaranteed rust-proof boning. Six heavy suspender web hose supporters. Two hooks and eyes below front clasp. Silk stitching below steels prevent them from breaking through the material. Wide lace and ribbon trimming. Length of back, 19½ inches; front clasp, 11½ inches long and over hips from waist line down, 14 inches. Shpg. wt., 1 lb. 14 oz.

STRICTLY LATEST STYLE
NATURAL FIGURE EFFECT
POSITIVELY WORTH $3.00
11F5638 PRICE EACH **$1.48**
SIZES, 19 to 26
Be Sure to Mention Size Wanted

If you want the very latest style in corsets buy this model. The lines of this corset closely follow the lines of the natural figure making it very comfortable for all figures. It is made very low in the bust and has the popular unboned free hip section, producing the much desired corsetless effect. Has two gores of broad elastic webbing inserted at the top which hold the top of the corset smooth and snug to the figure. Material is double basiste, light in weight, but very strong. Length of back, 17½ inches. Lenght over hips from waist down, 15 inches. Front clasp, 10½ inches long. Shpg. wt., 1 lb. 7 oz.

SHOWING NET PROTECTION BEHIND FRONT CLASPS

Warner's Rust-Proof
FRONT LACER
11F5642 PRICE EACH **$2.00**
SIZES, 19 to 32
Be Sure to State Size

This model fits perfectly and is very comfortable for all average and medium figures. A great improvement is the net protective shield behind the front laces which prevents the flesh from being caught between the laces. Material is light weight batiste and rust-proof double boning. Medium low bust. Front clasp, 10 in.: over hips from waist down, 14½ in. In back, 18 in. Shipping wt., 1 lb. 14 oz.

FRONT LACER
PERFECT FITTING
$2.50 RETAIL VALUE
11F5646 PRICE EACH **$1.48**
SIZES, 18 to 30
Don't forget to state size

Fashionable women are now wearing front-lacing corsets more than ever before, because of their perfect fit, comfort, style and strength. This model is exceptionally comfortable because of the ventilated mesh back and the broad elastic band which expands when sitting. Suitable for average figures, being low in bust, and long in back and over hips. Material is excellent quality, coutil and non-rustable boning. Length of back, 17 in. Front clasp, 12 in. Over hips from waist down, 13 in. Shpg. wt., 1½ lbs.

NEMO AND "STRONGSMYTH" REDUCERS THE BEST CORSETS FOR STOUT FIGURES

ELASTIC GORES

 **Nemo** TRIPLE STRIP | **LIMSHAPING SELF-REDUCING**

11F409 POSTAGE PREPAID **$4.00**

SIZES: 20 to 36. State Size

VERY STRONG NEMO REDUCING CORSET

Reduces the hips and abdomen by means of the broad elastic limb-shaping bands, which also produce a smooth effect and perfect comfort whether the wearer is sitting or standing. Is long in back and over hips, and medium low in bust. Material is very strong fine quality coutil and guaranteed rust-proof boning. Length of back, 18½ inches, front clasp, 12 inches; over hips from waist down, 13 inches. Postage prepaid.

 **DUPLEX SELF-REDUCING**

11F328 POSTAGE PREPAID **$3.00**

SIZES 20 to 36. State Size

The newest NEMO corset, has wide elastic bands in back extending below the steels which curve in when you sit down giving you ease and comfort. Front clasps curve in at the bottom supporting abdomen. Material is strong coutil and rust-proof toning. Medium low in bust and very long in back and over hips. Length of back 19½ inches; front clasp 13 inches; over hips from waist line 15 inches. Postage prepaid.

Nemo TRIPLE STRIP | **LASTICURVE-BACK SELF-REDUCING**

11F322 POSTAGE PREPAID **$3.00**

SIZES 20 to 36. State Size

Popular priced NEMO Corset. Gores of elastic webbing in the back expand when sitting, giving ease and comfort, and cling while standing giving a smooth and snug appearance. Material is very strong coutil, and guaranteed rust-proof boning, suitable for short and medium figures being medium low in bust, and long over hips. Length of back 17½ inches; front clasp 11½ inches; over hips from waist line down 12½ inches. Postage prepaid.

Nemo TRIPLE STRIP | **IN-CURVE BACK SELF-REDUCING**

11F508 POSTAGE PREPAID **$5.00**

SIZES: 20 to 36. State Size

THIS NEMO CORSET IS SO STRONG THAT YOU WILL FIND IT HARD WORK TO WEAR IT OUT

Wide bands of lastikops elastic webbing in back and elastic gores at the bottom, give the wearer perfect comfort while sitting, standing or walking, and also reduce the hips, abdomen and upper limbs. Material is excellent quality strong coutil and guaranteed rust-proof boning. Length of back, 19½ in.; front clasp, 12½ in.; over hips from waist down, 14 in. Postpage prepaid.

ABDOMINAL REDUCING

REGULAR $2.00 VALUE **11F5684** PRICE EACH **$1.39**

SIZES: 18 to 30. State Size

The elastic straps flatten the abdomen and give the wearer perfect comfort whether sitting or standing. Material is good strong coutil and rust-proof boning. Six supporters. Three hooks and eyes below front clasp. Very long in back and over hips. Length in back, 19 inches. Front clasp, 12 inches; over hips from waist down, 15 inches. Shipping weight, 1 lb. 9 oz.

BELT-REDUCER CORSET

GUARANTEED $3.00 VALUE **11F5690** PRICE EACH **$1.79**

SIZES: 19 to 36. Don't Forget to State Size

The reinforced belt and graduated front clasp control and flatten the abdomen and the wide elastic bands in back give the wearer absolute comfort and ease whether sitting or standing, and at the same time create a smooth, neat and stylish appearance. Very long in back and over hips, and medium low in bust. Material is strong coutil, and rust-proof double boning. Length of back, 18 in.; front clasp, 11¾ in. Over hips from waist down, 14 in. Shpg. wt., 1 lb. 14 oz.

OLD RELIABLE REDUCER

11F5686 SIZES: 19 TO 30 **$1.48**

11F5687 SIZES: 32 to 36 $1.74
11F5688 SIZES: 38 to 40 $1.97

Just the corset for women who cannot wear long corsets, especially those inclined to have a protruding abdomen. The stomach is supported and flattened by the wide spoon shaped front clasps and large hips are held in by the side lacings. Material is good strong coutil and rust-proof boning. Back is 15 in. Front clasp 13½ in. Shpg. wt., 1 lb. 10 oz.

ADJUSTABLE REDUCER

REALLY WORTH $3.00 **11F5694** PRICE EACH **$1.98**

SIZES: 20 to 36. State Size

Adjustable flaps and elastic bands over abdomen flatten and reduce the protruding stomach. Made of good strong coutil and rust-proof double boning. Long in back and over hips. Length of back, 16½ inches; front clasp, 13 inches; over hips from waist down, 11½ inches. Shipping weight, 2 lbs.

STUDY THIS PAGE CAREFULLY—EVERY NUMBER A BIG VALUE

Warner's Rust-Proof
11F5652 PRICE EACH **$1.00**
SIZES: 18 to 30. State Size.

The best value in the entire line of Warner's Rust-Proof Corsets. Latest low bust model, very long in back and over hips. Material is strong coutil and guaranteed "Rust-proof" double boning. Four strong supporters and draw strings to control bust, hook and eye below front clasp. Length of back, 19 inches; front clasp, 11½ inches. Over hips from waist down, 16½ inches. Shipping weight, 1 lb. 8 oz.

BELTED MODEL FOR FULL FIGURES
REGULAR $1.50 VALUE **11F5656** PRICE EACH **$1.19**
SIZES: 19 to 36. State Size.

Strictly up-to-date model for those who need a strong corset and still wish to retain a stylish appearance. Graduated front clasp widening at the bottom and reinforced belt over abdomen, flatten the abdomen and produce the popular straight front effect. Material is strong coutil and rust-proof double boning. Stylish low bust and very long in back and over hips. Length of back 19 inches; front clasp, 11½ inches; over hips from waist line down, 16 inches. Shpg. wt., 1 lb. 10 oz.

EMBROIDERED CORSET VERY HANDSOME MODEL
USUAL $1.50 VALUE **11F5660** PRICE EACH **98c**
SIZES: 18 to 30. State Size

The embroidered dots on this material and the silk embroidered trimming give this corset a very attractive style. Made in the stylish low bust model and is very long in back and over hips. Will fit the average figure perfectly. Material is strong coutil and non-rustable boning. Two hooks and eyes below front clasp. Length of back, 18 inches; front clasp, 11 inches; over hips from waist down, 15 inches. Shipping weight, 1 lb. 6 oz.

THOMSON'S Glove-Fitting
11F5664 PRICE EACH **$1.00**
SIZES: 18 to 30. State Size

Strictly up-to-date corset for average figures. Medium low in bust and very long in back and over hips. Material is strong coutil and non-rustable double boning. Rubber laces below front clasp. Silk stitching below steels. Length in back, 19 inches; front clasp 11½ inches; over hips from waist down, 15 inches. Shipping weight, 1 lb. 9 oz.

ADVERTISED $1.00 CORSET
11F5668 PRICE EACH **79c**
SIZES: 18 to 30. State Size

Great big value. Latest very low bust model, very long in back and over hips. Will fit average figure perfectly. Good strong coutil, guaranteed rust-proof boning, suspender web supporters, lace and ribbon trimand draw strings to control bust. Length of back, 19 inches; front clasp, 11 inches; over hips from waist down, 16 inches. Shipping weight, 1 lb. 5 oz.

VENTILATED NET LIGHT AND COOL
11F5670 PRICE EACH **49c**
SIZES: 18 to 30. State Size

Ventilated net, light weight, best for comfort. Will fit any figure. Medium bust and medium length in back and over hips. Length of back, 15½ inches; front steel, 10¾ inches; over hips from waist down, 9½ inches. Shipping weight, 1 lb.

TAPE GIRDLE FOR SLENDER FIGURES
11F5672 PRICE EACH **38c**
SIZES: 18 to 26. State Size

Very short. For girls and slender figures. Used while doing housework, exercising, etc. Allows body complete freedom of movement. 7-inch back, 10-inch front steel. Two hose supporters. Shipping wt., 9 oz.

SHORT CORSET FOR SHORT FIGURES
11F5678 PRICE EACH **45c**
SIZES: 18 to 30. State Size

A good model for those who cannot wear the long corsets. Full gored, taking care of large hips. Material is strong coutil. Back is 13 inches long, front clasp, 11 inches, and length over hips from waist down is 10 in. Shipping weight, 1 lb.

STYLISH LONG CORSET
11F5682 PRICE EACH **49c**
SIZES: 18 to 30. State Size

A good corset for every-day wear. Medium low bust. Long in back and over hips. Material is strong corset twill and is boned with watch spring steel. Length of back, 17½ inches; and front steel is 12½ inches long. Over hips from waist line down is 11½ inches. Shipping weight, 1 pound.

MATERNITY AND NURSING CORSETS, LADIES' AND CHILDREN'S WAISTS

NO CLASPS
NO HOOKS
NO EYELETS
NO STRINGS
NO HEAVY STEELS
NO PADDING

H. & W. NURSING AND MATERNITY CORSET
11F5710 PRICE EACH $1.89
SIZES, 20 to 36. State Size

Supplies a great need for expectant and convalescent mothers. The front and side laces can be adjusted as necessary, giving support to the body, and still enabling the wearer to preserve a neat appearance. Material is strong coutil and pliable non-rustable boning. Bust flaps fasten with tape, attached pearl buttons. Back, 16 inches long; Front clasp, 10 in. Shipping weight, 1 lb. 6 oz.

H. & W. MATERNITY ELASTIC FRONT
11F5714 PRICE EACH $2.98
SIZES, 20 to 36. State Size

A boon to the expectant mother, convalescent and invalid. Elastic panels in front and adjustable side-lacings give ease and comfort, and at the same time preserving a neat and stylish appearance. Material is strong coutil and non-rustable boning. Good length. Black, 17 inches; front clasp, 12 inches. Shipping weight, 1 lb. 8 oz.

PERFECT FORM AND CORSET COMBINED
REGULAR $1.50 VALUE
11F5715 PRICE EACH $1.09
SIZES, 18 to 30. State regular corset size

Produces a perfect figure for every woman. Gives a perfect bust to the flat chested woman. Throws the shoulders back naturally and expands the chest. Made of strong jean with lightly boned bust which will not cave in. Good length. Length of back, 15 inches; length over hips, 9½ inches. In ordering, state size the same as for any other corset. Shipping weight, 1 lb. 4 oz.

MATERNITY CORSET WAIST
COMFORTABLE BUTTON FRONT
GOOD $2.00 VALUE
11F5717 PRICE EACH $1.39
SIZES, 20 to 36. State size

A very comfortable corset for the expectant mother, at the same time retaining a neat and stylish appearance. A comfort for convalescents and invalids and will keep the figure in perfect proportions after confinement. Made of fine coutil and pliable non-rustable boning. Fastens in front with tape attached buttons. Good length. Back, 16½ inches. Shipping weight, 1 lb. 7 oz.

NURSING CORSET
FOR ALL FIGURES, GOOD VALUE
11F5713 PRICE EACH 98c
SIZES, 18 to 36. State Size

Good length, but not extreme, giving perfect comfort to the wearer and still retaining style. Is medium low in bust and long in back and over hips. Material is good quality coutil with non-rustable boning. Bust fastens with two glove clasps which are easily opened. Back is 16 inches long. Front clasp is 11½ inches long. Shipping weight, 1 lb. 4 oz.

H. & W. COMFORT CORSET WAIST
11F5723 PRICE EACH 98c
SIZES, 19 to 36. State waist measure

Combines the health and comfort of a waist and the style of the most up-to-date corset. Lightly boned. Adjustable shoulder straps. Good length. Back is 15 inches long. Has tape attached button-front. Material is double sateen. Shipping weight, 1 lb.

EXPANSION BUST CORSET WAIST
FOR GIRLS 9 TO 17 YEARS
11F5729 PRICE EACH 55c
SIZES, 19 to 28. State waist measure

An Ideal Garment for Growing Girls. Has plaited expansion bust, which adjusts itself to the natural bust development of the wearer. Material is strong sateen and pliable boning. Button front. Shipping wt., 10 oz.

CHILDREN'S WAIST
FOR AGES UP TO 12 YEARS
11F5736 PRICE EACH 48c
SIZES, 20 to 28. State waist measure

A very comfortable waist for growing children. Has very light pliable boning in the back, just enough to support the body. Fastens in front with tape attached buttons. Has adjustable shoulder straps. Material is strong jean. Shipping wt., 9 oz.

WOMEN'S WAISTS
COMFORT, STRENGTH, STYLE
11F5738 PRICE EACH 98c
SIZES, 20 to 36. Mention size

Old Reliable Corset Waist, especially desirable for the woman who "just can't wear the long corsets." Very lightly boned, but heavily corded, giving the body perfect support and real comfort at the same time. Good length. Back is 16 inches long. Has bust conforming top, and shoulder straps; clasp front. Material is double sateen. Shipping wt., 1 lb.

IIE561

IIE558

IIE562

IIE559

IIE560

SAHLIN
PERFECT
FORM
CORSET

IIE557   95c   IIE557

BACK VIEW

Sahlin Perfect Form 95c

11E557 This corset is made of a very strong, fine quality coutil, and is a perfect bust form and corset combined. Fastens without laces or hooks as shown in picture above. Is one of the best figure building corsets on the market today. Particularly fine for slender figures, giving a full bust effect without any pressure on the heart or lungs. Has adjustable straps over shoulder and acts as a shoulder brace. Has four elastic web hose supporters. This corset is made in three lengths, short, medium and long.
Sizes 30 in. bust with 18-20-22 inch waist measure.
32 in. bust with 20-22-24 inch waist measure.
34 in. bust with 22-24-26 in. waist measure.
36 in. bust with 22-24-26-28 in. waist measure.
38 in. bust with 24-26-28-30 waist measure.
40 in. bust with 28-30-32 waist measure.
In ordering give your actual waist meaure and the bust measure desired; also do not fail to give the length of your waist at side from arm pit to waist line.
If these measurements are correctly given this corset will assure you of a perfect figure. Color: white.
Price prepaid........................95c

Regular $1.50 Corset 95c

11E559 Corset made of very fine strong Janes cloth; lace trimmed, extra long skirt; low bust. A perfect fitting corset made with double boning both front and back. Wide single boning at sides, trimmed with strong hooks in front, laces down back; has 6 hose supporters of strong elastic web, adjustable. Length from waist line over hips, 15 inches. Front 16 in. Back 19 in. Color white only. Sizes 18 to 30.
Price prepaid........................95c

Nursing Corset 98c

11E561 Ladies' nursing corset made of a good quality Janes cloth, very light and strong. Has light weight flexible boning; medium long skirt; medium bust. Large button opening fastened with covered snaps. An excellent corset for convalescing mothers. Front length, 15 in.; back 16 in. Color, white only. Sizes 18 to 30.
Price prepaid........................98c

Reducing Corset 98c

11E558 An extra fine reducing corset made of a good quality strong Janes cloth; has double boning both front and back. Laces in back. Especially designed for short or stout figures. Straps at side pull up so as to support the abdomen without any strain whatever. Rust proof stays throughout. The corset is trimmed with 4 elastic web hose supporters, medium bust and skirt length. Front length 16½ in., back length 17 in. An extra fine regular $1.50 corset. Color, white only. Sizes 20 to 36.
Price prepaid........................98c

Extra Long Corset 98c

11E560 Here is a new long skirt model; has a medium high bust and an extra long skirt; made of good quality heavy Alexander cloth and non-rustable steels. Has double flexible boning both front and back, wide single boning at side, bottom of skirt is without bones. Skirt length from waist line over hips 18 inches; front 19½, back 21 in. An extra fine good fitting corset; color, white only. Sizes 18 to 30.
Price prepaid........................98c

Ladies' Maternity Corset Waist $1.45

11E562 Made of good quality soft coutil; fastens in front with strong buttons and taped button holes. Has adjustable lacing half way up front on either side and all the way up the side; lacing can be let out as desired, assuring comfort and good support. Has boning in front; two flexible bones on either side of back. Trimmed with four elastic hose supporters; length in front 14½ in., back 15 in. Color, white only. Sizes 20 to 30. When ordering, state size of present waist measure.
Price prepaid........................$1.45

Note: To get your actual corset size, take your waist measure over your corset and deduct 2 inches for spread of laces.

1914

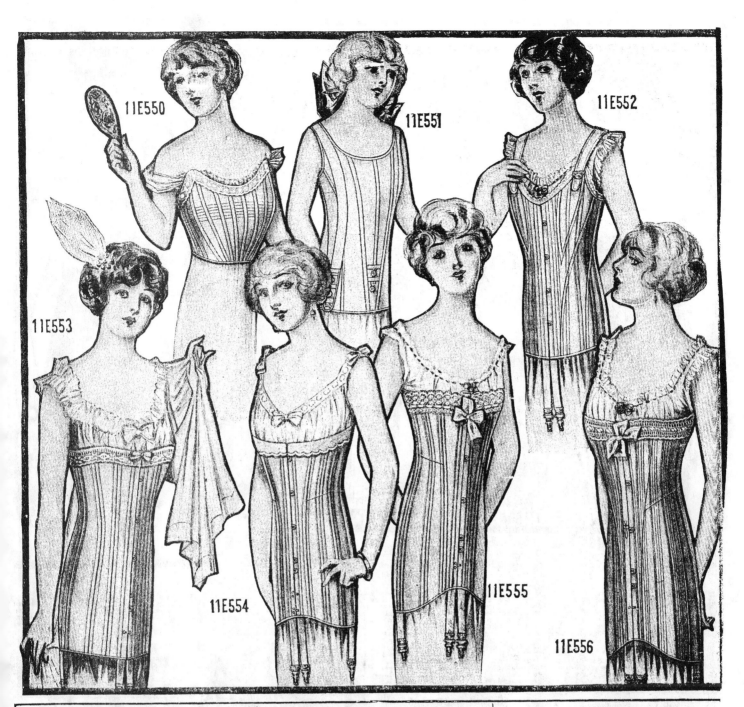

11E550

11E551

11E552

11E553

11E554

11E555

11E556

Ladies' Corset
49c

11E553 Ladies' or misses' corset made of a good quality batiste; has medium high bust and neatly trimmed around top with embroidery. Laces down back; good, strong double boning. It is not only substantial, but flexible and comfortable. Hooks in front, has four elastic web hose supporters. Front length 16½ in. Back 16½ in. **Color white only, sizes 18 to 30 in. Price Prepaid ..** 49c

Ladies' Long Hip Corset
65c

11E554 Ladies' corset made with a medium high bust and extra long hip; double boning throughout. Material used is a good quality Janes cloth. Laces in back, embroidery trimmed around top. **Color, white only.** Length 15 inches over hip from waist; 17 in. front, 18½ in. back. **Sizes 18 to 30 in. Price Prepaid ....** 65c

Ladies' Bust Form   48c

11E550 Ladies' bust form made of good quality muslin, strong flexible stays, trimmed around top with neat embroidery. Gives a perfect figure to any lady. In ordering state size bust desired. Sizes 32 to 44 in. Price Prepaid 48c

Child's or Misses' Waist 69c

11E551 A very fine quality child's or misses' waist, made of an excellent quality Janes cloth. Fastens down front with five large taped bone buttons; reinforced with wide tape at sides and over shoulders. Has three tapes running to point in back, is further trimmed with two bone buttons on each side and a holder for hose supporters. An exceptionally well made garment. **Sizes 20 to 27 in. waist measure. Price Prepaid** 69c

Misses' or Ladies' Waist 98c

11E552 The most desirable garment for ladies or misses. Stays are strong, yet flexible; has wide shoulder straps; fastens with neat buckle in front; laces down back. Fastens in front with hooks as shown. Has four strong elastic web hose supporters. The material used is batiste. **Sizes 18 to 28. Front length 14 in., back 15 in. Color, white only. Price Prepaid** 98c

Ladies' New Model Corset
89c

11E555 This is the famous style 150 corset, so widely advertised, made of a good quality Alexander cloth; neat silk bow in front; trimmed around top with a wide band of lace. Laces in back, has low bust and extra long over hips. 15 inches from waist line over hip; front 16¼ in., back 18½. Has four strong elastic web hose supporters. **Sizes, 18 to 30, color, white only. Price Prepaid ..** 89c

Ladies' Corset
98c

11E556 This corset is made of a good quality heavy batiste; embroidery trimmed; ribbon bow in the front; has triple boning front and back and is very strong and flexible. Extra long over hips. Length from waist over hips 15 inches; front 17 in.; back 19 in. **Sizes 18 to 30. Color, white only. Price Prepaid ....** 98c

---

TO GET YOUR ACTUAL CORSET SIZE TAKE WAIST MEASURE OVER YOUR CORSET AND DEDUCT 2 IN. FOR SPREAD OF LACES

Satisfaction Guaranteed
or Money Refunded

Corset Covers, Princess Slips and Muslin Underwear Priced Lower

SEND SAVAGE—MINNEAPO

11E568

11E567

11E566   11E564   11E563

Guaranteed 6 Months Corset
$1.55

11E563 We offer you this number, a ladies' up-to-date new style corset made of strong light weight Alexander cloth, and we guarantee it against the steels breaking or the front ripping for 6 months. Has double boning in front. Side and back has wide single boning, has a good flexible long skirt and bottom trimmed with 4 elastic web, adjustable hose supporters. Non-rustable steels, lace trimmed front. Length from waist over hips, 13 in. Front 16 in. Back 18 in. Guaranteed 6 months. Color white only; sizes, 18 to 30.
Price, prepaid.................. **$1.55**

Front Lace Corset
$1.45

11E565 This corset is made of good quality Janes cloth; embroidery trimmed around top and laces down front. Has 6 strong elastic web hose supporters; strong double boning; long skirt. A well made flexible corset we are sure will please you. Length from waist line over hips, 13 in. Back 18 in. Front 16 in. Color, white only. Sizes 18 to 30.
Price, prepaid.................. **$1.45**

Extra Fashionable Model
$1.95

11E567 Ladies' corset made of a good quality Alexander cloth, draw string at top; embroidery trimmed; has extra long skirt; medium bust; 6 elastic web hose supporters with covered buttons. Double boning. A well made fashionable corset, especially designed for slender figures. Length from waist line over hips, 15½ in.; front 20 in.; back 19½ in. A regular $3.00 value. Color, white only. Sizes 18 to 30.
Price, prepaid.................. **$1.95**

Armor Side Reducing Corset
$1.49

11E564 Ladies' reducing corset made with the armor side as shown; heavy double boning in front; non-rustable steels and wide single boning in the back. Adjustable tape sides; may be drawn to any position desired; giving good strong support to the abdomen without any strain whatsoever. The corsets is trimmed with 4 elastic web hose supporters and wide row of lace around top. Laces down back, fastens with clasp in front. An extra strong good wearing reducing corset. sizes 20 to 30. Color white only.
Price, prepaid.................. **$1.49**

Extra Long Corset
$1.65

11E566 Ladies' corset made with an extra long skirt so much desired this season. Elaborately trimmed with silk ribbon bow and wide lace trimming around top. Laces down back, has double boning which is strong and flexible. No boning at bottom of skirt. Length from waist line over hips 15 inches; front 15 in.; back 21½ in. An excellent value. Color, white only. Sizes 18 to 30.
Price, prepaid.................. **$1.65**

Our Popular Model
$2.19

11E568 A ladies' corset made of good quality Janes cloth with draw string of silk and lace trimming around top. Has a new patent feature which insures a perfect fitting figure. Double strong flexible boning in front, single boning back; non-rustable steels, medium long skirt and low bust. Length from waist line over hips, 15 in.; front 17 in.; back 16 in. A corset that ordinarily sells for not less than $3.50 and often as high as $4.00. Note the exceptionally low price. Color, white only. Sizes 18 to 30.
Price, prepaid.................. **$2.19**

NOTE: To get your actual corset size, take your waist measure over your corset and deduct 2 inches for spread of laces

11E565
BACK VIEW

11E565

NEW
FRONT LACE
CORSET
$1.45

1914

Inside Reasons for Corset Service

1914

WE show you here some of the inside reasons for "National" Corset Supremacy. Some of the carefulness of "National" Corset making that means so very much to you, not only in comfort but in actual service.

Study these pictures. See for yourself the inside reasons why you should wear only corsets of "NATIONAL" quality.

1. Full-length covering for steels
2. Outside covering of Corset
3. Heavy, soft metal tips on steels
4. Extra lining, covering lower end of steel

Outside covering of Corset

Full-length covering for steels

Moisture-proof lining

Strong, flexible steels, covered to prevent rusting

All steels have heavy, soft metal tips

Hose supporters of excellent quality elastic

Durable steels that give great strength and flexibility

Moisture-proof inner lining to insure greater service

Protected tips at top and bottom

Extra strong front steels

extra covering that means longer wear

Outer covering, serviceable and beautiful

2741 2742 $1.50

"NATIONAL" CORSET

GUARANTEE TAG

THIS "NATIONAL" CORSET IS MADE OF THE VERY BEST MATERIAL ESPECIALLY SELECTED FOR ITS SERVICE-GIVING QUALITIES. IT GIVES THE PROPER SUPPORT AND IS COMFORTABLE BECAUSE IT IS CONSTRUCTED ON THE MOST SCIENTIFIC LINES.

WE GUARANTEE IT TO GIVE SATISFACTORY WEAR OR REPLACE IT WITH ANOTHER CORSET FREE OF CHARGE.

National Cloak & Suit Co.
New York City

Read other side

A "NATIONAL" Bargain

41—Why not order this "NATIONAL" Guaranteed corset and test for yourself its charm and style, its grace-giving s and its remarkable service? Examine the splendid material, d quality Coutil, firm and evenly woven, strong and durable.

And note the superior workmanship, the boning, the dainty mmings and every small detail of fit and finish. Here is, ed, a corset worthy of the "NATIONAL" Guarantee Tag, ich says that your corset must give satisfactory service.

This model is made with medium low bust, suitable for rage figures, either medium or stout, requiring extra abdominal port. Two bias reverse abdominal straps with hose support-attached provide perfect support and give the graceful, erect position ich displays the lines of the suit or gown to the best advantage. The n and flexible boning insures permanency of shape, holding the figure in rect lines without binding or discomfort.

This corset is moderately long in back and over the hips, but the boning minates at just the right depth to insure perfect comfort when sitting. e top is attractively trimmed with dainty lace threaded with satin baby bon and finished with a bow. Four durable hose supporters. WHITE UTIL only. SIZES: 18 to 30. Read "How to Order Corsets" on page 177.

This corset is an extraordinary value at $1.50—it is a regular $2.00 value. if you feel that you should not pay more than $1.00 for a corset, turn age 179, Style No. 2750. There is a corset for $1.00 that is one of the best es ever offered. We recommend, however, that you pay 50 cents more order this corset, style No. 2741, price $1.50. The extra 50 cents will g you a full dollar's worth of extra corset value.

OUR PRICE, Two for $2.90; each $1.50
—and we pay postage and expressage.

42—"NATIONAL" Guaranteed Corset, same as No. 2741, but le with medium high bust for *tall figures,* medium or stout. WHITE UTIL only. SIZES: 18 to 30.

OUR PRICE, Two for $2.90; each $1.50
—and we pay postage and expressage.

Beauty and Service

IT was to give proper lines to the suit or dress, to bring out the lines and beauty of a "NATIONAL" Suit or Dress that the "NATIONAL" Corset was designed.

That was their inspiration—that is the reason for their being made. Therefore, in their making the whole hought has been, How good can a corset be made? Above we show you how "NATIONAL" Corsets are made. We show you inside reasons for their superiority and longer service. But it is on the basis of appearance that we wish to advise you to try one "NATIONAL" Corset.

So anxious are we to have "NATIONAL" Garments worn over perfect "NATIONAL" Corsets, so anxious we to have you enjoy the full beauty of your dresses and suits, that were it possible, we would give you a "NATIONAL" Corset with every dress or suit.

Of course this is plainly impossible, but we have done the next best thing. We have put so much quality into every "NATIONAL" Corset, so much of service as well as of beauty, and have made the prices so low, that not one of our customers can afford to do bout a "NATIONAL" Corset.

e word more. Pay as much for your corset as you can. Bus as good a corset as you can afford. It will pay in longer service and increased satisfaction.

On our advice and protected by our "NATIONAL" Corset Guarantee, just order one "NATIONAL" Corset and see.

"National" Corsets

2756
2757—$2.00
Reducing Corset

Famous "NATIONAL" $2.00 Corset

The Best $2.00 Corset Ever Made

Here is Real Beauty and Grace

This is a "NATIONAL" Corset Figure

Your Best Aid to a Good Figure

2756—Your corset, not your figure, is the foundation of your dress. How necessary, then, that you have a correctly designed, proper fitting corset.

This new "NATIONAL" Guaranteed Improved Reducing Corset is an excellent model to give you the lines demanded by the present fashions.

It is made with medium low bust, suitable for *average figures, medium or stout*, and the adjustable abdominal straps and elastic bands at each side hold the abdomen in correct position, and yield easily when sitting.

Strongly boned and fitted with broad front steels. Ribbon-run lace trims the top. Six extra strong hose supporters attached. WHITE COUTIL only. SIZES: 19 to 36. Read "How to Order Corsets" on this page.

Don't economize on your corset. Pay as much as you can, because the best corset is always the cheapest in the end.

*OUR PRICE, Two for $3.88; each $2.00
—and we pay postage and expressage.*

2757—Same as No. 2756, but made with medium high bust for *tall figures, medium or stout.* WHITE COUTIL only. SIZES: 19 to 36.
*OUR PRICE, Two for $3.88; each $2.00
—and we pay postage and expressage.*

HOW TO ORDER CORSETS
If you know what size corset you wear, and it is the right size for you, order your "NATIONAL" Corset by that size. If you do not know, or are not quite sure, you will find it a very simple matter to get a perfect-fitting corset the "NATIONAL."

Just order by size, not by waist measure. The correct size of your corset is three inches smaller than your waist measure taken over your dress. If your waist measure is 23 inches, order a corset Size 20; if your waist measure is 28 inches, order Size 25; and so on. Front Lacing Corsets, Nos. 2720, 2765, and 2784, shown on Page 181, should be ordered Size *one inch smaller than* your waist measure. Corset Waist No. 2764 and 2775, on page 179, should be ordered Size *two inches* smaller than your waist measure. Maternity Corsets, Nos. 2739 and 2740, shown on page 180, and Nos. 31201, 31202, 31203, 31204, and 31205, shown on page 168, should be ordered Size *two inches* smaller than your waist measure.

Charm and Gracefulness
Come with a "NATIONAL" Corset

ANALYZE beauty of form. Try a figure of natural beauty in an ordinary corset and see how its beauty is spoiled. Try the average figure in a "NATIONAL" Corset and see the figure made beautiful—see for yourself whence comes beauty of form.

Madam, the corset is the foundation of your dress. The lines of the corset are the lines of your figure. If your corset has proper lines, if it is a "NATIONAL" Corset, it gives to your figure lines of Grace and Beauty.

Make no mistake about your corset. Try a "NATIONAL" Corset and see for yourself the difference. You can never appreciate the difference until you try one "NATIONAL" Corset.

The "NATIONAL" Corset is simply the outcome of our pride in "NATIONAL" Suits and Dresses. "NATIONAL" Corsets are made to bring out the full beauty of our outer garments. They are created for this purpose and no other. They were created because it is our ambition to have every customer of the "NATIONAL" distinctive in appearance; to have every "NATIONAL" Suit and Dress show its full beauty of design.

Therefore, try one "NATIONAL" Corset. Try one corset that is made not primarily to sell, but made to add beauty to the figure. Try one "NATIONAL" Corset and see for yourself that "Charm and Gracefulness come with a 'NATIONAL' Corset."

1914

1914

Style H-2800 is for the average figure. The materials are pink, attractively arranged. The upper part is fancy brocade and the skirt is of plain material, satin finished. The trimming is lace feather-stitched on fancy ribbon. The front length is 17 inches; the 10 inch front clasp has white enameled eyelets. The entire length of back is 21½ inches; the back wires are 16½ inches long with featherbone below.

Style H-703 is for the average figure. Made of a fancy batiste, finished at top with lace edged with a fancy pink ribbon. Two medallions in front. Very low bust, with long skirt. Length of front is 16½ inches. 10 inch front clasp has white enameled eyelets below, laced with elastic lacer. Length of back 20 inches; 15½ inch back wires; featherbone below. Three pairs of supporters. Sizes, 20 to 32.

THE surest way for you to get exactly what you want in a corset is to ask for Le Revo, Society's Corset.

You'll see a real creation; a garment which possesses all the features demanded by Fashion, and the excellence demanded by good taste and knowing what you want.

Le Rêvo, Society's Corset, is made with just one idea: to produce as fine a corset as it is possible to make. The designs come from Paris; the materials are imported, the best we can find; the workmanship is costly.

Le Rêvo Corsets are for women who buy slowly, carefully, expecting the best in every detail and demanding it. They cost more than the kind bought by the woman who is satisfied with anything; of course.

Le Rêvo
Society's Corset

The Kabo Corset Company

New York   Chicago   San Francisco

IF you buy your corsets carefully; if you know where to look for the good points of the best corsets; if you know why one corset gives you style and comfort, while another at the same price does not, then go to your dealer and ask him to show you the various models of Le Rêvo, Society's Corset.

You'll find your corset among them; yours because it will meet every requirement you would make if you stood by and directed the making of it. Le Rêvo corsets are made for women who know that the finest materials, the most skilled labor, the most accurate knowledge of style are things that cost money and are worth it. They are all in Le Rêvo Corsets.

Buy a Le Rêvo corset and you'll be sure to be entirely satisfied; if you become dissatisfied for any reason at any time your dealer is authorized by us to refund your money and charge it to us.

Le Rêvo
Society's Corset

The Kabo Corset Company

New York   Chicago   San Francisco

1914

1914

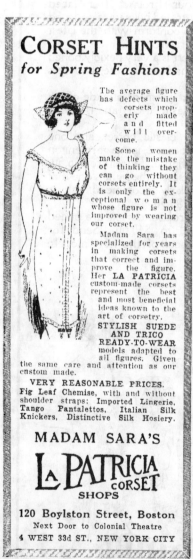

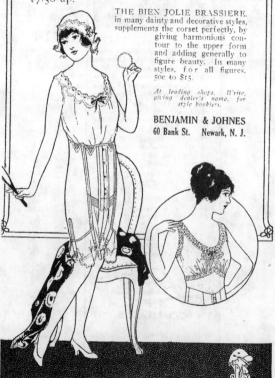

The Natural Figure

A woman can give her figure no greater praise than to say,

"*I buy Redfern Corsets and they fit me perfectly*"

Redfern Corsets

are modelled on women of perfect figure who, although of varying measurements are naturally well proportioned.

The natural figure is not straight up and down, hipless, boneless, spineless—the corset curves to just the extent that the correctly built woman is curved.

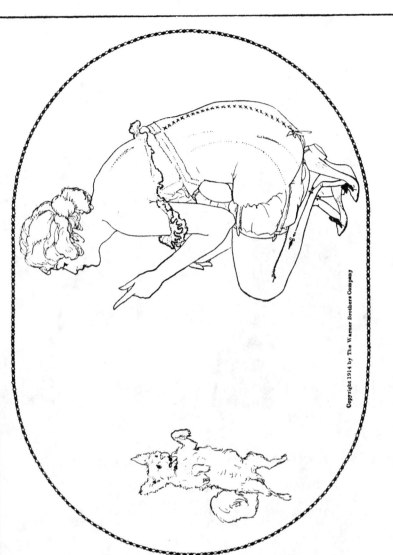

Copyright 1914 by The Warner Brothers Company

You are always comfortable in a Redfern. Freedom shows in every pose, and healthful support is assured by the supple boning rightly placed.

Whatever your figure, there is a Redfern style for you, and the leading stores are pleased to assist you in your selection by careful personal fittings.

THREE TO FIFTEEN DOLLARS THE PAIR

AT HIGH CLASS SHOPS

1914

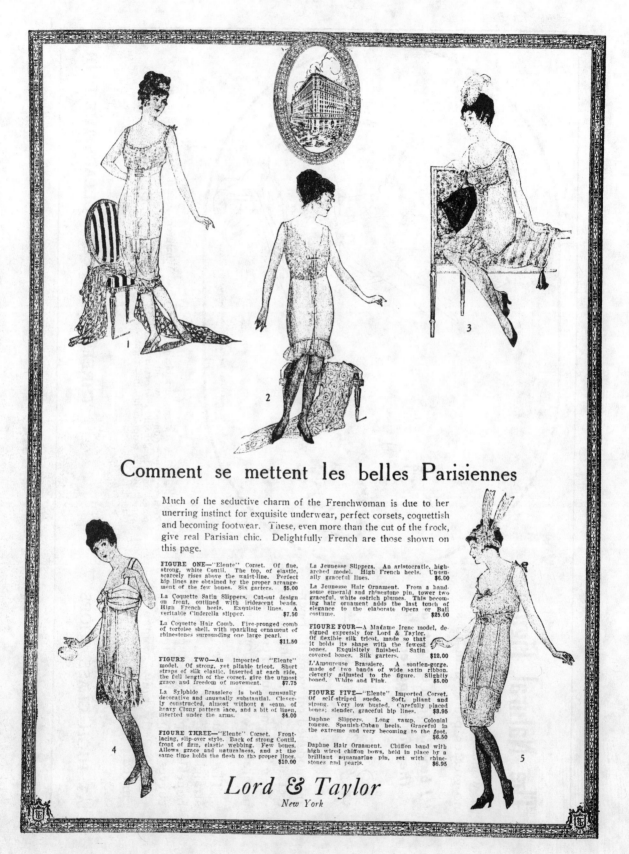

Comment se mettent les belles Parisiennes

Much of the seductive charm of the Frenchwoman is due to her unerring instinct for exquisite underwear, perfect corsets, coquettish and becoming footwear. These, even more than the cut of the frock, give real Parisian chic. Delightfully French are those shown on this page.

FIGURE ONE—"Elente" Corset. Of fine, strong, white Contil. The top, of elastic, scarcely rises above the waist-line. Perfect hip lines are obtained by the proper arrangement of the few bones. Six garters. **$5.00**

La Coquette Satin Slippers. Cut-out design on front, outlined with iridescent beads. High French heels. Exquisite lines. A veritable Cinderella slipper. **$7.50**

La Coquette Hair Comb. Five-pronged comb of tortoise shell, with sparkling ornament of rhinestones surrounding one large pearl. **$11.50**

FIGURE TWO—An imported "Elente" model. Of strong, yet pliable tricot. Short straps of silk elastic, inserted at each side, the full length of the corset, give the utmost grace and freedom of movement. **$7.75**

La Sylphide Brassiere is both unusually decorative and unusually substantial. Cleverly constructed, almost without a seam, of heavy Cluny pattern lace, and a bit of linen, inserted under the arms. **$4.00**

FIGURE THREE—"Elente" Corset. Front-lacing, slip-over style. Back of strong Contil, front of firm, elastic webbing. Few bones. Allows grace and naturalness, and at the same time holds the flesh to the proper lines. **$10.00**

La Jeunesse Slippers. An aristocratic, high-arched model. High French heels. Unusually graceful lines. **$6.00**

La Jeunesse Hair Ornament. From a handsome emerald and rhinestone pin, tower two graceful, white ostrich plumes. This becoming hair ornament adds the last touch of elegance to the elaborate Opera or Ball costume. **$25.00**

FIGURE FOUR—A Madame Irene model, designed expressly for Lord & Taylor. Of flexible silk tricot, made so that it holds its shape with the fewest bones. Exquisitely finished. Satin covered bones. Silk garters. **$12.00**

L'Amoureuse Brassiere. A soutien-gorge, made of two bands of wide satin ribbon, cleverly adjusted to the figure. Slightly boned. White and Pink. **$5.00**

FIGURE FIVE—"Elente" Imported Corset. Of self-striped suede. Soft, pliant and strong. Very low busted. Carefully placed bones; slender, graceful hip lines. **$8.95**

Daphne Slippers. Long vamp. Colonial tongue. Spanish-Cuban heels. Graceful in the extreme and very becoming to the foot. **$6.50**

Daphne Hair Ornament. Chiffon band with high wired chiffon bows, held in place by a brilliant aquamarine pin, set with rhinestones and pearls. **$6.95**

Lord & Taylor
New York

1914

Our Perfect Fitting C/W Corsets at Special Prices

1915

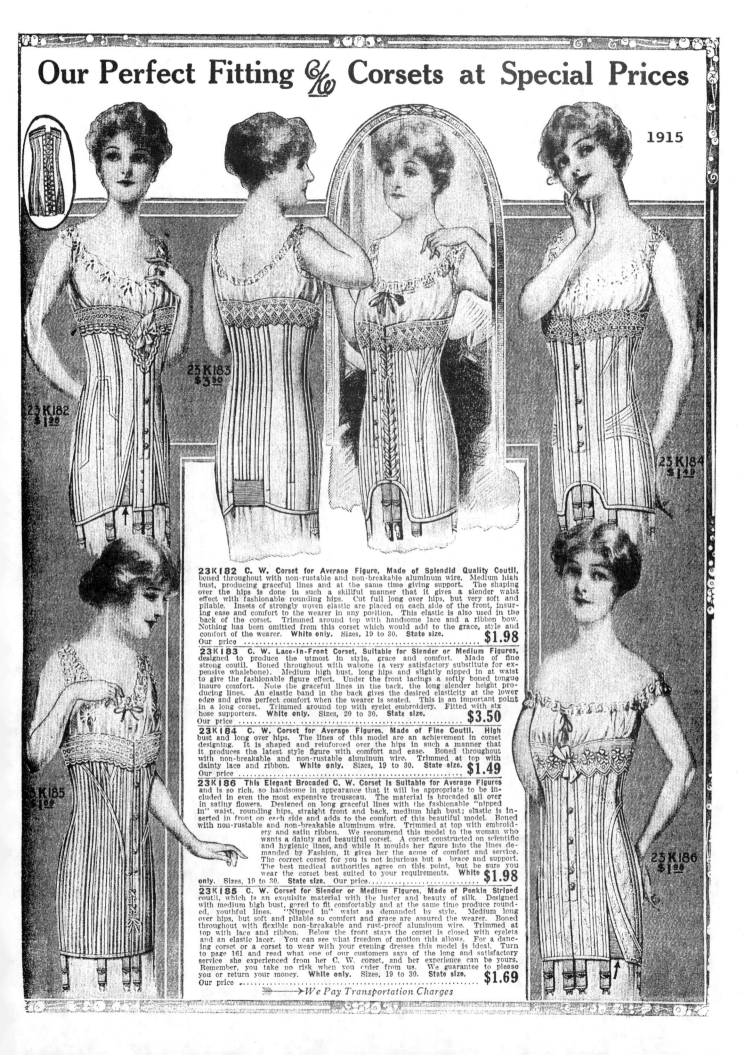

23K182 C. W. Corset for Average Figure, Made of Splendid Quality Coutil, boned throughout with non-rustable and non-breakable aluminum wire. Medium high bust, producing graceful lines and at the same time giving support. The shaping over the hips is done in such a skillful manner that it gives a slender waist effect with fashionable rounding hips. Cut full long over hips, but very soft and pliable. Insets of strongly woven elastic are placed on each side of the front, insuring ease and comfort to the wearer in any position. This elastic is also used in the back of the corset. Trimmed around top with handsome lace and a ribbon bow. Nothing has been omitted from this corset which would add to the grace, style and comfort of the wearer. White only. Sizes, 19 to 30. State size.
Our price **$1.98**

23K183 C. W. Lace-In-Front Corset, Suitable for Slender or Medium Figures, designed to produce the utmost in style, grace and comfort. Made of fine strong coutil. Boned throughout with wabone (a very satisfactory substitute for expensive whalebone). Medium high bust, long hips and slightly nipped in at waist to give the fashionable figure effect. Under the front lacings a softly boned tongue insure comfort. Note the graceful lines in the back, the long slender height producing lines. An elastic band in the back gives the desired elasticity at the lower edge and gives perfect comfort when the wearer is seated. This is an important point in a long corset. Trimmed around top with eyelet embroidery. Fitted with six hose supporters. White only. Sizes, 20 to 30. State size.
Our price **$3.50**

23K184 C. W. Corset for Average Figures, Made of Fine Coutil. High bust and long over hips. The lines of this model are an achievement in corset designing. It is shaped and reinforced over the hips in such a manner that it produces the latest style figure with comfort and ease. Boned throughout with non-breakable and non-rustable aluminum wire. Trimmed at top with dainty lace and ribbon. White only. Sizes, 19 to 30. State size. **$1.49**
Our price

23K186 This Elegant Brocaded C. W. Corset is Suitable for Average Figures and is so rich, so handsome in appearance that it will be appropriate to be included in even the most expensive trousseau. The material is brocaded all over in satiny flowers. Designed on long graceful lines with the fashionable "nipped in" waist, rounding hips, straight front and back, medium high bust; elastic is inserted in front on each side and adds to the comfort of this beautiful model. Boned with non-rustable and non-breakable aluminum wire. Trimmed at top with embroidery and satin ribbon. We recommend this model to the woman who wants a dainty and beautiful corset. A corset constructed on scientific and hygienic lines, and while it moulds her figure into the lines demanded by Fashion, it gives her the acme of comfort and service. The correct corset for you is not injurious but a brace and support. The best medical authorities agree on this point, but be sure you wear the corset best suited to your requirements. White **$1.98**
only. Sizes, 19 to 30. State size. Our price ....

23K185 C. W. Corset for Slender or Medium Figures, Made of Penkin Striped coutil, which is an exquisite material with the luster and beauty of silk. Designed with medium high bust, gored to fit comfortably and at the same time produce rounded, youthful lines. "Nipped in" waist as demanded by style. Medium long over hips, but soft and pliable so comfort and grace are assured the wearer. Boned throughout with flexible non-breakable and rust-proof aluminum wire. Trimmed at top with lace and ribbon. Below the front stays the corset is closed with eyelets and an elastic lacer. You can see what freedom of motion this allows. For a dancing corset or a corset to wear with your evening dresses this model is ideal. Turn to page 161 and read what one of our customers says of the long and satisfactory service she experienced from her C. W. corset, and her experience can be yours. Remember, you take no risk when you order from us. We guarantee to please you or return your money. White only. Sizes, 19 to 30. State size.
Our price **$1.69**

>>>→ **We Pay Transportation Charges**

Very Special Prices for High Class C/W Corsets

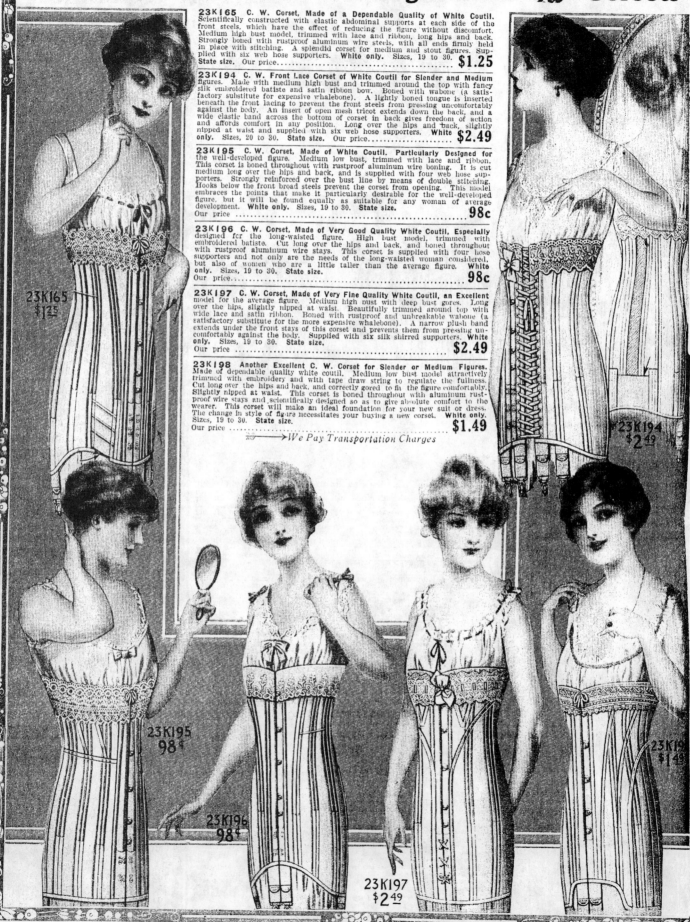

23K165 C. W. Corset, Made of a Dependable Quality of White Coutil. Scientifically constructed with elastic abdominal supports at each side of the front steels, which have the effect of reducing the figure without discomfort. Medium high bust model, trimmed with lace and ribbon, long hips and back. Strongly boned with rustproof aluminum wire steels, with all ends firmly held in place with stitching. A splendid corset for medium and stout figures. Supplied with six web hose supporters. **White only. Sizes, 19 to 30. State size. Our price.................. $1.25**

23K194 C. W. Front Lace Corset of White Coutil for Slender and Medium figures. Made with medium high bust and trimmed around the top with fancy silk embroidered batiste and satin ribbon bow. Boned with wabone (a satisfactory substitute for expensive whalebone). A lightly boned tongue is inserted beneath the front lacing to prevent the front steels from pressing uncomfortably against the body. An insert of open mesh tricot extends down the back, and a wide elastic band across the bottom of corset in back gives freedom of action and affords comfort in any position. Long over the hips and back, slightly nipped at waist and supplied with six web hose supporters. **White only. Sizes, 20 to 30. State size. Our price....................... $2.49**

23K195 C. W. Corset, Made of White Coutil. Particularly Designed for the well-developed figure. Medium low bust, trimmed with lace and ribbon. This corset is boned throughout with rustproof aluminum wire boning. It is cut medium long over the hips and back, and is supplied with four web hose supporters. Strongly reinforced over the bust line by means of double stitching. Hooks below the front broad steels prevent the corset from opening. This model embraces the points that make it particularly desirable for the well-developed figure, but it will be found equally as suitable for any woman of average development. **White only. Sizes, 19 to 30. State size. Our price 98c**

23K196 C. W. Corset, Made of Very Good Quality White Coutil, Especially designed for the long-waisted figure. High bust model, trimmed with embroidered batiste. Cut long over the hips and back, and boned throughout with rustproof aluminum wire stays. This corset is supplied with four supporters and not only are the needs of the long-waisted woman considered, but also of women who are a little taller than the average figure. **White only. Sizes, 19 to 30. State size. Our price 98c**

23K197 C. W. Corset, Made of Very Fine Quality White Coutil, an Excellent model for the average figure. Medium high bust with deep bust gores. Long over the hips, slightly nipped at waist. Beautifully trimmed around top with wide lace and satin ribbon. Boned with rustproof and unbreakable wabone (a satisfactory substitute for the more expensive whalebone). A narrow plush band extends under the front stays of this corset and prevents them from pressing uncomfortably against the body. Supplied with six silk shirred supporters. **White only. Sizes, 19 to 30. State size. $2.49**

23K198 Another Excellent C. W. Corset for Slender or Medium Figures. Made of dependable quality white coutil. Medium low bust model attractively trimmed with embroidery and with tape draw string to regulate the fullness. Cut long over the hips and back, and correctly gored to fit the figure comfortably. Slightly nipped at waist. This corset is boned throughout with aluminum rustproof wire stays and scientifically designed so as to give absolute comfort to the wearer. This corset will make an ideal foundation for your new suit or dress. The change in style of figure necessitates your buying a new corset. **White only. Sizes, 19 to 30. State size. Our price $1.49**

→We Pay Transportation Charges

℅ Corsets Are Shapely and Wear Splendidly

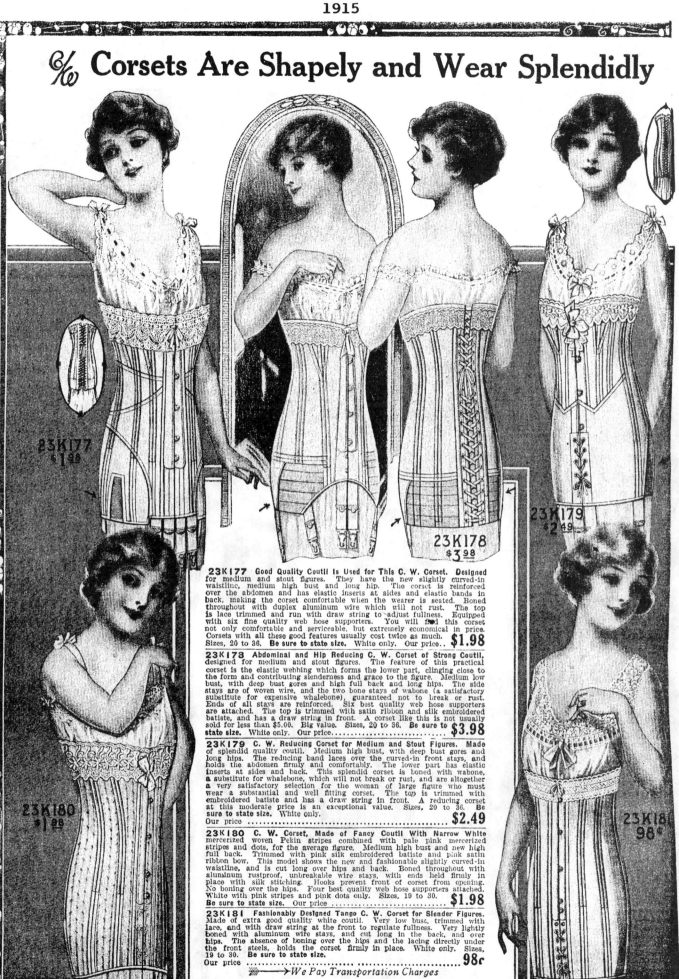

23K177 Good Quality Coutil Is Used for This C. W. Corset. Designed for medium and stout figures. They have the new slightly curved-in waistline, medium high bust and long hip. The corset is reinforced over the abdomen and has elastic inserts at sides and elastic bands in back, making the corset comfortable when the wearer is seated. Boned throughout with duplex aluminum wire which will not rust. The top is lace trimmed and run with draw string to adjust fullness. Equipped with six fine quality web hose supporters. You will find this corset not only comfortable and serviceable, but extremely economical in price. Corsets with all these good features usually cost twice as much. Sizes, 20 to 36. **Be sure to state size.** White only. Our price.. **$1.98**

23K178 Abdominal and Hip Reducing C. W. Corset of Strong Coutil, designed for medium and stout figures. The feature of this practical corset is the elastic webbing which forms the lower part, clinging close to the form and contributing slenderness and grace to the figure. Medium low bust, with deep bust gores and high full back and long hips. The side stays are of woven wire, and the two bone stays of wabone (a satisfactory substitute for expensive whalebone), guaranteed not to break or rust. Ends of all stays are reinforced. Six best quality web hose supporters are attached. The top is trimmed with satin ribbon and silk embroidered batiste, and has a draw string in front. A corset like this is not usually sold for less than $5.00. Big value. Sizes, 20 to 36. **Be sure to state size.** White only. Our price................ **$3.98**

23K179 C. W. Reducing Corset for Medium and Stout Figures. Made of splendid quality coutil. Medium high bust, with deep bust gores and long hips. The reducing band laces over the curved-in front stays, and holds the abdomen firmly and comfortably. The lower part has elastic inserts at sides and back. This splendid corset is boned with wabone, a substitute for whalebone, which will not break or rust, and are altogether a very satisfactory selection for the woman of large figure who must wear a substantial and well fitting corset. The top is trimmed with embroidered batiste and has a draw string in front. A reducing corset at this moderate price is an exceptional value. Sizes, 20 to 36. **Be sure to state size.** White only.
Our price **$2.49**

23K180 C. W. Corset, Made of Fancy Coutil With Narrow White mercerized woven Pekin stripes combined with pale pink mercerized stripes and dots, for the average figure. Medium high bust and new high full back. Trimmed with pink silk embroidered batiste and pink satin ribbon bow. This model shows the new and fashionable slightly curved-in waistline, and is cut long over hips and back. Boned throughout with aluminum rustproof, unbreakable wire stays, with ends held firmly in place with silk stitching. Hooks prevent front of corset from opening. No boning over the hips. Four best quality web hose supporters attached. White with pink stripes and pink dots only. Sizes, 19 to 30. **Be sure to state size.** Our price **$1.98**

23K181 Fashionably Designed Tango C. W. Corset for Slender Figures. Made of extra good quality white coutil. Very low bust, trimmed with lace, and with draw string at the front to regulate fullness. Very lightly boned with aluminum wire stays, and cut long in the back, and over hips. The absence of boning over the hips and the lacing directly under the front steels, holds the corset firmly in place. White only. Sizes, 19 to 30. **Be sure to state size.**
Our price **98c**

⟫⟫⟫ →We Pay Transportation Charges

Newest Styles in ℅ Corsets—Perfect Fitting

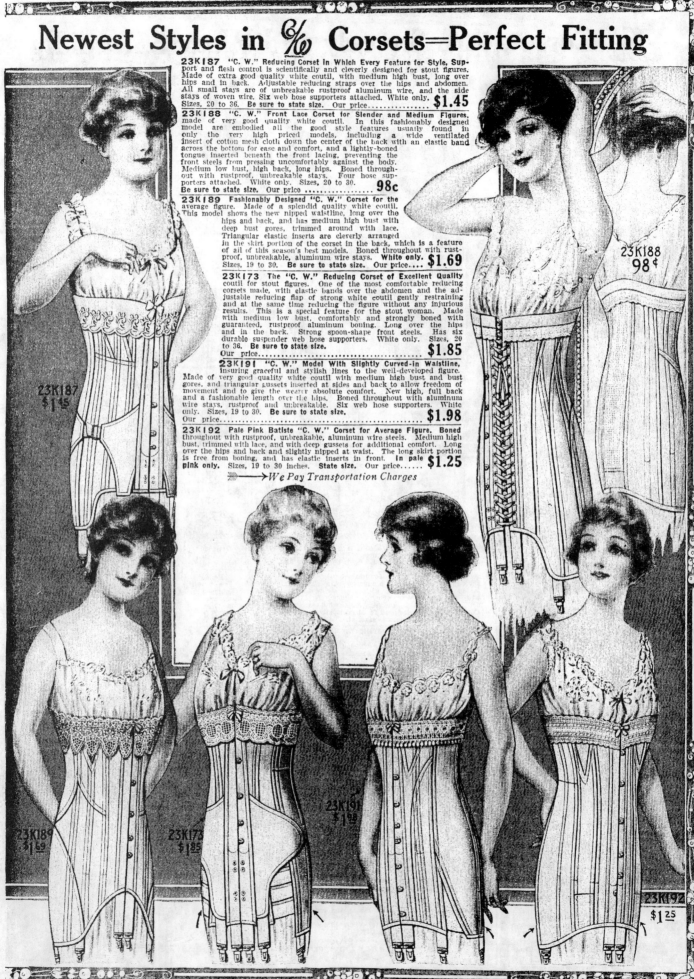

23K187 "C. W." Reducing Corset in Which Every Feature for Style, Support and flesh control is scientifically and cleverly designed for stout figures. Made of extra good quality white coutil, with medium high bust, long over hips and in back. Adjustable reducing straps over the hips and abdomen. All small stays are of unbreakable rustproof aluminum wire, and the side stays of woven wire. Six web hose supporters attached. White only. Sizes, 20 to 36. Be sure to state size. Our price................. **$1.45**

23K188 "C. W." Front Lace Corset for Slender and Medium Figures, made of very good quality white coutil. In this fashionably designed model are embodied all the good style features usually found in only the very high priced models, including a wide ventilated insert of cotton mesh cloth down the center of the back with an elastic band across the bottom for ease and comfort, and a lightly-boned tongue inserted beneath the front lacing, preventing the front steels from pressing uncomfortably against the body. Medium low bust, high back, long hips. Boned throughout with rustproof, unbreakable stays. Four hose supporters attached. White only. Sizes, 20 to 30. Be sure to state size. Our price.................... **98c**

23K189 Fashionably Designed "C. W." Corset for the average figure. Made of a splendid quality white coutil. This model shows the new nipped waistline, long over the hips and back, and has medium high bust with deep bust gores, trimmed around with lace. Triangular elastic inserts are cleverly arranged in the skirt portion of the corset in the back, which is a feature of all of this season's best models. Boned throughout with rustproof, unbreakable, aluminum wire stays. White only. Sizes, 19 to 30. Be sure to state size. Our price.... **$1.69**

23K173 The "C. W." Reducing Corset of Excellent Quality coutil for stout figures. One of the most comfortable reducing corsets made, with elastic bands over the abdomen and the adjustable reducing flap of strong white coutil gently restraining and at the same time reducing the figure without any injurious results. This is a special feature for the stout woman. Made with medium low bust, comfortably and strongly boned with guaranteed, rustproof aluminum boning. Long over the hips and in the back. Strong spoon-shape front steels. Has six durable suspender web hose supporters. White only. Sizes, 20 to 36. Be sure to state size. Our price................. **$1.85**

23K191 "C. W." Model With Slightly Curved-in Waistline, insuring graceful and stylish lines to the well-developed figure. Made of very good quality white coutil with medium high bust and bust gores, and triangular gussets inserted at sides and back to allow freedom of movement and to give the wearer absolute comfort. New high, full back and a fashionable length over the hips. Boned throughout with aluminum wire stays, rustproof and unbreakable. Six web hose supporters. White only. Sizes, 19 to 30. Be sure to state size. Our price................. **$1.98**

23K192 Pale Pink Batiste "C. W." Corset for Average Figure. Boned throughout with rustproof, unbreakable, aluminum wire steels. Medium high bust, trimmed with lace, and with deep gussets for additional comfort. Long over the hips and back and slightly nipped at waist. The long skirt portion is free from boning, and has elastic inserts in front. In pale pink only. Sizes, 19 to 30 inches. State size. Our price...... **$1.25**

→*We Pay Transportation Charges*

23K187
$1.45

23K188
98¢

23K189
$1.69

23K173
$1.85

23K191
$1.98

23K192
$1.25

Corsets Will Give You the New Style Figure

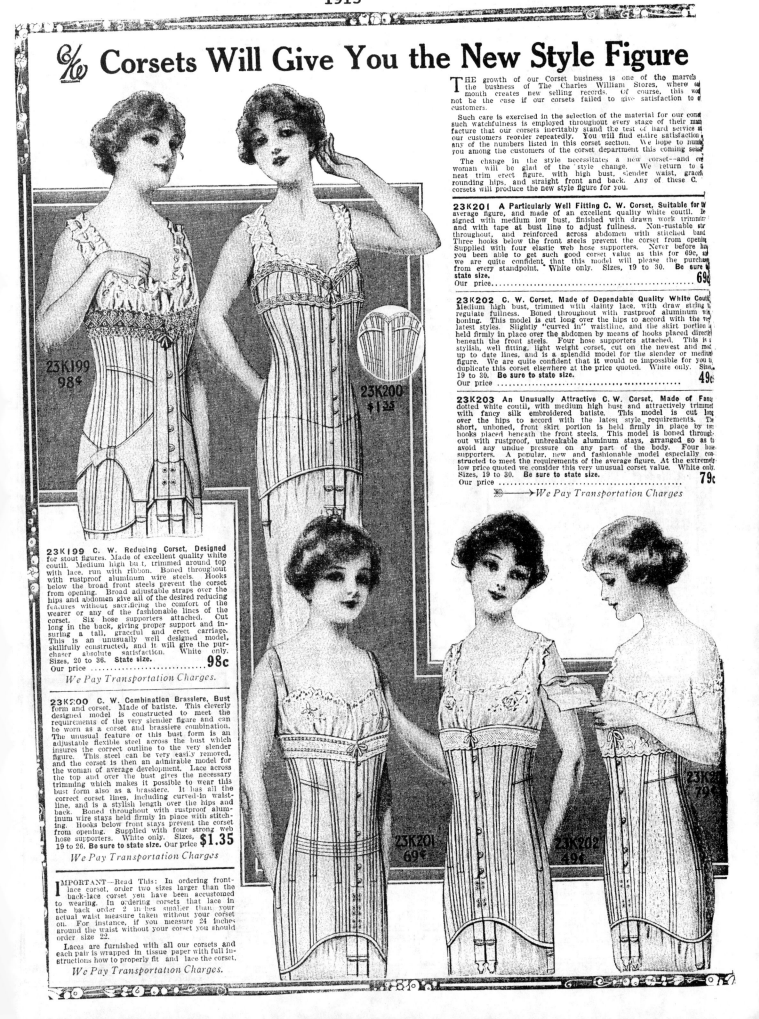

THE growth of our Corset business is one of the marvels the business of The Charles William Stores, where each month creates new selling records. Of course, this would not be the case if our corsets failed to give satisfaction to our customers.

Such care is exercised in the selection of the material for our corsets such watchfulness is employed throughout every stage of their manufacture that our corsets inevitably stand the test of hard service and our customers reorder repeatedly. You will find entire satisfaction in any of the numbers listed in this corset section. We hope to number you among the customers of the corset department this coming season.

The change in the style necessitates a new corset—and every woman will be glad of the style change. We return to the neat trim erect figure, with high bust, slender waist, gracefully rounding hips, and straight front and back. Any of these C. W. corsets will produce the new style figure for you.

23K201 A Particularly Well Fitting C. W. Corset, Suitable for the average figure, and made of an excellent quality white coutil. Designed with medium low bust, finished with drawn work trimming and with tape at bust line to adjust fullness. Non-rustable steel throughout, and reinforced across abdomen with stitched band. Three hooks below the front steels prevent the corset from opening. Supplied with four elastic web hose supporters. Never before have you been able to get such good corset value as this for 69c, and we are quite confident that this model will please the purchaser from every standpoint. White only. Sizes, 19 to 30. Be sure to state size.
Our price..69c

23K202 C. W. Corset, Made of Dependable Quality White Coutil. Medium high bust, trimmed with dainty lace, with draw string to regulate fullness. Boned throughout with rustproof aluminum wire boning. This model is cut long over the hips to accord with the very latest styles. Slightly "curved in" waistline, and the skirt portion is held firmly in place over the abdomen by means of hooks placed directly beneath the front steels. Four hose supporters attached. This is a stylish, well fitting, light weight corset, cut on the newest and most up to date lines, and is a splendid model for the slender or medium figure. We are quite confident that it would be impossible for you to duplicate this corset elsewhere at the price quoted. White only. Sizes, 19 to 30. Be sure to state size.
Our price..49c

23K203 An Unusually Attractive C. W. Corset, Made of Fancy dotted white coutil, with medium high bust and attractively trimmed with fancy silk embroidered batiste. This model is cut long over the hips to accord with the latest style requirements. The short, unboned, front skirt portion is held firmly in place by two hooks placed beneath the front steels. This model is boned throughout with rustproof, unbreakable aluminum stays, arranged so as to avoid any undue pressure on any part of the body. Four hose supporters. A popular, new and fashionable model especially constructed to meet the requirements of the average figure. At the extremely low price quoted we consider this very unusual corset value. White only. Sizes, 19 to 30. Be sure to state size.
Our price..79c

→ *We Pay Transportation Charges*

23K199 98¢

23K200 $1.35

23K199 C. W. Reducing Corset, Designed for stout figures. Made of excellent quality white coutil. Medium high bust, trimmed around top with lace, run with ribbon. Boned throughout with rustproof aluminum wire steels. Hooks below the broad front steels prevent the corset from opening. Broad adjustable straps over the hips and abdomen give all of the desired reducing features without sacrificing the comfort of the wearer or any of the fashionable lines of the corset. Six hose supporters attached. Cut long in the back, giving proper support and insuring a tall, graceful and erect carriage. This is an unusually well designed model, skillfully constructed, and it will give the purchaser absolute satisfaction. White only. Sizes, 20 to 36. State size.
Our price...98c

We Pay Transportation Charges.

23K200 C. W. Combination Brassiere, Bust form and corset. Made of batiste. This cleverly designed model is constructed to meet the requirements of the very slender figure and can be worn as a corset and brassiere combination. The unusual feature of this bust form is an adjustable flexible steel across the bust which insures the correct outline to the very slender figure. This steel can be very easily removed, and the corset is then an admirable model for the woman of average development. Lace across the top and over the bust gives the necessary trimming which makes it possible to wear this bust form also as a brassiere. It has all the correct corset lines, including curved-in waistline, and is a stylish length over the hips and back. Boned throughout with rustproof aluminum wire stays held firmly in place with stitching. Hooks below front stays prevent the corset from opening. Supplied with four strong web hose supporters. White only. Sizes, 19 to 26. Be sure to state size. Our price **$1.35**

We Pay Transportation Charges

IMPORTANT—Read This: In ordering front-lace corset, order two sizes larger than the back-lace corset you have been accustomed to wearing. In ordering corsets that lace in the back order 2 inches smaller than your actual waist measure taken without your corset on. For instance, if you measure 24 inches around the waist without your corset you should order size 22.

Laces are furnished with all our corsets and each pair is wrapped in tissue paper with full instructions how to properly fit and lace the corset.

We Pay Transportation Charges.

23K201 69¢

23K202 49¢

23K203 79¢

Comfortable Styles in Correct Maternity Garments

Brassiere
25K2784
49¢

Flannelette
25K2781
98¢

Cotton Messaline
25K2785
98¢

C. W. Maternity and Nursing Corset, Made of White Strong Coutil $1.49

25K2779 This Very Practical Maternity and nursing corset is made of strong white coutil lace trimmed around top. The bust is medium high, the hips medium long, and the fit generally one of perfect ease and comfort. Side laces and laces over the abdomen adjusts the corset to the figure very readily and in such a manner that pressure at any point can be instantly relieved. Nursing flaps, which are arranged to fasten conveniently with snap fasteners, make the corsets more practical and economical, since they are thereby adapted to longer wear. These splendid corsets are boned throughout with non-rustable aluminum wire stays and fitted with two hooks below the front stays to keep the corset from opening. Four hose supporters attached. For corsets assuring such long and useful service and so substantially made, the price charged is extremely reasonable. We are sure you will be pleased if you order this C. W. maternity corset as you will find it very comfortable, convenient in every way, and economically priced. Sizes, 20 to 36. White only. Be sure to state size.
Our price....................$1.49

——➤ *We Pay Transportation Charges.*

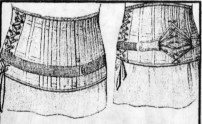

42K1200 Maternity Brace, Made of Coutil, scientifically constructed. Raises the body upward and backward, supporting it above the waist on the spine, and preventing congestion of the vital organs. Soft adjusting back lace. The two side outlets are double laced to fit the hips exactly, and can be let out from four to six inches. This practical maternity brace will be found ideally comfortable and a most satisfactory support. Hose supporters are not supplied with this brace, but may be attached as illustrated.

42K1200 Sizes, 30 to 38. Our price..$2.69
42K1202 Sizes, 40 to 46. Our price..$2.89
42K1204 Sizes, 48 to 56. Our price..$3.00

How to measure: Take measurements over the undergarments. Give number of inches around waistline and number of inches around hips, measuring hip 8 inches below waistline.

——➤ *We Pay Transportation Charges*

25K2781 Maternity Kimono, Made of Fine Quality Flannel- ette, in attractive floral pattern. This pretty kimono is designed on Empire lines, and has an elastic run through waistline which adjusts the waist to the figure very comfortably and conveniently. The long, broad collar is prettily shaped and trimmed with a stylish knife plaiting of satin ribbon, matching in color the general tone of the material. A similar plaiting heads the wide cuff, and a bow of the ribbon trims the waistline. This is a very pretty and practical garment and will be found extremely useful and generally becoming. The price asked is so moderate that it would be worth while to order two or three of these convenient garments at one time. It is an ideal kimono for hospital use, soft and warm and may be slipped on and off in an instant. Sizes, 34 to 44 inches bust measure. Be sure to state size.
25K2781 Navy Blue.
25K2782 Gray.
25K2783 Copenhagen Blue.
Our price...................98c

25K2785 Cotton Messaline Is the Serviceable Material Used for this maternity petticoat, closing at side-front. The waist size is adjusted in back by means of a clever arrangement of eyelets, with a hook each side. When the first eyelet is used, the back presents the appearance of a double box plait, the depth of the plaits being reduced as the hooks are moved gradually toward the last eyelets. The deep flounce is prettily plaited and cord tucked. Lengths, 36 to 44 inches. Be sure to state length.
25K2785 Black.
25K2786 Navy Blue.
Our price...................98c

25K2784 Maternity Brassiere, Made of Strong White Batiste. Boned at just the proper intervals to insure comfort. Easily adjusted to fit by the clever arrangement of the side laces. Trimmed with neat hemstitched scalloped embroidery. Sizes, 32 to 48 inches bust measure. Be sure to state size.
Our price...................49c

NOTE—In ordering Maternity Garments it is advisable that you be careful to order them full large, larger than you normally need.

——➤ *We Pay Transportation Charges on All Maternity Garments.*

C. W. Practical Nursing Corset, Made of Durable Coutil 98c

25K2780 This Perfect Fitting Nursing C. W. corset is made of strong white coutil, and designed on the new lines, with the addition of the nursing feature, the flaps fastening conveniently with snap fasteners. The bust is medium high, the hips long enough to hold the figure in comfortably, and the waistline sufficiently defined to conform to the new fashion lines. Boned with aluminum wire stays, the front is fastened below the stays with two hooks to prevent the corset from opening. Four hose supporters attached. There is no reason why the nursing corset should not be as carefully made and perfectly fitted as any other, and we have carried out this idea in designing this corset. It is as well made as our regular corsets and conforms in every particular to the lines demanded for gowns, suits and outer garments generally this season. The price for such desirable quality, is very moderate. This corset will be found to be very soft and comfortable. Sizes, 19 to 30. White only. Be sure to state size. Our price...........98c

HOW TO ORDER—Order two sizes smaller than your actual waist measure without corsets. For instance, if your waist measure is 24 inches, order size 22 corset.

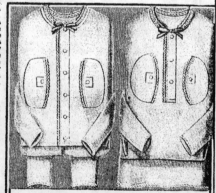

15K1425 Nursing union suit of splendid quality combed white cotton. Medium weight. Button closed nursing feature. Ankle length. Sizes, 32 to 38 inches.
15K1425 High Neck; long sleeves.
15K1427 Low neck; sleeveless.
Our price........75c

15K1411 Nursing vest of splendid quality combed cotton. Medium weight. Button closed nursing feature. Pure white. Sizes 32 to 38 inches bust measure.
15K1411 High Neck; long sleeves.
15K1413 High Neck; sleeveless.
Our price......35c

——➤ *We Pay Transportation Charges*

A PRACTICAL "FIGURE-BUILDING" CORSET.

This new model from the Wright Formette Co. is designed particularly for the slender woman who is not blessed with sufficient figure to appear smart in the popular new military modes. It is lightly though firmly boned and lends a beautiful contour over which the severe military lines of the new costumes appear to advantage.

1915

1915

A GOOD SPRING MODEL FROM THE MODART LINE.

An almost equally proportioned corset designed for the figure with medium and large hips and bust, and also when the hip line is high. Of fine imported coutil with wide elastic section across the boning at the top of back. From the Modart Corset Co.

A WELL-DESIGNED SPECIALTY CORSET.

This practically adjustable and easy-fitting model shows an original touch in the designing of the hip and waist lines. It is tastefully trimmed and is one of the especially successful models of the H. & W. Co.

A LUXURIOUS MODEL DESIGNED FOR EASE.

This model is one of the newest creations of the "Jurna" line. The deep elastic gores in the bust and back give that freedom and comfort which is so much desired in present day fashions. Fancy silk batiste in both white and pink as well as white coutil are used in the construction of this model. From the E. C. McWatty Co., Inc.

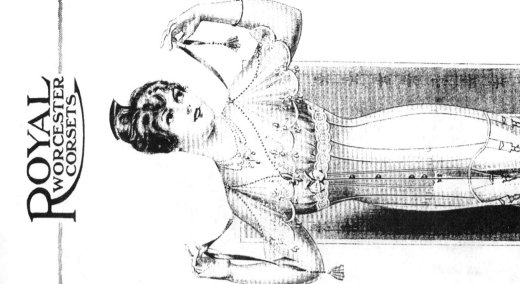

ROYAL
WORCESTER CORSETS

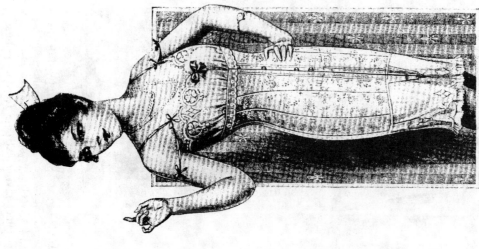

Style 550—Average Figure

Destined to be extremely popular because of its wonderful fitting qualities, handsome appearance, and new style features. This model will appeal to most everyone. Medium low bust and medium skirt. Broché, white or pink: Sizes 19 to 30. Style 525 on same pattern.

PRICE $1.50

1916

ROYAL
WORCESTER CORSETS

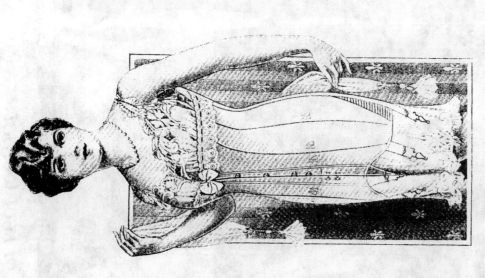

Style 637—Full Figure

A popular style that has proven itself to be right for the majority of figures of this type. Gives graceful curves. Medium high bust. Medium skirt with elastic inserts. Embroidery trimmed. Coutil. Sizes 22 to 36.

PRICE $2.50

ROYAL WORCESTER CORSETS

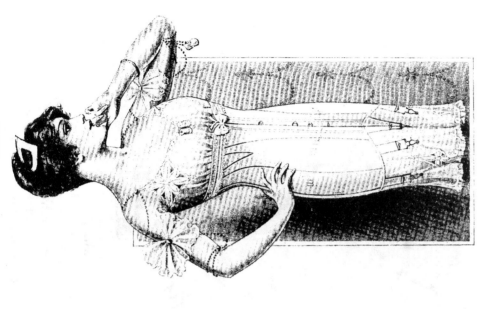

Style 563—Short Waisted — Average Figure

The designer conceived several new features and perfected them in this handsome garment. Medium bust with deep material gores at sides. Medium length skirt. Attractively trimmed. Coutil. Sizes 19 to 30.

PRICE $2

1916

ROYAL WORCESTER CORSETS

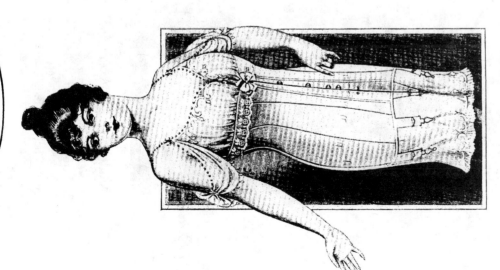

Style 526—Full Figure

Seldom does one see, at the price, a model that will equal this in style, value and fit. It corsets the full figure perfectly and is very comfortable. Medium bust. Graduated clasp. Coutil. Sizes 22 to 36.

PRICE $1.50

BonTon CORSETS

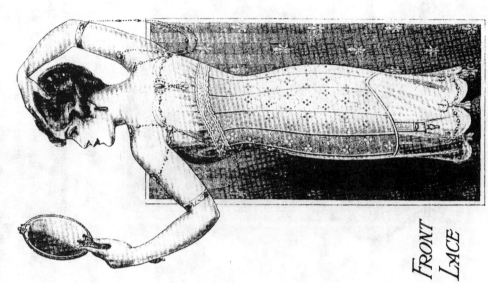

FRONT LACE

Model 1047—Average and Medium Tall Figures

A conspicuous feature is the unique panel back—a scientific achievement in corset designing. Charming lines at back and over hips. Medium bust. *Wundabohn boning.* Silk figured broché, white, pink or blue. Sizes 20 to 30.

PRICE $6.50

BonTon CORSETS

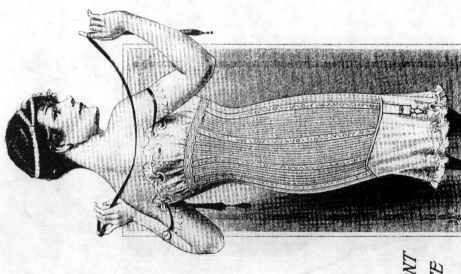

FRONT LACE

Model 1032—Average Figure

If you prefer Tricot, this is a corset you will revel in. Clings to the form but is extremely supple and comfortable. Excellent for warm weather wear. Note the exquisite back. Medium low bust. Silk braid trimmed. *Wundabohn boning.* White or pink. Sizes 19 to 28.

PRICE $5

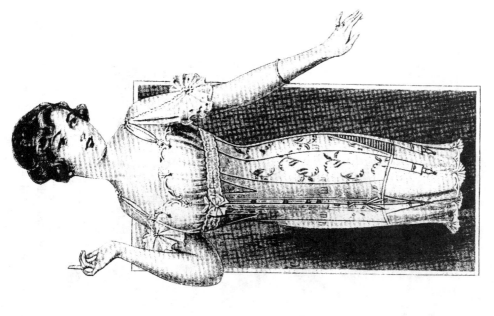

BonTon CORSETS

Model 857—Average Figure

A leading model and an excellent value. Medium bust. The skirt being cut away gives freedom in walking. Elastic hip inserts. Trimmed with silk embroidered batiste banding. *Wundabohn boning.* Figured coutil, white or pink. Sizes 19 to 30.

1916

BonTon CORSETS

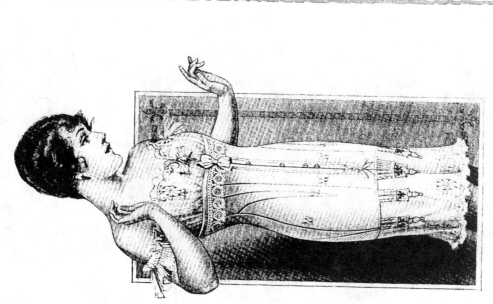

Model 982—Average and Slender Average Figures

This corset reflects the touch of the master designer and is a masterpiece. Close fitting but perfectly comfortable. Medium high bust. Artistically trimmed. Medium skirt. *Wundabohn boning.* Imported coutil. Sizes 19 to 30.

BonTon CORSETS

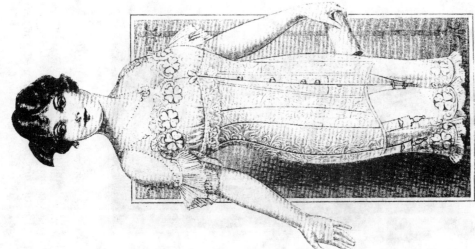

Model 912—Full Figure

At the first wearing you realize its complete comfort, for it is cut low under bust and arms and higher in front and back. Then too, it controls and shapes the form fashionably. Medium bust and rather short skirt. *Wundabohn boning.* Broché, white or pink. Sizes 22 to 36.

PRICE $5

1916

BonTon CORSETS

Model 1077—Average Figure

FRONT LACE

A "de luxe" corset of Parisian design, reflecting all the new and practical features. Gives exquisite long lines at back and sides. Medium bust with ample fullness, and slightly higher at back. Elastic insert. *Wundabohn boning.* Silk moire batiste, white or pink. Sizes 20 to 30.

PRICE $1?

ROYAL
WORCESTER CORSETS

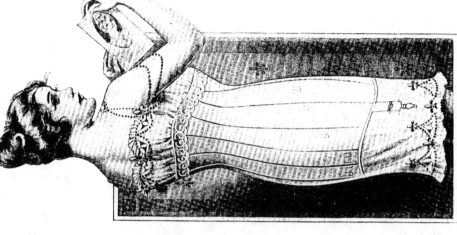

FRONT LACE

Style 746—Full Figure

If your purse is limited and you want a high grade, perfect fitting, front lace corset, this one will meet every requirement. Medium bust. Sateen jean. Sizes 22 to 36.

1916

ROYAL
WORCESTER CORSETS

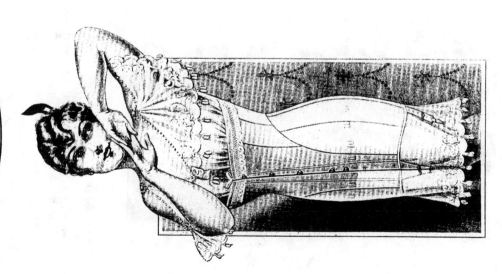

Style 424—Full Figure

Here is a model without an equal, considering its quality, style and workmanship. Shapes the figure as Fashion decrees. Medium high bust, long skirt. Coutil, white or gray. Sizes 19 to 36.

PRICE $1

ROYAL WORCESTER CORSETS

FRONT LACE

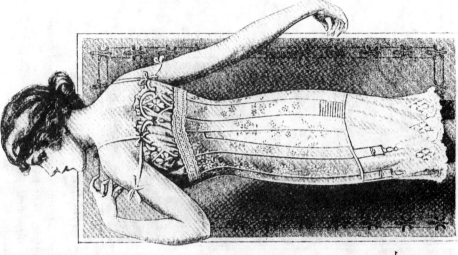

Style 765—Petite and Slender Figures

Aside from the convenience of front lacing which is preferred by many, this model emphasizes all the newest style features. Medium bust with deep cloth gores, which are also at hips. Panel back with elastic insert. Broché, white or pink. Sizes 18 to 28.

PRICE $2

1916

ROYAL WORCESTER CORSETS

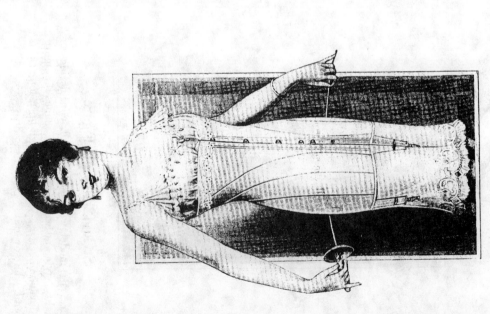

Style 446—Average and Well Developed Average Figures

In this corset you quickly attain the graceful, stylish contour which every woman admires. Excellent value. Medium high bust. Even length skirt. Coutil. Sizes 19 to 30.

PRICE $1

ROYAL WORCESTER CORSETS

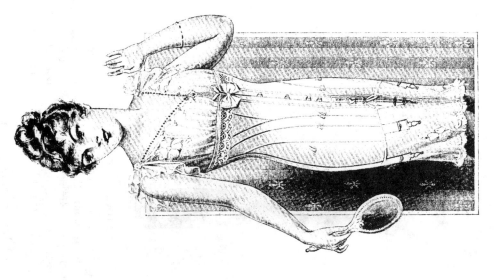

Style 646—Average Figure

Gives the wearer an individual air and style. Ideal for walking as the skirt is rather short and curves up at front and back, assuring comfort. Medium bust. Coutil. Sizes 19 to 30.

PRICE $2.50

1916

ROYAL WORCESTER CORSETS

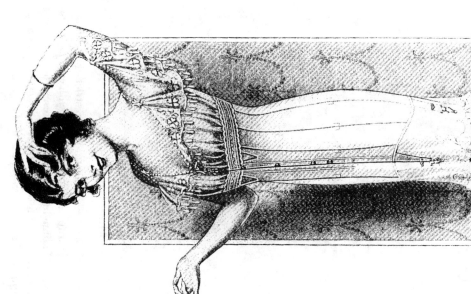

Style 482 — Petite and Slender Figures

An ideal corset for these types, giving stylish lines and necessary support, although it is lightly boned. Only the corset cloth touches the hip bones. Medium low bust. Coutil. Sizes 18 to 28.

PRICE $1

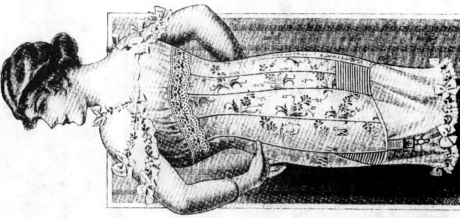

BonTon CORSETS

FRONT LACE

Model 1068—Full Figure

An ultra-modish corset designed with the idea of perfectly controlling the fullness of the figure at every point. It does this to a nicety. Medium bust. Elastic inserts at hips and back. *Wundabohn boning.* Silk figured broché, white or pink. Sizes 22 to 36.

Model 1057 on same pattern at $8.

PRICE $10

1916

BonTon CORSETS

Model 921—Full Figure

Has all the newest features to restrict the well developed form, yet accomplishes it with ease and comfort. Medium bust with deep gores. The skirt gores also add to its fitting qualities. *Wundabohn boning.* Imported sateen. Sizes 22 to 36.

PRICE $6.50

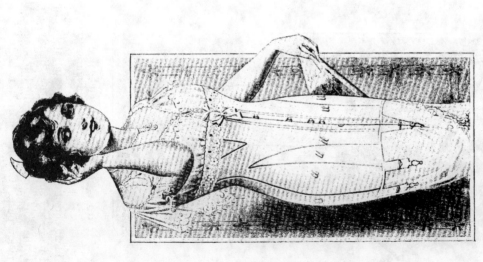

BonTon CORSETS

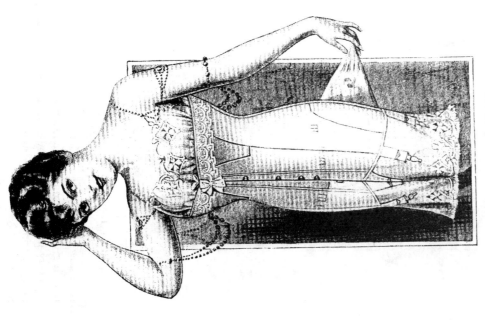

Model 845.-- Full Figure

Has wonderful shaping power, as it moulds the flesh into symmetrical lines and perfectly controls abdomen. Medium high bust with ample fullness. Embroidery trimmed. *Wundabohn boning.* Coutil. Sizes 22 to 36.

Model 927 on same pattern at $5.

PRICE $3.50

1916

BonTon CORSETS

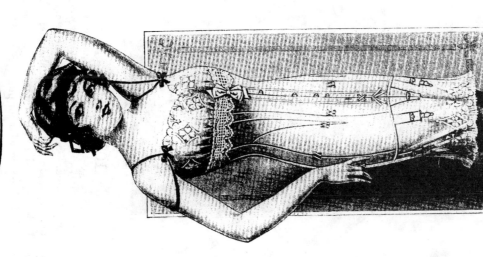

Model 956— Average Figure

A stylish, graceful figure is the pearl beyond price. This corset creates a beautiful contour and is supremely comfortable. Medium high bust. Rich, attractive trimming. *Wundabohn boning.* Imported batiste. Sizes 19 to 30.

PRICE $8

BonTon CORSETS

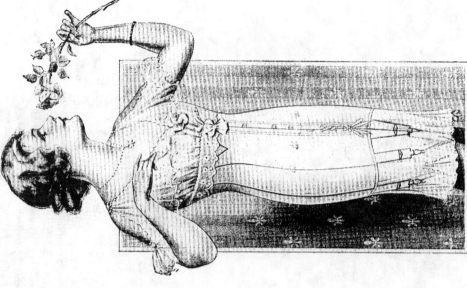

PRICE $3.50

Model 855—Average and Slender Average Figures

Note how perfectly this corset fits and what stylish lines it gives. An unmatchable value at a price that fits every purse. Medium bust. Braid and silk embroidery trimmed. *Wundabohn boning.* Coutil. Sizes 19 to 30.

1916

BonTon CORSETS

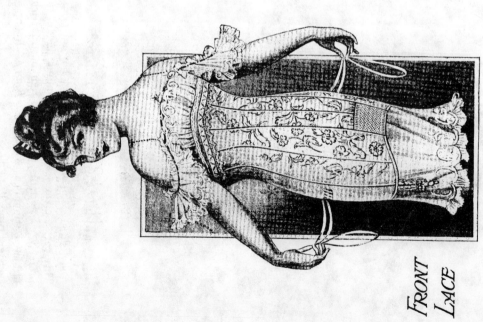

FRONT LACE

PRICE $15

Model 1087—Full Figure

Its inimitable style and exquisite appearance will be keenly appreciated. Scientifically designed to control abdomen, thighs and the flesh at shoulders. Medium high bust. Daintily trimmed. *Wundabohn boning.* Silk brocade, white or pink. Sizes 22 to 36.

BonTon CORSETS

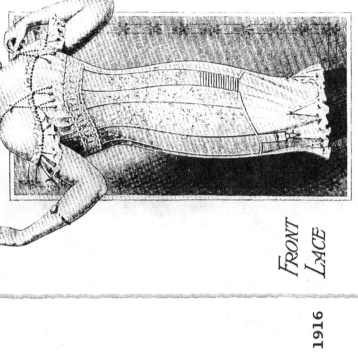

FRONT LACE

Model 1030—Average Figure

Several new features make this an unusual corset. Cut semi-circular at top of back and cleverly designed to give that much desired roundness to the form. Medium bust. Deep cloth gores over hips. *Wundabohn boning.* Broché, white, pink or blue. Sizes 19 to 30.

PRICE $5

1916

BonTon CORSETS

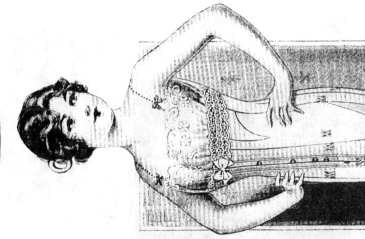

Model 978—Average Figure

While designed for evening wear, this luxurious corset may be worn at any hour of the day. It sets off the most expensive gown and gives the figure an exclusive air. Medium bust. Elastic inserts. Elaborately trimmed. *Wundabohn boning.* Silk batiste. Sizes 19 to 30.

PRICE $10

BonTon CORSETS

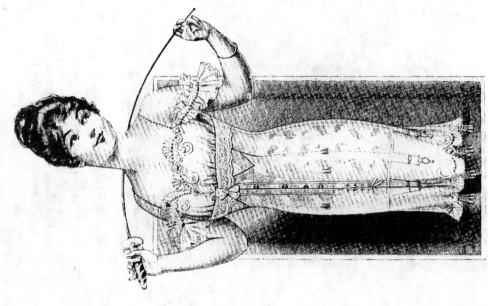

Model 910 — Average and Tall Figures

To perfectly fit these types of figure requires skill, and this is an unusual conception. Gives graceful, long lines and flat back effect. Medium high bust. *Wundabohn boning.* Broché, white or pink. Sizes 19 to 30.

Model 909 on same pattern, and of fancy batiste.

PRICE $5

1916

BonTon CORSETS

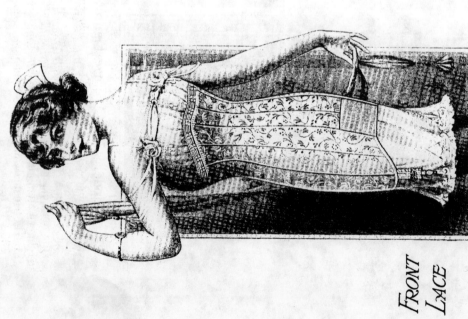

FRONT LACE

Model 1055 — Average Figure

This has proven to be one of the most popular of the Front Lace corsets. It fits beautifully and gives a graceful contour. Medium bust. Elastic insert at back. *Wundabohn boning.* Silk figured broché, white or pink. Sizes 20 to 30. Other models on same pattern are 1016 at $3.50, 1044 at $5 and 1095 at $20.

PRICE $8

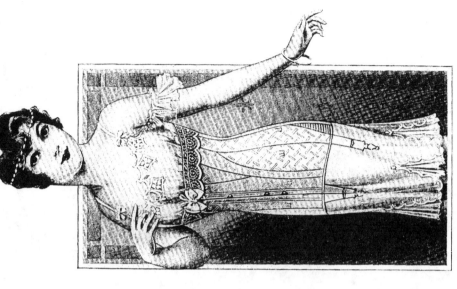

Model 851—Petite and Slender Figures

Accentuates those lithe lines and graceful undulating curves you so much admire. Medium low bust. Only the corset cloth touches the hip bones, which insures extra comfort and freedom. Elastic inserts. *Wundabohn boning.* Etamine broché, white or pink. Sizes 18 to 28.

PRICE $3.50

1916

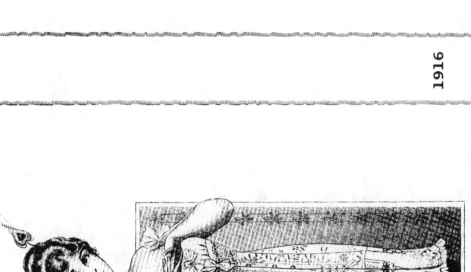

Model 998—Average Figure

This might well be termed the "corset de luxe" for it not only delineates correct style but reveals the touch of the master hand and expresses thoughts of the artistic mind. Gives an incomparably beautiful figure. Medium low bust. Silk hose supporters and exquisite trimming. *Wundabohn boning.* Brocaded silk batiste, white or white and pink. Sizes 19 to 30.

PRICE $20

BonTon CORSETS

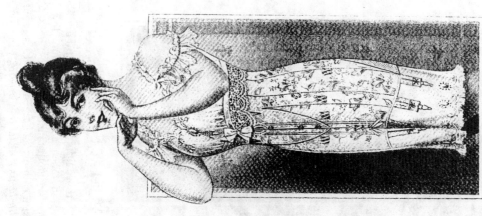

Model 990—Average Figure

At social functions and evening events you naturally want to look your prettiest. This corset will give your figure an artistic and exclusive effect. Medium low bust. Elastic inserts. Silk hose supporters and rich trimming. *Wundabohn boning.* Silk brocade. Sizes 19 to 30.

(PRICE) $15

1916

BonTon CORSETS

FRONT LACE

Model 1014   Average and Well Developed Figures

If you would be smartly gowned and have a distinctive, stylish figure, wear this corset with its charming closed back. Medium low bust. Elastic inserts at back and hips. *Wundabohn boning.* Coutil. Sizes 19 to 30.

(PRICE) $3.50

BonTon CORSETS

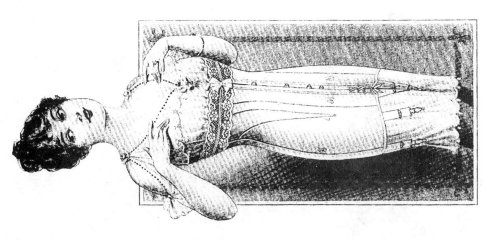

Model 930—Average and Well Developed Figures

Few corsets surpass the perfection of this as it insures the graceful, smooth lines decreed by Dame Fashion. Medium high bust. Note the unusual shape of the gores. Handsome trimming. *Wunda-bohn boning*. Coutil. Sizes 19 to 30.

PRICE $6.50

1916

BonTon CORSETS

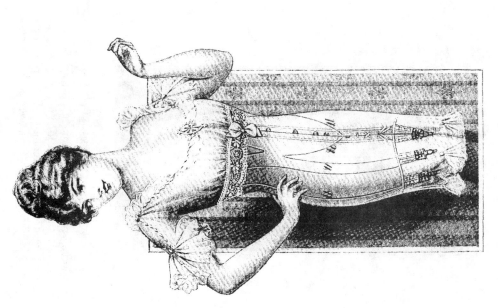

Model 965—Average Figure

Aside from being designed for evening wear, it accentuates the prevailing stylish curves and gives correct poise. Medium bust. Richly trimmed. *Wundabohn boning*. Imported coutil. Sizes 19 to 30.

PRICE $10

BonTon CORSETS

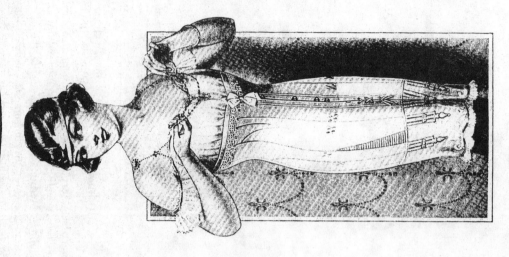

Model 948—Average Figure

All the pretty curves and gracefulness of the new mode are admirably expressed. Medium bust. Deep elastic inserts. Plush lined clasp. *Wundabohn boning.* Imported coutil. Sizes 19 to 30.

1916

BonTon CORSETS

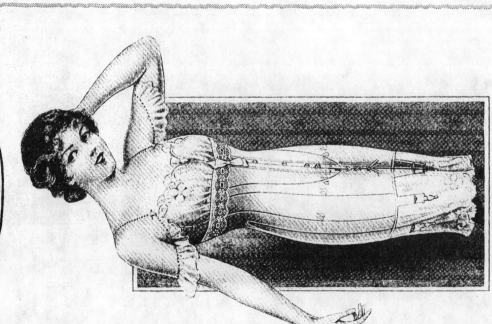

Model 875—Average Figure

Free hip space and ample room at bust are features which make this corset ideal for the figure requiring unusual freedom. Medium bust. Satin ribbon and Oriental lace trimming. *Wundabohn boning.* Coutil. Sizes 19 to 30.

Other models, same pattern, are 924 & 928 at $6.50.

AN ATTRACTIVE "LA VICTOIRE" MODEL

One of the well-made and daintily designed corsets featured in the "La Victoire" line. Flexibility is one of the strongest features of this model. From George C. Batcheller & Co.

1918

SOME NEW "FERRIS" MODELS

The illustration shown above portrays four of the many attractive models included in the new Spring line of the Ferris Bros. Corset Co.

1918

TWO CHARMING MODELS FROM THE BIEN JOLIE LINE

At the left, a front-lace, lightly boned corset for the woman with a slender figure. At the right, a misses' model with shoulder straps crossing in the back. This corset is cut high in the back and is topless in the front. Both of these garments are included in the new Bien Jolie line of "Grecian-Treco" corsets featured by Benjamin & Johnes.

1918

1918

A NEW "R & G" MODEL FOR SPRING

One of the attractively designed models featured in the 1918 line of R & G corsets for the Spring and Summer of 1918. From the R & G Corset Co., Inc.

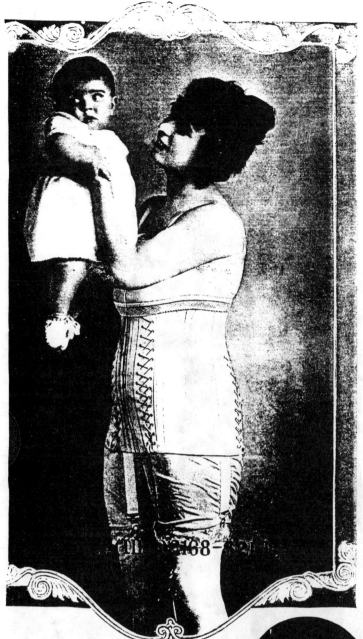

Maternity

There are "H. & W." Corset Waists

in styles to meet every need.

Prices from
$8.50 to $39.00

The H. & W. Company

The House of Brassieres

Newark, N. J.

Selling Agents

Geo. C. Batcheller & Co., 130 Fifth Ave., N.Y.
301 West Monroe St., Chicago, Ill.

B. F. Wellington, 121 Geary Street
San Francisco, Cal.

1918

Misses' Waists

Style 548 — Price, $12 doz. (Seated figure) — Made of jeans, sizes 19 to 30.
Style 444 — Price, $12 doz. (Standing figure) — Made of batiste, sizes 19 to 30.

Maternity Waist

Style 2115 — Price, $15 doz. Maternity waist, with back, hip and side front lacing. Coutil, sizes 20 to 30.

Maternity Waist

Style 2161 — Price, $18 doz. Maternity waist, with back, hip lacing. Supporting band over abdomen. Coutil, sizes 20 to 30.

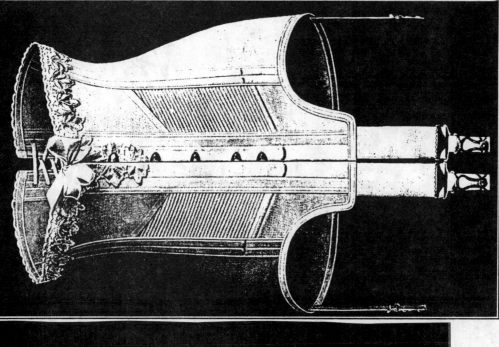

An attractive corset of Grecian Treco. This model is inset with corded treco over the abdomen, thus giving the body additional support at that point. It is cut very low in front, which makes it especially suitable for athletic wear. From Benjamin & Johnes.

1918

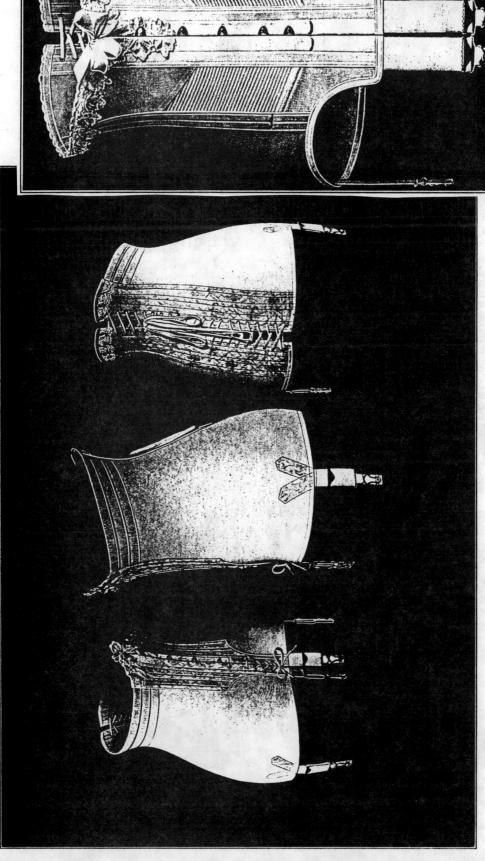

A NEW GRECIAN-TRECO MODEL

This corset is made with an elastic top and has a strip of rich brocade down the front and back. A feature of this corset is the absolutely free hip, there being no boning used except in the front and back. This is one of the new garments which will be featured in the Bien Jolie line of Grecian-Treco creations for the season of 1918. From Benjamin & Johnes.

1920s & 1930s

"NATIONAL" Maternity Corsets

No Article of Maternity Wear is So Important as Your Corset

YOUR health, comfort and happiness largely depend upon the corset you wear during the maternity period. An ordinary corset, no matter how perfect, is unsuited and may even be harmful.

The "NATIONAL" Maternity Corset is the work of the most skilled designers, the result of years of practical experience in corset designing.

To give you a corset that supports without binding—to construct a corset easily adjustable at all times to the changing figure—to preserve your health, comfort and happiness—such is the purpose, the ideal, of the "NATIONAL" Maternity Corset.

How well we have succeeded is proven by thousands of mothers who, keeping in mind the future health and happiness of their child have worn "NATIONAL" Maternity Corsets.

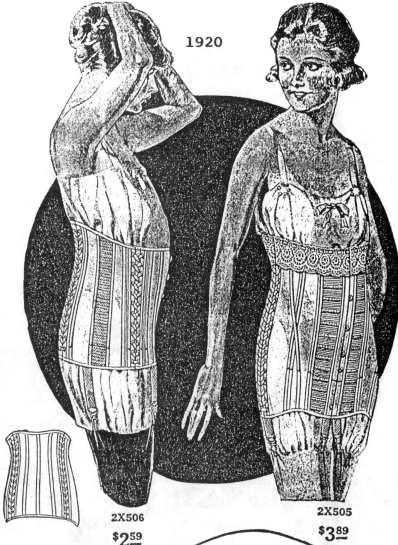

1920

2X506
$2 59

2X505
$3 89

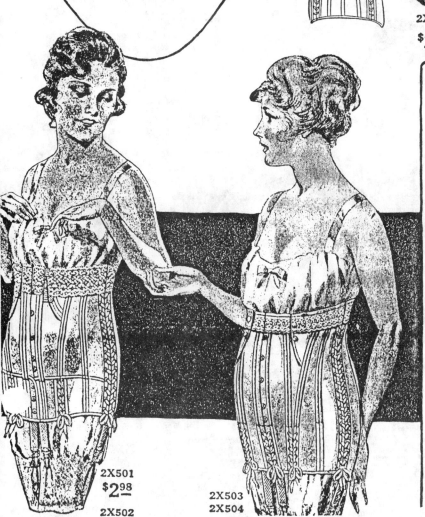

2X501
$2 98
2X502

2X503
2X504

Maternity and Nursing Corset

2 X 501—"NATIONAL" Guranteed Maternity and Nursing Corset; taped buttons below front clasp. Side lacings and abdominal lacings permit perfect adjustment; side lacings have gusset to protect flesh. Flexible non-rustable boning. Four hose supporters.

WHITE COUTIL. SIZES: 20 to 36. Order size two inches smaller than present waist measure taken over dress. State corset size .... OUR PRICE. $2.98
Postage 4¢ extra.

2 X 502—Same as Number 2 X 501, but without nursing feature.
OUR PRICE. $2.89
Postage 4¢ extra.

Maternity and Nursing Corset

2 X 503—"NATIONAL" Guaranteed Maternity and Nursing Corset with laces below front clasps. Adjustment as required is easily made by means of side lacings, abdominal lacings and back lacing.

Side lacings have cloth gussets to protect flesh. Flexible aluminum-finished boning. Four hose supporters.

WHITE COUTIL. SIZES: 20 to 36. Order size two inches smaller than present waist measure taken over dress. State corset size .... OUR PRICE. $2.79
Postage 4¢ extra.

2 X 504—Same as Number 2 X 503, but without nursing feature.
OUR PRICE. $2.79
Postage 4¢ extra.

Our Best Maternity Corset

2 X 505—Here is one of the best maternity corsets made—a "NATIONAL" Guaranteed Maternity Corset of good quality Coutil. Scientifically constructed to promote health and comfort.

Elastic panels in front together with side and back lacings, make possible easy and comfortable adjustment to the changing figure. Side lacings have gusset to protect flesh. Flexible non-rustable aluminum-finished boning. Four hose supporters.

WHITE COUTIL. SIZES: 20 to 36. Order size two inches smaller than present waist measure taken over dress. In ordering state corset size...OUR PRICE. $3.89
Postage 4¢ extra.

Maternity or Surgical Abdominal Corset

2 X 506—Maternity or Surgical Abdominal Corset with wide elastic webbing inserts on each side. Gives splendid support and provides for expansion by four lacings in addition to the elastic inserts.

Cloth gussets under lacings protect the flesh. Lightly boned with non-rustable boning. Four hose supporters.

WHITE COUTIL. SIZES: 24 to 38 (even sizes only). Order size two inches smaller than present waist measure taken over dress if wanted either for maternity wear or as a surgical abdominal corset. In ordering be sure to state corset size.
OUR PRICE. $2.59
Postage 4¢ extra.

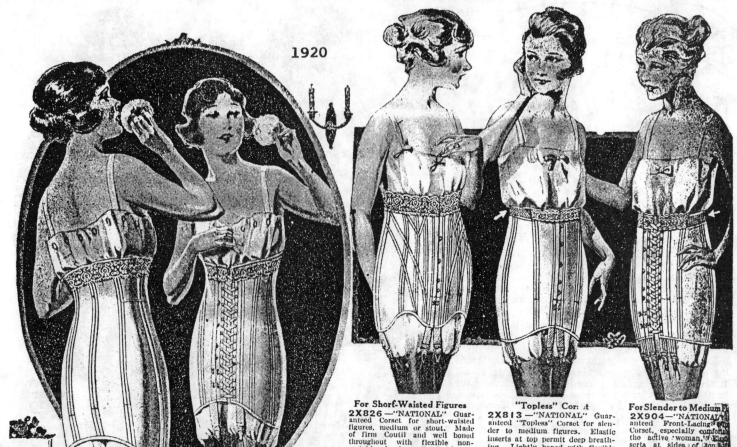

1920

For Short-Waisted Figures

2X826—"NATIONAL" Guaranteed Corset for short-waisted figures, medium or stout. Made of firm Coutil and well boned throughout with flexible non-rustable aluminum-finished stays. Gored bust and gored hips. Bust 4½ inches above waist-line; 11½-inch front clasp. Four hose supporters.

WHITE ONLY. SIZES: 20 to 36. Order corset size three inches smaller than waist measure taken over dress. State corset size .... Postage 4c extra. **$1.98**

"Topless" Corset

2X813—"NATIONAL" Guaranteed "Topless" Corset for slender to medium figures. Elastic inserts at top permit deep breathing. Lightly boned with flexible non-rustable stays. 9-inch front clasp. Entire length of back 17½ inches; side length 18¼ inches. Four hose supporters.

WHITE COUTIL. SIZES: 19 to 30. Order corset size three inches smaller than waist measure taken over dress. State corset size .... Postage 4c extra. **$1.89**

For Slender to Medium

2X904—"NATIONAL" Guaranteed Front-Lacing Corset, especially comfort the active woman. Elastic serts at sides of top, boned with non-rustable 9-inch front clasp; full back, 17 inches; side 18¼ inches. Six hose supporters.

WHITE COUTIL. to 30. Order corset inch smaller than wa taken over dress. S size......OUR PRICE Postage 4c extra

$1.89 Regular Value $2.50

Front Lacing Corset
for Slender to Medium Figures

2X814—Here's a remarkably well shaped, well made "NATIONAL" Guaranteed Front-Lacing Corset for only $1.89. The regular value for equally good quality is $2.50.

This corset of good quality Coutil is a very comfortable model designed on stylish, graceful lines, made with the popular long skirt and is well boned. It gives splendid support, yet is so flexible that it permits perfect freedom.

Has medium low bust which can be adjusted to slender figures by means of drawstring at top. Flexible, non-rustable, aluminum-finished boning. Height of bust above waist-line 4½ inches; front clasp 11 inches long. Four hose supporters.

WHITE ONLY. SIZES: 19 to 30. Order corset size one inch smaller than waist measure taken over dress. State corset size. Regular value $2.50........OUR PRICE, $1.89
Postage 4¢ extra.

Mrs. Ray G. Buckingham of Tacoma, Washington, writes:

"Received my goods a few days ago. Wish to say the Brassieres were very nice and the long cloth was the best I have ever seen for the price. I know from experience how well your goods wear. My catalogue is loaned to all my neighbors and I tell all my friends of the values I receive from you."

We never publish a letter without the writer's permission.

Miss Estelle Durham of Honea Path, South Carolina, writes:

"I was charmed with everything I ordered. I was expecting to be, though, for I have ordered from you before. The 'NATIONAL' is universally recognized as the House of Bargains and Styles. I am always glad to recommend the 'NATIONAL' to anyone."

White or Pink Brocade Slender to Medium

2X855—Guaranteed Front-Lacing Corset for slender to medium figures. Band of open mesh tricot in back finished at bottom with elastic webbing. Flexible non-rustable aluminum-finished boning. Bust 4½ inches above waist-line; 10-inch front clasp. Six hose supporters.

White or flesh-pink Brocade. SIZES: 19 to 32.

White or Pink Brocade "Topless" Corset

2X875—"NATIONAL" Guaranteed Corset of Brocade with elastic inserts at top. Flexible non-rustable aluminum-finished boning. Length of back, 15 inches. Front clasp 9 inches long. Four hose supporters.

COLORS: white or flesh-pink. SIZES: 20 to 30. Order size three inches smaller than waist meas-

For Medium to Full Figures

2X878—"NATIONAL" Guaranteed Front-Lacing Corset. Made with long skirt and reinforced with a sewed-in abdominal belt. Elastic webbing at side fronts. Flexible non-rustable boning. Medium bust, 4 inches above waist-line; 11-inch front clasp.

WHITE COUTIL. SIZES: 20 to 32. Order corset size one inch smaller than

For Slender to M Figures

2X625—You this "NATIONAL anteed Front-Lacing model obtainable price. Made of white Jean and boned with flex rustable stays, inches above 11-inch front clasp

SIZES: 20 to der size three inch

1920

$1⁶⁹ Regular Value $2⁰⁰

For Slender to Medium Figures, $1.69

2X824—This "NATIONAL" Guaranteed Corset of firmly woven Coutil is a great favorite with our customers. Hips are cut long, are carefully proportioned and correctly boned to give perfect comfort.

Flexible, non-rustable, aluminum-finished boning. Height of bust above waist-line 4½ inches; front clasp 11 in. long, two hooks below. Six hose supporters.

WHITE ONLY. SIZES: 19 to 30. Order corset size three inches smaller than waist measure taken over dress. State corset size. Value $2.00.

SPECIAL PRICE. $1.69
Postage 4¢ extra.

---

pless"Corset $1¹⁹ White Jean

2X606—"NATIONAL" guaranteed "Topless" Corset. popular for athletics; also a good model for the slender woman or young girl who we good hip support with ability and perfect freedom the waist-line. Four hose supporters.

Made of White Jean; elastic gores at sides. Light flexible boning. 10 inches long. SIZES: 19 to 30. Order corset size three inches smaller than waist measure taken over dress. State corset size.

Postage 3¢ extra. $1.19

Corset Waist $2³⁹ for Women

2X603—"NATIONAL" Guaranteed Corset Waist for the woman who needs figure support but does not wish a heavily boned corset. Corded and lightly boned with flexible non-rustable stays. Buttons in front; laces in back. Front measures 14½ inches. Four hose supporters.

WHITE COUTIL ONLY. SIZES: 20 to 36. Order corset waist size two inches smaller than waist measure taken over dress. State corset waist size.

OUR PRICE. $2.39
Postage 3¢ extra.

Bust-Forming $1⁹⁸ Corset

2X766 — "NATIONAL" Bust-Forming Corset with well proportioned bust built out with featherbone. It gives graceful curves to slender, flat-chested figures. Crosses in back and is held firmly in place at waist-line by the adjustable strap. Flexible non-rustable boning. Four hose supporters.

WHITE BATISTE ONLY. SIZES: 19 to 30. Order corset size three inches smaller than waist measure taken over dress. State corset size.

OUR PRICE. $1.98
Postage 3¢ extra.

Bust-Forming $2³⁹ Corset

2X832—"NATIONAL" Guaranteed Bust-Forming Corset lightly boned over bust to give graceful lines to flat-chested figures. Gives all the necessary support of a corset. Adjustable shoulder straps. Laces in back. 10-inch front clasp; hook below. Four hose supporters.

WHITE BATISTE. SIZES: 19 to 30. Order corset size three inches smaller than waist measure taken over dress. Be sure to state corset size.

OUR PRICE. $2.39
Postage 4¢ extra.

For Girls and Misses

$1⁶⁹
Front Lacing "Topless" Corset

2X925—"NATIONAL" Guaranteed Front-Lacing "Topless" Corset—ideal for general wear. A two-inch elastic webbing band at top permits freedom of movement.

Circular sectional sides fit smoothly over hips. Non-rustable aluminum-finished boning. 9-inch clasp. Length of sides 15 inches. Four hose supporters.

---

p Confiner 83c White Jean

2X901—"NATIONAL" guaranteed Hip Confiner for or general wear. Permits perfect freedom. Made of quality Jean, firmly bound and lower edge. Lightly Closes in front with a inch clasp; laces in back. th at sides 11 inches. in rear 8½ inches.

Misses' and Girls' $1²⁹ Corset Waist

2X902—"NATIONAL" Guaranteed Corset Waist of good quality Jean—ideal for misses and growing girls. Firm cording and light flexible boning. Has soft plaited bust pockets; adjustable shoulder straps. Buttons in front; laces in back. Two hose supporters.

WHITE. SIZES: 19 to 28.

For Misses and Growing Girls $1⁴⁹

2X604—"NATIONAL" Guaranteed Corset for misses and growing girls. It gives excellent figure support, yet permits perfect freedom. Corded and lightly boned with flexible non-rustable stays. Height of bust above waist-line 3½ in.; 9-inch font clasp. Four hose supporters.

WHITE BATISTE with lace-

Young Girls' $1¹⁹ Corset Waist

2X775 "NATIONAL" Guaranteed Corset Waist hygienically designed for growing girls. Made of firm Jean, corded and very lightly boned. Adjustable shoulder straps take weight of clothing from hips. Taped buttons. Buttons in front; laces in back. Two hose supporters.

WHITE ONLY. SIZES: 19

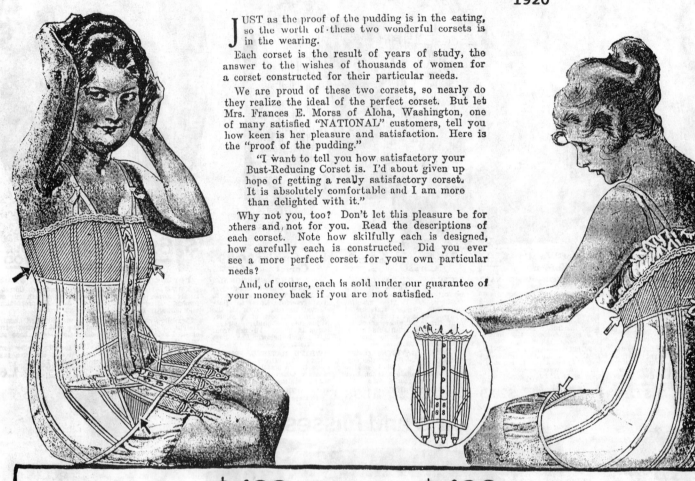

Reducing Corsets

1920

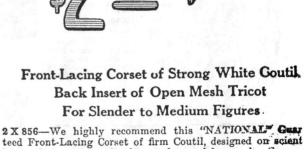

$2^{45}

For Medium to Full Figures, $2.49 up

2X792—"NATIONAL" Guaranteed Reducing Corset carefully designed to give stylish lines and guaranteed to give satisfactory wear.

Non-elastic straps pull strong double tabs over abdomen, gently reducing without discomfort. Corset is well boned over abdomen and hose supporters hold tabs firmly in place. Flexible non-rustable boning. Height of bust above the waist-line, 5 inches; 12-inch graduated front clasp. Six hose supporters.

WHITE COUTIL. Order corset size three inches smaller than waist measure taken over dress. State corset size.

SIZES: 20 to 32........PRICE..........$2.49
SIZES: 34 to 42........PRICE..........2.69

Postage on each 4¢ extra.

Our Finest Reducing Corset, $5.98

2X870—To women with stout or medium figures requiring a very strong corset, we recommend this "NATIONAL" Guaranteed Reducing Corset of good quality Coutil. Bands of heavy elastic webbing lace over abdomen and double the reducing power without uncomfortable pressure.

Reinforced bias bands of Coutil with six hose supporters attached hold abdomen in correct position. Non-rustable boning. Bust 4½ inches above waist-line. 11½-inch graduated front clasp.

WHITE. SIZES: 20 to 36. Order corset size three inches smaller than waist measure taken over dress. State corset size. $5.98

Postage 5¢ extra.

For Stout Figures, $3.98

2X610—Splendid "NATIONAL" Guaranteed Reducing Corset for women of stout figure and prominent abdomen. Bands of elastic webbing increase the reducing power without unhealthful or uncomfortable pressure and the reinforced abdominal belt (see small picture) holds the abdomen in correct position.

Front hose supporters keep the belt firmly in place. Flexible non-rustable boning. Height of bust about 4¾ inches above waist-line. 11-inch graduated front clasp. Four hose supporters.

For Medium to Full Figures, $2.98

2X907—This "NATIONAL" Guaranteed Corset is a splendid model for reducing abdomen and hips without discomfort. Designed for full or stout figures or for medium figures requiring a strong corset.

A wide band of elastic webbing hooks over the abdomen, gives splendid support and preserves straight front lines. Flexible non-rustable boning. Bust 4 inches above waist-line. 10-inch front clasp. Six hose supporters.

Front-Lacing Corset of Strong White Coutil, Back Insert of Open Mesh Tricot
For Slender to Medium Figures

2X856—We highly recommend this "NATIONAL" Guaranteed Front-Lacing Corset of firm Coutil, designed on scientific lines. It is an exceedingly popular model worn by thousands of our customers, to whom it has given complete satisfaction.

Small picture shows ventilating back of open mesh tricot. Elastic webbing band at bottom of tricot insert holds corset firmly to figure.

Flexible non-rustable boning; bust 4½ inches above waist-line; 10-inch front clasp. Six hose supporters.

WHITE. SIZES: 19 to 32. Order corset size one inch

Why You Should Wear "NATIONAL" Corsets

TO preserve the lines that Nature gave or to give to those who lack—this is the ideal, the inspiration, of the NATIONAL" Corset.

It is not, therefore, a commercial corset rely—not made for profit alone—but with purpose.

It is made with a designer's ideal, a designer's hope, that worn over this perfect set, every "NATIONAL" Dress and might display in full the lines, the style, grace that every "NATIONAL" garment is designed to possess.

To bring out in full the charm of your NATIONAL" Dress or Suit—to preserve the figure the lines that Nature gave, or give to those who lack.

Truly, here is the corset for you!

For in buying a "NATIONAL" Corset not only profit by this ideal embodied its making, but you get more actual worth and satisfaction than you can otherwise get.

Because we put more into the corset—value, better materials and workmanship in order that it fill its ideal, that it may be its purpose of adding to the beauty, style and grace of your "NATIONAL" dresses and Suits.

Just wear one "NATIONAL" Corset and for yourself that this grace and beauty figure really may be yours.

How "NATIONAL" Corsets Are Made

A—Extra strong front steels prevent breaking over abdomen.

B—Outside covering of corset of very durable material.

C—Extra covering for non-rustable boning to give additional strength.

D—Cover for non-rustable boning.

E—Protected tips for boning.

F—Strong hose supporters.

Why "NATIONAL" Corsets Are Comfortable

All "NATIONAL" Corsets are so boned that the corset may be bent double, as illustrated. As flexible a corset as this is sure to be comfortable.

Our Guarantee
Your Money Back if You Want It

Corsets like everything else at the "NATIONAL" may be returned if not satisfactory your money refunded.

HOW TO ORDER CORSETS

Order by corset size not by waist measure. each description for the number of inches

$4.98

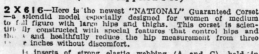

"NATIONAL" Guaranteed
Hip and Thigh Reducing Corset
The Very Newest Idea in Corsetry
(Patent Applied For)

2X616—Here is the newest "NATIONAL" Guaranteed Corset—a splendid model especially designed for women of medium to full figure with large hips and thighs. This corset is scientifically constructed with special features that control hips and thighs and healthfully reduce the hip measurement from three to four inches without discomfort.

The inserts of strong elastic webbing (A and C), hold in superfluous flesh over hips and at back, yet expand when sitting or bending over. The reduction is further increased by back lacing (B), below which is a strong elastic duplex garter (D), holding the corset down firmly. Note the comfortably cut medium low bust (E); the reinforced sewed-in abdominal belt (F), which, together with the strong spoon clasp (G), holds the abdomen in correct position and gives straight front lines.

Note also the two small figures which illustrate the difference in the figure lines—the bulging hip lines given by an ordinary corset and the trim graceful lines that the "NATIONAL" Guaranteed Hip and Thigh Reducing Corset make possible.

Flexible non-rustable boning. Six hose supporters. Height of bust 4 inches above waist-line; 11-inch spoon clasp.

Good quality White Coutil, trimmed with ribbon-run lace.

SIZES: 24 to 36. Order corset size three inches smaller

Guaranteed for Six Months

Reducing Corsets

HERE are four splendid Reducing Corsets guaranteed for six months' satisfactory wear or a new corset free.

We can guarantee these "NATIONAL" Corsets because, in addition to being correctly designed to give stylish figure lines, they are specially constructed to give the maximum of service.

Firmly woven durable materials; flexible non-rustable boning; strong front steels; extra reinforcement where the greatest strain comes; exceptional comfort because they are constructed on scientific lines—these are some of the features of these "NATIONAL" Reducing Corsets. These are the real reasons for their superiority and longer service. These are the reasons why they will withstand the strain to which a reducing corset is usually subjected.

The "NATIONAL" guarantees each of the four corsets shown on this page to give you six months' wear from date of purchase.

If for any reason your corset does not give you six months of perfect corset satisfaction, return it and we will give you a new corset free.

> Six Months'
> Wear
> Guaranteed

Low Bust Reducing Corset for Medium to Stout Figures $3⁴⁰

2 X 619 — We recommend this splendid new "NATIONAL" Six Months' Guaranteed Reducing Corset to women of stout figure and large abdomen who prefer a low bust corset giving plenty of room for easy breathing.

Elastic band top gives complete freedom above the waist, and the forced coutil bands hold the abdomen in correct position.

Elastic inserts at either side of the lower edge give expansion necessary for comfort in sitting. Two elastic hose supporters. Non-rustable boning. Elastic top 3 inches above waist-line. 9¾-inch graduated front clasp.

WHITE COUTIL. SIZES: 24 to 36. Order corset size three inches smaller than waist measure taken over dress. State corset size. Read our Six Months' Guarantee.

OUR PRICE,
Postage 4¢ extra. $3.49

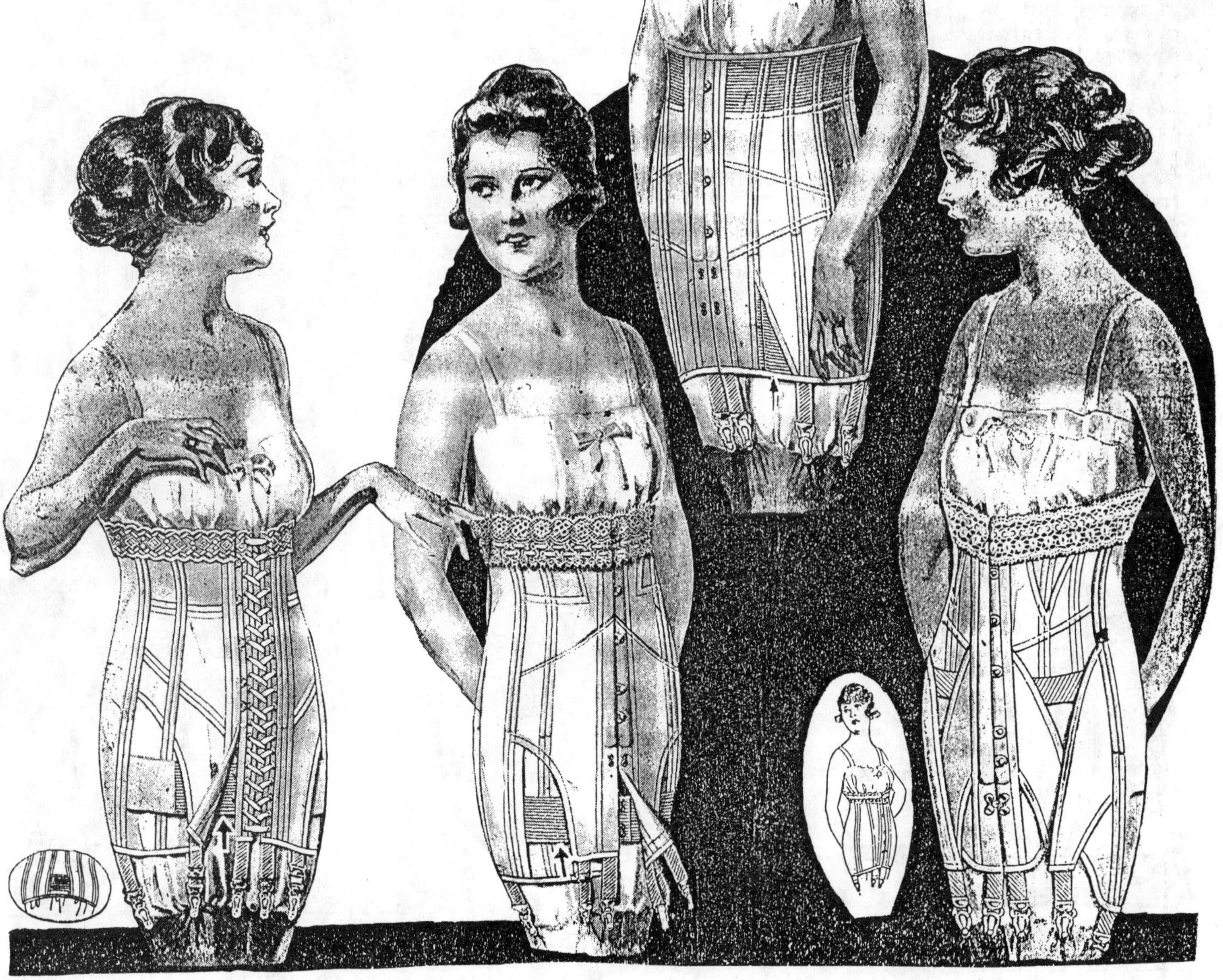

2 X 619
$3⁴⁹

1920

Woven Wire-Boned Corsets

Woven Wire Boning Makes Corset Flexible—Gives Perfect Support

Guaranteed Unbreakable Non-Rustable

TO you who have worn a "NATIONAL" Guaranteed Corset with woven wire boning these corsets need no introduction. You know how much real corset satisfaction, there is for you in "NATIONAL" Corsets.

But to you who have never worn them, we say: try one of these corsets. Find out for yourself how comfortable, flexible and serviceable are "NATIONAL" Corsets with woven wire boning.

"NATIONAL" Woven Wire Boning is composed of fine wires woven together as pictured. Instead of breaking when you bend over, this boning bends with you no matter which way you turn, and gives the utmost flexibility to the corset while affording absolute and comfortable support. It is guaranteed unbreakable and non-rustable.

Note the Diagram of Corset pictured below and see the superior way these corsets are made in order to give the best service.

G—protected tips prevent boning from cutting through material.
H—woven wire boning gives strength and flexibility.
I—extra strong front steel.
J—boning covered to prevent rusting.
K—extra covering for boning.
L—outer covering, very strong.

2X867
$3.98

2X905
$2.98

2X854
$2.59
up

2X868
$2.98
up

1920

YOUR MID-SUMMER CORSET is Here LOOK at These LOW PRICES!

Newest French Girdle

Asst. Materials

Bargain!
4A1270
97¢

Challenge VALUE! Worth $2.00
4A1272 $1.33

Coutil

Extra Value
4A1273
$1.39

Elastic Girdle

PHILIPSBORNS Famous Reducer
4A1203
$2.00 Everywhere
$1.46

Brocade Worth $1.25
4A1269
89¢

4A1270 Here is the new French girdle or semi-corset which is the newest idea in corsetry. Made of fancy brocaded corset material with wide inserts of elastic webbing at sides. Made extra long at back to conceal shape of form. See miniature of back. Ideally comfortable for slender to medium figures.
COLOR: Pink. SIZES: 22, 24, 26 or 28. (State uncorseted waist measure.)
PRICE, PREPAID to your home 97c

4A1273 For sports, dancing and general wear, this new Philipsborn's elastic girdle is an ideal choice. It is made entirely of wide bands of elastic webbing with light boning at the sides and front. See miniature for back view. One of the most comfortable girdles ever designed for slender to medium figures. To introduce this new girdle to our customers, we have priced it very low. COLOR: Pink. SIZES 23 to 32. (State uncorseted waist measure.)
PRICE, PREPAID to your home $1.39

4A1203 A great sale offering—this Philipsborn's reducing corset—now $1.46 This is a back-lacing corset well made throughout of very strong coutil and boned with extra strong boning. Non-elastic straps pull the reinforced double coutil tabs over the abdomen giving the stout woman a more slender appearance. Hose supporters hold tabs firmly in place. Height and slenderness to the full figure. COLOR: White. Sizes 20 to 36. (ORDER 2 inches smaller than waist measure taken over dress.)
PRICE, PREPAID to your home $1.46

4A1272 Special sale of corsets in splendid assorted materials. Bought at a sacrifice price. Every corset worth at least $2.00. Our price $1.33. The materials include fancy, stripes, brocades, and also solid color materials. All are front-lacing models featuring tongues under the lacings. Elastic insert at back. Big values. COLOR: Pink. SIZES: 20 to 30. (Order one inch smaller than waist measure taken over dress.)
PRICE, PREPAID to your home Special $1.33

4A1269 A very desirable new corset at a special low price. This is a back-lacing model made of good quality brocaded corset material. It is designed with the free unboned hip, which relieves any uncomfortable pressure on the sensitive hip bone. The elastic top about three inches above the waist-line gives the fashionable low bust-line and adds to the comfort of the corset. Worth $1.25. COLOR: Pink. SIZES: 20 to 28. (Order two inches smaller than waist measure taken over dress.)
PRICE, PREPAID to your home 89c

CHICAGO, ILL. ★

PHILIPSBORN'S "EVERDAINTY" Underwear is Chosen by Millions of Women as the Best in Quality, Style, and Service.

early 20's

EVERYTHING PREPAID

BACK BUTTONING MODEL Extra Value

Three Big Values – Typical of Philipsborn's

Brocade Corsetlette

Coutil Worth $1.00

Worth $1.25

4A1274 89¢

4A789 37¢

4A793 87¢

4A795 88¢

4A1255 87¢

4A1274 Here is a new style corset girdle which you are sure to like. It is made of coutil with wide elastic sections at sides and elastic band around the top. Long tabs with garters attached conceal the figure lines at the back. COLOR: White. SIZES: 22 to 24, 26, 28, 30 uncorseted waist measure.
PRICE, PREPAID to your home. 89c

4A789 Combination Brassiere and garters of a firmly woven summer tricot. COLOR: Pink. SIZES: 32 to 48 bust.
PRICE, PREPAID to your home 37c

4A793 Mercerized brocaded cotton corset-lette with elastic webbing and brassiere top. Garters. COLOR: SIZES: 32 to 48 bust.
PRICE, PREPAID to your home 87c

4A795 New style corsetlette of brocaded cotton. Extra long over the hips. Brassiere top. Garters. COLOR: Pink. SIZES: 32 to 48 bust.
PRICE, PREPAID to your home 88c

4A1255 Bargain extraordinary. PHILIPSBORN'S coutil corset for average figures. Boning is close set and substantial. Medium high bust and skirt. COLOR: White. SIZES: 20 to 30. (Order corset two inches smaller than waist measure taken over a dress.)
PRICE, PREPAID to your home 87c

Elastic Girdle

Misses Model

For Stout Women

Hip Confiner

4A1218 83¢

4A1204 94¢

4A1211 84¢

4A1215 $2.38

BARGAIN!

4A1208 48¢

4A1218 Very special at this money-saving price — a favorite style corset girdle and hip confiner. Made of good quality coutil with side inserts of elastic webbing. A splendid style for the woman who does not like the average corset. COLOR: Pink. SIZES: 20 to 28. (Order two inches smaller than waist measure taken over dress.)
PRICE, PREPAID to your home 83c

4A1204 Popular low bust corset of coutil. COLOR: Pink. SIZES: 20 to 28. (Order two inches smaller than regular waist measure taken over dress.)
PRICE, PREPAID to your home 94c

4A1211 Lightly boned jean corset for misses. COLOR: White. SIZES: 20 to 28. (Order two inches smaller than regular waist measure taken over dress.)
PRICE, PREPAID to your home 84c

4A1215 Reducing corset of coutil with elastic belt. COLOR: White. SIZES: 22 to 36. (Order two inches smaller than regular waist measure taken over dress.)
PRICE, PREPAID to your home $2.38

4A1208 A very special bargain in a corset girdle or hip confiner. Made of good quality coutil with boning at front and back only. Will give good wear. COLOR: White. SIZES: 23 to 40. (State uncorseted waist measure.)
PRICE, PREPAID to your home 48c

See PHILIPSBORN'S New Summer Suits for Women in this Catalog. Offered in a Variety of Styles and Materials at Bargain Prices

early 20's

★PHILIPSBORN'S

41660 98¢
31651 $1.19
31652 $1.89
31653 $2.19
31654 $1.59

41660 For sports, dancing, negligee or bathing is this comfortable girdle corset belt of **Pink Coutil.** The top and sides are elastic for flexibility. Very lightly boned. Belt hooks in front and has four hose supporters, two in front and two in back. Order natural uncorseted waist measurement. Sizes 23 to 35. Price 98¢

31651 Very long in the back is this corset of **White Coutil.** An excellent model for the slender or medium figure. Non-rustable boning. Hooks below front steel; four hose supporters. Trimmed at top. Order size **two inches** smaller than waist measurement over dress. Sizes 19 to 30. Price **$1.19**

31652 Elastic webbing at sides, top and bottom for flexibility is the feature of this corset of strong **Pink or White Coutil.** Lightly boned; hook below front steel. Good for average and slender figures. Order size **two inches** smaller than waist measurement over dress. Sizes 20 to 28. Price **$1.89**

31653 Lacefront **White Coutil** corset with long slender lines. Smooth fitting back with elastic webbing strap. Finished with trimming at top; light non-rustable boning; four strong hose supporters. Excellent value. Order size **one inch** smaller than waist measurement over dress. Sizes 21 to 28. Price **$2.19**

31654 Here is a corset that gives supple lines and yet firm support to the hips. Of strong **Pink Coutil** it has an elastic top, giving freedom to waist line. An excellent model for young girls, slender or average figures. Order size **two inches** smaller than waist measurement over dress. Sizes 20 to 26. Price **$1.59**

41651 39¢
41652 59¢
41653 49¢
41650 59¢
41654 49¢
41655 69¢
41656 39¢
41657 $1.29

41650 This is the new idea Bandeau Corset, a combination of Brassiere and Corset. Can be used as a brassiere or corset. Of **Pink Cotton Brocade,** with two hose supporters in front. Hooks in back. Popular for athletics, housewear, etc. A very useful model. Sizes 32 to 46. Price . . . . 59¢

41651 Fasten-in-front Brassiere of sturdy **White Cambric,** reinforced under arms. Eyelet embroidery trimmed. Back and armholes edging finished. Sizes 32 to 46. 39¢

41652 A Bandeau of **Satin striped Pink Brocade.** Lightly boned sides and back. Elastic insert in back. Sizes 32 to 44. 59¢

41653 This fasten-in-front Brassiere of **White Cambric** is an excellent model for slender and full figures. Trimmed with Cluny pattern lace. Sizes 32 to 46. 49¢

41654 A **Pink Cotton Brocade** fasten-in-back Baudeau has a special feature-elastic webbing across the front waistline to help reduce the diaphragm. Sizes 32 to 46. Price . . . . 49¢

41655 Very new is the Bandeau of lace. This fasten-in-back model is heavy **Cluny pattern lace** with a strip of fancy Brocade. Sizes 32 to 44. Price . . . . 69¢

41656 Specially designed for the low bust corset is this Bandeau of **Pink or White Brocade** Rubber insert in the back. Boning under arms. Back closing. Sizes 32 to 41. Price . . . . 39¢

41657 New style Brassiere or Bandeau Corset of **Pink Cotton Brocade.** Can be used as a corset for slender women or brassiere for larger women. Made with wide elastic bands over the hips which insure a trim fit. Four hose supporters. Hooks in back. Sizes 32 to 46. Price $1.29

Our liberal guarantee protects you fully!

1922

THE HAMILTON GARMENT CO.

Woven Wire Boned COMFORT CORSETS

2C905
Front Lacing
$2.15

Strong Coutil Corset
$2.15

Woven Wire Boning

Woven Wire Boning bends in every direction and gives utmost flexibility to the corset while affording absolute and comfortable support. This boning is guaranteed non-rustable and unbreakable.

Low Bust Long Hip

2C785—Women of medium to full figures can acquire stylish straight lines by wearing this new "NATIONAL" Guaranteed Reducing Corset with woven wire boning. It is a low bust model made with an elastic webbing band at top of front which controls the diaphragm while providing comfortable expansion. The boning is guaranteed unbreakable and non-rustable and makes the corset both firm and flexible. Double material in front is scientifically shaped so as to comfortably reduce the abdomen and hold in the thighs. Inserts of elastic webbing at lower edge in back.

9-inch graduated front clasp. WHITE COUTIL. Order size three inches smaller than waist measure taken over dress.

All Sizes: 23 to 28; also 30.
Postage 5¢ extra. **$2.98**
Even Sizes: 32 to 36.
Postage 5¢ extra. **$3.39**

2C905—A splendid corset for medium to slender figures is this favorite Front-Lacing "NATIONAL" Guaranteed Corset. Woven Wire Boning gives flexibility to corset and is guaranteed unbreakable and non-rustable.

Center back has ventilating band of open mesh tricot with elastic webbing at lower edge which holds skirt snugly to figure. Bust 4 inches above waist-line. Front clasp 11 inches long.

WHITE COUTIL. All Sizes: 20 to 28; also 30 and 32. Order corset size two inches smaller than waist measure taken over dress.
OUR PRICE,
Postage 5¢ extra. **$2.15**

2C785
$2.98 up

Our Favorite Reducing Model $3.49

Reducing Corset with Elastic Webbing Belt For Medium to Full Figure

2C934—This favorite "NATIONAL" Guaranteed Reducing Corset will give your figure graceful lines. Woven Wire Boning gives flexibility and is guaranteed unbreakable and non-rustable. Wide bands of heavy elastic webbing and reinforced belt over abdomen give smooth-fitting front and comfortable support.

Elastic inserts over hips give trim lines and provide comfortable expansion. Bust 4 inches above waist-line. 11-inch graduated front clasp.

WHITE COUTIL. All Sizes: 22 to 28; also Even Sizes: 30, 32, 34 and 36. Order size three inches smaller than waist measure taken over dress.
Postage 5¢ extra. **$3.49**

Extra Strong Corset For Medium to Full Figures

2C868—If you require an extra strong corset and want one that will give you the correct lines for a trim and attractive figure, then order this "NATIONAL" Guaranteed Corset. The Woven Wire boning in this corset of firm, strong Coutil will bend in any direction. It gives utmost flexibility while affording comfortable support.

This boning is guaranteed unbreakable and non-rustable. Sewed-in belt of self-material is cut crosswise so corset cannot stretch out of shape across abdomen. Bust 4 inches above waist-line; four hose supporters. 11-inch clasp. WHITE.

All Sizes: 20 to 28; also Even Sizes: 30, 32, 34 and 36. Order size three inches smaller than waist measure taken over dress.
OUR PRICE,
Postage 5¢ extra. **$2.15**

2C854
Long Hip Corset
$1.98

Favorite Long Hip Corset For Slender to Medium Figures

2C854—This "NATIONAL" Guaranteed Corset is an exceedingly popular model worn by thousands of our customers to whom it has given complete satisfaction. The woven wire boning makes this corset very strong, yet exceedingly flexible. This boning is guaranteed unbreakable and non-rustable.

Corset is made of firm White Coutil and is cut long over hips. Boning terminates at just the right depth for comfort when sitting. Six hose supporters. Bust 4 inches above waist-line. Front clasp 11 inches long, with two hooks below.

WHITE. All Sizes: 20 to 28; also Even Sizes: 30, 32, 34 and 36. Order corset size three inches smaller than waist measure taken over dress.
OUR PRICE,
Postage 5¢ extra. **$1.98**

Low-Bust Coutil Corset For Slender to Medium Figures

2C712—As a foundation for trim smartness, women of slender to medium figures will find this Low-bust Corset with elastic webbing top an ideal model. And the guaranteed woven wire boning makes it exceptionally flexible.

Corset is made of firm pink Coutil with wide band top of pink elastic webbing. It gives freedom above waist and splendid support through the hips and abdomen. Inserts of elastic webbing at lower edge hold the corset trimly to the figure and provide comfortable expansion. 7½-inch front steel. Four hose supporters.

PINK ONLY. All Sizes: 20 to 28; also 30. Order corset size three inches smaller than waist measure taken over dress.
OUR PRICE,
Postage 5¢ extra. **$1.59**

2C712
Low Bust Model
$1.59

Here is A Corset for Every Figure

An Excellent Reducing Corset For Medium to Stout Figures

2 C 619—To women of medium or stout figure and large abdomen who prefer a low bust and large abdomen we thoroughly recommend this "NATIONAL" Reducing Corset. It is made with an elastic band top which gives freedom above waist. Reinforced coutil bands hold the abdomen in correct position and elastic inserts at either side of the lower edge allow for expansion. Six hose supporters. Non-rustable boning. Elastic top 3 inches above waist-line. 9¾-inch graduated front clasp.
WHITE COUTIL. All Sizes: 20 to 28; also Even Sizes: 30, 32, 34 and 36. Order corset size three smaller than waist measure taken over dress...... OUR PRICE. Postage 5¢ extra. **$2.19**

Medium Bust $1.23

Extra Strong Corset

2C619 Low Bust Reducing Corset $2.19

A Satisfactory Reducing Corset for Medium to Stout Figures

2 C 810—If you need a reducing corset and good abdominal support you will find this "NATIONAL" Guaranteed Reducing Corset a most satisfactory selection. It is made with elastic abdominal band and reinforcement of coutil cut so it will not stretch and finished with six strong hose supporters which also help flatten the abdomen. Elastic bands at each side-back. Non-rustable boning. Bust 2½ inches above waist-line. 10¾-inch front clasp.
WHITE COUTIL. All Sizes: 21 to 28; also Even Sizes: 30, 32, 34 and 36. Order corset size three inches smaller than waist measure taken over dress....... Postage 5¢ extra. **$2.29**

2C810 Elastic Abdominal Band Reducing Corset $2.29

2 C 647—The double skirt means double wear for this Guaranteed Corset of White Coutil for slender to medium figures. Lined below waist with a strong white cotton material, giving extra strength. Picture displays inner lining ripped free to show the construction. Medium low bust about 3 in. above waist-line. Non-rustable duplex boning. 9½-in. front steels. All Sizes: 20 to 28; also 30 to 36 in even sizes. Order size three inches smaller than waist measure taken over dress...... Postage 5¢ extra. **$1.39**

2 C 814—We offer you good value in this well made "NATIONAL" Guaranteed Front-Lacing Corset for only $1.23. It is a stylish, comfortable model for slender to medium figure and is made of good quality Coutil. Has flexible non-rustable boning. Height of bust above waist-line inches; front clasp 11 inches.
WHITE. All Sizes: 20 to 28 also size 30. Order size two inches smaller than your waist measure taken over your dress.
OUR PRICE. **$1.23**
Postage 5¢ extra.

An Excellent Corset for Slender to Medium Figures

2 C 625—Here's extra big value in a "NATIONAL" Guaranteed Corset for only 87 cents. This well made corset for slender to medium figures is made of serviceable White Coutil and lightly boned with flexible, non-rustable stays. Bust 3½ above waist-line; 11-inch front clasp. Four hose supporters. ALL SIZES: 20 to 28; also size 30. Order size three inches smaller than waist measure taken over dress.
OUR PRICE. Postage 5¢ extra. **87¢**

Be Sure to Give Your Correct Corset Size

Low Bust Brocade Corset

9-Inch Elastic Girdle

2C625 Medium Bust 87¢

Elastic Band Top $1.00

"Topless" Corset of Pink Brocade

2 C 784—Our 35th Anniversary Special— "Topless" Corset of Pink Cotton Brocade for only 59¢. This model is very popular with slender women or girls who want good hip support with freedom above waist-line. Elastic webbing band at top of front gives the freedom and expansion necessary for comfort. Lightly boned with non-rustable boning. Laces in back. 7-inch front clasp.
All Sizes: 20 to 28; also 30. Order size three inches smaller than waist measure taken over dress.
35TH ANNIVERSARY SALE PRICE, 59¢
Postage 5¢ extra.

Anniversary Special 2C784 59¢

Front-Lacing "Topless" Corset

2 C 925—Women of slender to medium figure find this "NATIONAL" Guaranteed Front-Lacing "Topless" Corset an exceptionally comfortable model. It is made of White Coutil and has a 2-inch band of elastic webbing at the top which provides comfortable expansion. Circular sectional sides fit smoothly over the hips. Non-rustable boning. 9-inch clasp; length of sides 15 inches.
All Sizes: 20 to 28; also size 30. Order size two inches smaller than waist measure taken over dress.
OUR PRICE, $1.00
Postage 5¢ extra.

Front-Lacing $1.00

Diaphragm Reducing Corset $1.09

2 C 779—For slender to medium figures. If you have a large diaphragm this new and very comfortable low top corset will remedy the condition. A band of elastic webbing is hooked across the diaphragm (see small view); corset is then hooked over band. Allows perfect freedom in breathing. Non-rustable boning. Elastic inserts at sides of top. Four hose supporters. 6½-inch front clasp.
PINK COUTIL. All Sizes: 21 to 28; also 30. Order corset size three inches smaller than waist measure over dress........ Postage 5¢ extra. **$1.09**

2C779

2 C 778—If you of slender to medium figure want to be most comfortably corseted, try this favorite Wrap-around Girdle of strong Elastic Webbing, lightly boned at sides. Shaped sections at front and sides are of pink coutil. (For construction of back see small view.) No lacings—just wrap around and hook. 9 inches long. Four hose supporters.
PINK. SIZES: 22 to 32. In ordering give your corseted waist measure..... **$1.00**
Postage 5¢ extra.

$1.00

Girdle Belt 89¢

2 C 690—For either for or dancing or general w this new light flexible Gir Belt is ideally comforta It is designed for slender medium figures and is ve pliable. Made of Pink Cou with side inserts and to wide pink elastic webbi Light, flexible boning. Exp in front. No lacing. Dep in front 6 inches.
SIZES: 22 to 34; even siz In ordering give your corse waist measure.
OUR PRICE. **89¢**
Postage 5¢ extra.

Be Sure to Give Correct Corset Size

1923

Approved Models for Expectant Mothers

Our Best Maternity Corset

[305]—"NATIONAL" Guaranteed Maternity Corset of good quality Coutil, ... panels in front together with ... back lacings, make possible ... comfortable adjustment to ... figure. Side lacings have ... to protect flesh. Flexible non-... aluminum-finished boning, 12-... clasp with two hooks below. ... ALL Sizes: 20 to 28; also ... 30 to 36. Order size 2 inches ... than present waist measure ... over dress.......... $2.59
Postage 5¢ extra. **$2.59**

Maternity or Surgical Corset
2 C 506—Maternity or Surgical Abdominal Corset with wide elastic webbing on each side. Gives splendid support and provides for expansion by four lacings in addition to the elastic. Small view shows the smooth-fitting back. Cloth gussets under lacings protect the flesh. Lightly boned with non-rustable boning. 9-inch clasp.
WHITE COUTIL. SIZES: 24 to 38 (even sizes only). Order size two inches smaller than present waist measure taken over dress if wanted either for maternity wear or as a surgical abdominal corset.
Postage 5¢ extra. **$1.98**

Maternity and Surgical Abdominal Corset

59¢ Maternity Brassiere

Pink Coutil Maternity Brassiere with Adjustable Side Lacings
7 C 823—This well designed Brassiere of firmly woven Pink Coutil is equally good for maternity wear and for women with extra full bust. It is cut to give excellent support to the large figure. Comfortable adjustment is easily made by the lacing at each side. Invisible front closing. Give bust measure. SIZES: 34 to 54 bust.
OUR PRICE, **59¢**
Postage 2¢ extra.

Back Closing

2 C 505 **$2.59**

2 C 506 **$1.98**

Low Bust Maternity Corset

For Stylish Maternity Dresses See Page 80

... Bust Maternity Corset ... Elastic Front Panels
[519]—This Low Bust Maternity Corset gives splendid support ... provides for expansion by ... front panels and side lac-... with elastic laces. Gussets ... lacings protect the flesh. ... boned with flexible non-... boning. 8½-inch flexible ... clasp.
... COUTIL. All Sizes: 24 ... also 30 to 36 in even sizes. ... size two inches smaller than ... waist measure taken over ..... OUR PRICE. $1.79
Postage 5¢ extra. **$1.79**

Our New Maternity Corset Bandeau $1.49

Elastic Abdominal Belt

Front

Maternity Corset Bandeau with Elastic Abdominal Belt
2 C 521—The elastic abdominal belt is an excellent new feature of this Maternity Corset Bandeau—a well liked combination of corset and brassiere. Adjustment to the changing figure is made by the full-length side lacings. Cloth gussets under lacing protects flesh. Tape shoulder straps. Hooks in back. Four hose supporters. Fancy weave Pink Cotton Corset Cloth.
SIZES: 34 to 48 bust. Give bust measure........ $1.49
Postage 3¢ extra. **$1.49**

... Low Bust Maternity Corset with Elastic Abdominal Belt
[C 520]—Especially comfortable and well ... "NATIONAL" Guaranteed Maternity ... of good quality Coutil. Elastic belt ... across abdomen together with the side and ... back elastic lacings make easy and comfort-... adjustment to figure. Side lacings have ... Flexible non-rustable boning. Low ... with elastic at front top. Four hose sup-... 7½-inch clasp with three hooks below.
PINK. All Sizes: 24 to 28; also even sizes: ... 36. Order size two inches smaller than ... waist measure taken over dress.
OUR PRICE. $2.39
Postage 5¢ extra. **$2.39**

New Elastic Belt

2 C 520 **$2.39**

2 C 758 **$1.98**

Approved Materno Comfortier
New Corset Bandeau with Elastic Panels and Lacings
2 C 758—The new Materno Comfortier, a practical combination of corset and brassiere. Easy adjustment to the changing figure is made by triangular panels of elastic webbing at side-front and side-back (see small picture) and by side lacings with elastic laces. Elastic shoulder straps. Not boned yet gives splendid support. Hooks in front. Four hose supporters. PINK COUTIL. SIZES: 34 to 48 bust. In ordering give bust measure........... $1.98
Postage 3¢ extra. **$1.98**

1923

"NATIONAL" REDUCING CORSETS
Priced to Save You Money

2 C 782—"NATIONAL" Guaranteed Reducing Corset with adjustable outside reducing belt and lacing side sections that give stylish flat lines and help reduce prominent hips. Elastic inserts at front and flexible top steel (see small picture below) control flesh at diaphragm. Non-rustable duplex boning; six hose supporters. 8½-inch graduated front clasp. All lacings must be opened before corset is put on.
Pink Coutil. Order corset size 3 inches smaller than waist measure taken over dress.
All Sizes: 24 to 28; also 30.
Post. 5¢. **$2.89**
Even Sizes: 32 to 42.
Postage 5¢ extra. **$3.25**

Reducing Corset with Bust-Reducing Brassiere
2 C 928—This Patented Reducing Corset with attached Bust-Reducing Brassiere is designed for tall women of stout or medium figure and full bust. Corset is of strong White Coutil. Brassiere section of fine quality Elastic Webbing supports the bust and reduces it without discomfort. Elastic inserts at lower edge. 12-inch front clasp.
All Sizes: 24 to 28; also Even Sizes: 30, 32, 34 and 36. Order size three inches smaller than waist measure over dress.
Post. 5¢ extra..... **$3.69**
2 C 607—Same style corset as above but to fit medium stout figure. Two inches shorter waisted; 9½-inch front clasp. Same sizes as above. Order size three inches smaller than waist measure over dress.
Postage 5¢ extra. **$3.69**

Bust Reducing Brassiere and Corset Combined

2C774 Abdominal Reducing Corset **$2.89 up**

2 C 782 Abdominal Hip and Back Reducing Corset **$2.89 up**

2C928 2C607 **$3.69**

2C746 $1.69

Abdominal Reducing Corset in Low Bust Style
For Medium to Full Figures
2 C 774—Fashionable straight figure lines are now possible to women of medium to full figure with large abdomen. This "NATIONAL" Guaranteed Corset in low bust style gives the flat abdomen, straight back and slender hip lines so essential to today's dress styles, with no sacrifice of comfort.
An inside belt of 5-inch elastic webbing lifts the abdomen to correct position. Reinforcing outer sections of strong coutil on either side, with elastic hose supporters attached, further reduce the abdomen and give smooth lines. (See small view.) Elastic inserts at top in front. Flexible non-rustable boning. 8-inch spoon clasp.
White or Pink Coutil. Order size three inches smaller than waist measure over dress. State color desired.
All Sizes: 24 to 28; also 30...... **$2.89**
Postage 5¢ extra.
Even Sizes: 32 to 36. OUR PRICE. **$3.09**
Postage 5¢ extra.

Low Bust Adjustable Hip Reducing Corset
For Women of Stout Figure and Large Abdomen
2 C 746—If you of stout figure and large abdomen want a comfortable low bust corset that gives stylish lines, order this "NATIONAL" Guaranteed Reducing Corset. Elastic inserts at top give comfortable expansion and freedom above waist-line. Straps of extra strong non-elastic tape pull reinforced double coutil tabs over abdomen, reducing without discomfort. Corset is well boned over abdomen and hose supporters hold tabs in place. Flexible non-rustable boning. 8¾-inch graduated front clasp.
WHITE COUTIL. All Sizes: 22 to 28; also Even Sizes: 30 to 36. Order size three inches smaller than waist measure taken over dress......OUR PRICE. **$1.69**
Postage 5¢ extra.

Elastic Belt **$2.89 up**

Abdominal Reducing Corset
With Elastic Inner Belt
2 C 622—Women of medium to stout figure with large abdomen will be delighted with the stylish lines given by this scientifically constructed "NATIONAL" Guaranteed Corset. A wide inner belt of elastic webbing lifts the abdomen to its correct position, holds it there without uncomfortable pressure and reduces the abdominal measurement several inches.
Belt attached to inside of corset, leaving outside perfectly smooth (see small picture). Flexible non-rustable [...]
10-inch s[...]
Good [...]ite Coutil.
also Ev[...] 32, 34 and
size thre[...]maller than wa[...]
over dres[...]
......OUR PRICE. $[...]
Postage 5¢ extra.

1923

Fashion's Ideal Corset Bandeaux

For All Figures — For All Occasions

Fancy Brocade

2 C 750—Our 35th Anniversary Special price is only $1.39 for this Corset Bandeau. It is made of Pink Mercerized Cotton Brocade and combines a brassiere with a hip-confiner and gives excellent figure lines.

Upper part holds the bust same as a brassiere. Lower part with wide inserts of heavy elastic webbing holds the flesh firmly and confines the hips. The elastic provides the necessary expansion.

Extra long cut back (see small view) gives straight lines. Not boned; hooks in back. Tape shoulder straps. Four garters. PINK. SIZES: 32 to 48 bust. Give bust measure.
35th Anniversary Special Price, $1.39
Postage 3¢ extra.

2 C 612—Our picture shows you the novel construction of this excellent Corset Bandeau of strong Pink Cotton Brocade. It is a brassiere and girdle in one and gives all the support needed by the average figure, at the same time giving graceful lines with perfect comfort.

Front girdle sections lace at center front. Elastic insert at sides give required expansion. Brassiere portion hooks in front over the corset girdle (see small front view). Girdle is lightly boned in front. Four hose supporters. Tape shoulder straps.
SIZES: 32 to 48 bust. Give bust measure...... $1.69
Postage 3¢ extra.

2 C 612 Two-in-One Bandeau and Girdle Combined $1.69

Two-in-One Combination Brassiere and Rubber Girdle $1.79

Bandeau Brassiere and Corset Combined $1.89

Pink Cotton Brocade 45¢

Fancy Weave 69¢

Bust and Diaphragm Reducing Corset Bandeau $1.25

Combination Brassiere-and-Elastic Girdle

2 C 769—Thousands of women are delighted with our new Combination Brassiere and Elastic Girdle—a two-in-one garment that gives stylish figure lines and graceful contour to the bust. It supports and confines the hips, while affording perfect freedom of movement.

The brassiere is made of fancy figured cotton material and is lightly boned in the back. Tape shoulder straps. The attached corset section, 8½ inches deep, is made of strong elastic webbing and is lightly boned with flexible, non-rustable stays. Hooks down the side; no lacing. Four hose supporters.
PINK. SIZES: 32 to 48 bust. In ordering give bust measure.
Postage 3¢ extra. $1.79

Women who know the worth of the new Corset Bandeau are delighted with this front closing Brassiere with Hip Confiner.
Of Pink Mercerized Cotton the Upper part holds bust same as a brassiere. Lower part holds in by inserts of heavy elastic webbing and back (see small view) lightly boned at sides and back in front. Tape shoulder straps. Four garters.
PINK ONLY.
32 to 48 bust. In ordering give bust measure.
OUR PRICE, $1.89
Postage 3¢ extra.

2 C 754—One of our most popular Corset Bandeaux is this well shaped, well made model of firmly woven Pink Mercerized Cotton Brocade. This bandeau is a very comfortable style for athletic wear and for wear when doing housework. It gives excellent support to the bust and holds down the abdomen, at the same time permitting freedom of movement. Not boned. Front is long and held firmly by two garters. Tape shoulder straps. Hooks under arms.
PINK ONLY. SIZES: 32 to 48 bust. Give bust measure.
OUR PRICE, 45¢
Postage 3¢ extra.

2 C 755—This trim-fitting, comfortable Corset Bandeau is made of good quality cotton material in fancy weave. It is cut on brassiere lines, with extra long front with two detachable garters which hold the bandeau firmly to the figure, giving the desirable straight lines.

It is lightly boned and hooks in the back, where a narrow elastic webbing panel (see small picture) provides the necessary expansion. Tape shoulder straps. PINK ONLY.
SIZES: 32 to 48 bust. In ordering give bust measure.
OUR PRICE, 69¢
Postage 3¢ extra.

Bust-and-Diaphragm Reducing Corset Bandeau

2 C 611—You of medium to full figure who have large bust and surplus flesh over the diaphragm can greatly improve your figure lines by wearing this new Corset Bandeau. It is made of Pink Pekin Stripe, a strong cotton corset cloth that gives splendid service.

Wide inserts of heavy elastic webbing over the bust and diaphragm hold the flesh. A boned cloth section and elastic webbing inserts over the abdomen gives flat lines. Hooks in back. Tape shoulder straps. Four garters.
PINK. SIZES: 32 to 48 bust. Give bust measure.
OUR PRICE, $1.25
Postage 3¢ extra.

1923

1923

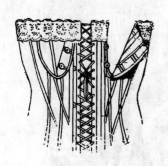

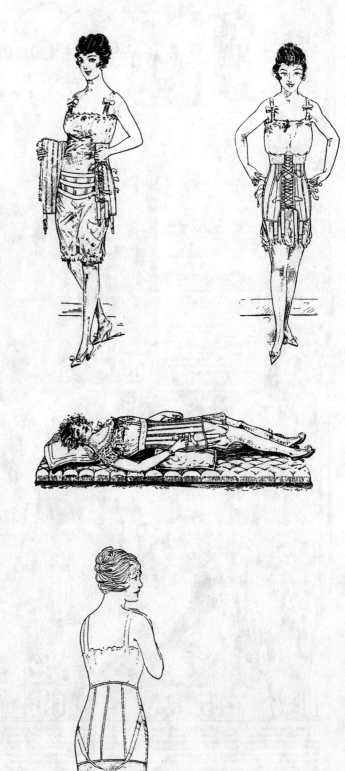

1923

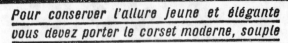
1924

1930

Cool - Transparent - Light - Strong

Shadow* Garments—Originated

by

Warner's

Made by the Creators, who know How

!

Half the Weight Twice as Strong

!

Because they are made of imported French voile, of long staple Egyptian cotton—they CANNOT stretch out of shape. And by years of experience, we KNOW how to make them.

Because the voile is used double thickness, actual tests prove them stronger and more durable than ordinary brocades and coutils—yet they weigh *half* as much.

They launder as easily as the daintiest lingerie!

They keep their crisp coolness under the most trying conditions!

They assure the lines of the Mode to discriminating women and have constantly increased in popularity for the last three years!

Shadow* Garments are now to be had in several of our most successful Princess Contour designs—and the demand for them this summer will mean sure profits during the hot months.

We assure prompt deliveries if you place your order early. Each season the orders on Shadow* Garments have more than doubled, and we are ready for the demand this season, when ALL women are Corset Conscious!

There are Shadow* Garments for all figure types -- from the heavily boned underbelt Corselette* and Wrap-Around* for the stout woman, to the light little wisp demanded by the slim Sub-Deb.

At all Prices from $15.00 to $66.00 the dozen. Write for illustrated price list.

THE WARNER BROTHERS COMPANY, Factories: Bridgeport, Conn.

NEW YORK, 200 Madison Avenue
CHICAGO, 367 West Adams Street
SAN FRANCISCO, 28 Geary Street

LONDON, 16 Portland Place
PARIS, 14 Boul. Poissoniere
BRUSSELS, 214 Ave. Rogier
Other branches all over the world.

HAMBURG, 38 Glashutten Str.
BARCELONA, 11 Rambla de Cataluna
MELBOURNE, 3 Howard St.

*Trade Mark Reg. U. S. Pat. Off.

Above is illustrated Rengo Belt style No. 931, a corset-brassiere combination made of brocade. It has a side-hook adjustable belt, with six hose supporters, and is made in sizes 36 to 50 at $36 per dozen.

Rengo Belts

Made by CROWN CORSET CO.   295 Fifth Avenue, New York

1930

De Bevoise
introduces "*American Princess*"
Styled in France — Custom Made in America

A distinct departure from domestic corset lines is the new American Princess series now introduced by De Bevoise. These luxuriously beautiful garments are custom made only, from exquisite imported materials.

Above, at left — No. 971, corsette of soft charmeuse lined with soft radium. Extremely long over hips and back.

Low cut—only one inch above waist-line at back. Tiny French tucks give shape and mold figure contours. Inserts of imported, lightweight, hand-loomed elastic. Flounce of Alençon lace—top edged with rose point. Detachable tab in pantie effect. $196.00 a dozen.

Center—No. 968—American Princess girdle, 16 inch length, entirely of Alençon lace, lined with soft peach char-

meuse. Light boning over abdomen; two tiny bones at back to support waistline. Six inch flounce. $120.00 a dozen.

Right—No. 974—Corsette of double glove silk jersey — clinging closely to the figure. French bust pockets—ideal for sports wear. $108.00 a dozen.

CHAS. R. DE BEVOISE COMPANY
1270 Broadway, at 33rd Street, N.Y.C.

1930

Style 954—A corset-brassiere combination made of tutone material with four panels of mercerized knitted elastic, diaphragm support and jersey top. Six hose supporters. Made in sizes 34 to 44 at $36 per dozen.

Made by the CROWN CORSET CO., 295 Fifth Ave., New York

1930

Corsés para bebé

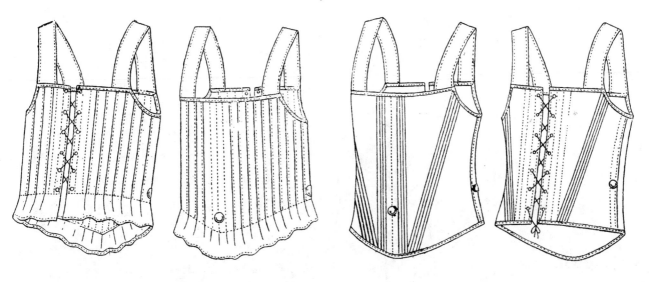

1934

Corsé de niña

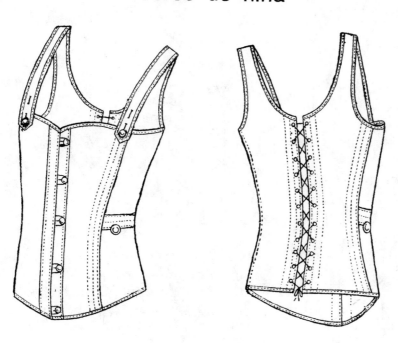

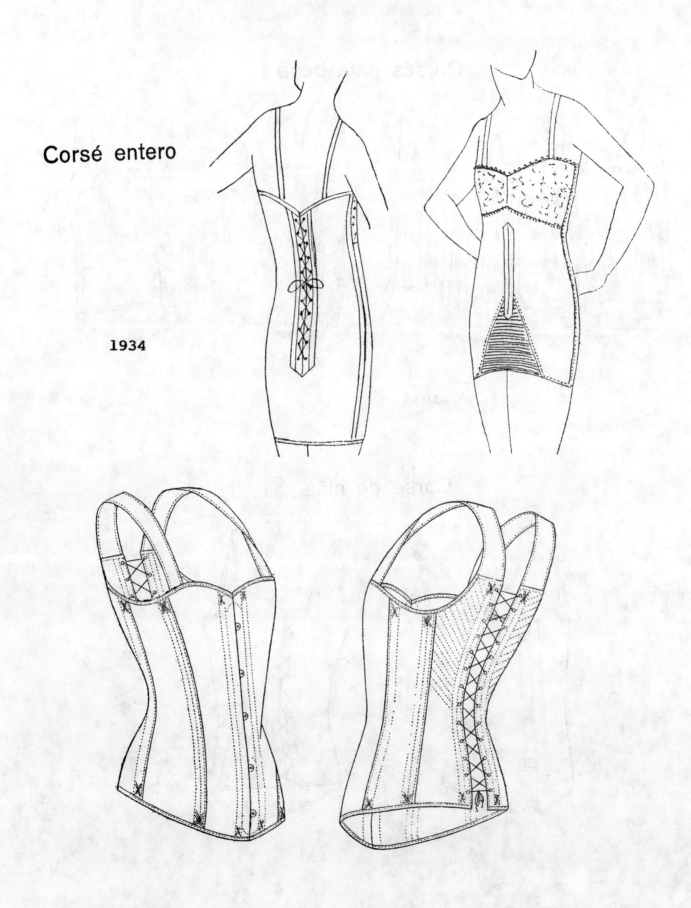

Corsé entero

1934

Titles published by R.L. Shep

ART OF CUTTING & HISTORY OF ENGLISH COSTUME (1887)
by Edward Giles.

THE BOOK OF COSTUME: or Annals of Fashion (1846)
by The Countess of Wilton. Annotated Edition.

CIVIL WAR ERA ETIQUETTE: Martine's Handbook & Vulgarisms
in Conversation.

CIVIL WAR LADIES: Fashions and Needle-Arts of the Early 1860's
from *Peterson's Magazine 1861 and 1864*; and additional hair styles and hair
jewelry from Campbell's *Self-Instructor in the Art of Hair Work 1867*.

DRESS & CLOAK CUTTER: Women's Costumes 1877-1882
by Charles Hecklinger. Rev. & Enlarged Edition.

THE HANDBOOK OF PRACTICAL CUTTING on the Centre Point System
(1866) by Louis Devere.

THE LADIES' GUIDE TO NEEDLE WORK (1877) by S. Annie Frost.

THE LADIES' SELF INSTRUCTOR in Millinery & Mantua Making,
Embroidery & Applique (1853).

EDWARDIAN LADIES' TAILORING: The Twentieth Century System of
Ladies' Garment Cutting (1910) by J.D. Hopkins.

TAILORING OF THE BELLE EPOQUE: Vincent's System of Ladies' Garment
Cutting (1903) by W.D.F. Vincent.

LATE GEORGIAN COSTUME: The Tailor's Friendly Instructor (1822)
by J. Wyatt & The Art of Tying The Cravat (1828) by H. Le Blanc.

THE LADIES' HAND BOOK OF FANCY AND ORNAMENTAL WORK —
Civil War Era — by Florence Hartley.

EDWARDIAN HATS: The Art of Millinery (1909) by Mme. Anna Ben-Yusuf.

CIVIL WAR COOKING: The Housekeeper's Encyclopedia
by Mrs. E. F. Haskell.

THE COMPLETE GUIDE TO PRACTICAL CUTTING (1853)
by Edward Minister & Son.

FREAKS OF FASHION: The Corset & The Crinoline (1868)
by William Berry Lord.

ART IN DRESS (1922) by P. Clement Brown.

For more information and prices, write to:

R.L. Shep, Box 668, Mendocino, CA 95460 USA